A SHORT HISTORY C

MALYN NEWITT

A Short History of Mozambique

HURST & COMPANY, LONDON

First published in the United Kingdom in 2017 by
C. Hurst & Co. (Publishers) Ltd.,
41 Great Russell Street, London, WC1B 3PL
© Malyn Newitt, 2017
All rights reserved.
Printed in the United Kingdom by Bell & Bain Ltd, Glasgow

A Cataloguing-in-Publication data record for this book
is available from the British Library.

ISBNs: 9781849048330

This book is printed using paper from registered sustainable
and managed sources.

www.hurstpublishers.com

CONTENTS

ACKNOWLEDGMENTS

I am very grateful to Dr Abdulcarimo Ismail, Dr Joel das Neves Tembe, Dr Gerhard Liesegang and Dr Liazzat Bonate for their help during a recent visit to Mozambique. Dr Corrado Tornimbeni read and commented on two of the chapters and I greatly appreciate his advice and his collaboration for over more than a decade. I would also like to thank the two anonymous reviewers whose comments on the MS I found of great value. The two maps were drawn by Sebastian Ballard.

ABBREVIATIONS

ANC	African National Congress
CAIL	Complexo Agro-industrial do Vale do Limpopo
COREMO	Comité Revolucionária de Moçambique
EIU	Economist Intelligence Unit
FDI	Foreign Direct Investment
GDs	Grupos Dinamizadores
GEs	Grupos Especiais
GEPs	Grupos Especiais Paraquedistas
HDI	Human Development Index
IMF	International Monetary Fund
MDM	Movimento Democrático de Moçambique
MFA	Movimento das Forças Armadas
MNR	Mozambique National Resistance (later known as Renamo)
MPLA	Movimento Popular de Libertação de Angola. The ruling party in Angola since independence
MUD	Movimento Unido Democrático
NGO	Non-Governmental Organisations
ONUMOZ	United Nations Operation in Mozambique
PARP	Poverty Reduction Action Plan
PCP	Partido Comunista Português
PIDE	Polícia Internacional e de Defesa do Estado

ABBREVIATIONS

RGS	Royal Geographical Society
SADC	Southern African Development Community
SME	Small and medium enterprises
SWAPO	South West Africa People's Organisation
UMCA	Universities Mission to Central Africa
UNITA	União Nacional para a Independência Total de Angola. The principal opposition party in Angola founded by Jonas Savimbi
WNLA	Witwatersrand Native Labour Association
ZANU	Zimbabwe African National Union

GLOSSARY

aldeamentos	protected villages created as part of a counterinsurgency strategy by the Portuguese
amendoim	groundnuts
aringa	large fortified stockade in Zambesia
assimilados	Africans who had acquired full Portuguese citizenship
bairros	shanty towns
barracas	street markets
cadernetes	passes
cantinas/cantineiros	rural stores/storekeepers
carreira da India	the voyage from Portugal to India
cartaz	pass purchased from the Portuguese allowing merchants to trade in the Indian Ocean
chefe de posto	the lowest ranking official in the colonial administration
chibalo	forced labour for the state
chicunda	clients or slaves of Portuguese prazo senhors
cipais	police
colonatos	planned agricultural settlements

GLOSSARY

colonos	African peasants – especially those on the prazos
concelhos	urban administrative areas
cooperantes	foreign aid workers, mostly from the Eastern bloc countries
curador	An official appointed to supervise migrant workers on the Rand
curandeiro	traditional doctors
curva	payment made by the Portuguese to be allowed free access to the Karanga fairs
dona	lady. Particularly referring to female holders of prazo leases
engagé labour	labour recruited under contract for the French Indian Ocean islands
fazendas	plantations in Brazil
feira	fair. Particuarly used for gold fairs
gergelim	sesame
guias da marcha	passes issued in post-civil war Mozambique, especially in Manica
indígenas	persons classified as 'natives' without full citizenship rights
indigenato	regulations defining the rights and obligations of natives (indígenas)
luane	rural estate in Zambesia
macuti town	the part of Mozambique Island inhabited by Africans
mapa cor-de-rosa	Rose-coloured map
modus vivendi	agreement signed in 1901 between Britain and Portugal to supply labour to the Rand
mussoco	head tax levied in Zambesia
não-indígena	anyone not categorised as indígena
palmatoria	a wooden paddle with holes. Used to beat

GLOSSARY

	the hands as a punishment. Used in Brazil and Africa.
planos de fomento	development plans
povo	the common people
postos militares	military posts. The smallest subdivision of local government
prazos	land grants in Zambesia
régulos	traditional authorities in colonial and post-colonial Mozambique
roças	plantations producing cocoa and coffee in São Tomé and Príncipe
sertanejos	backwoodsmen
toucas	embroidered caps worn by Muslim men
Washington Consensus	a term which came into use after 1989 to describe the prevailing policies of the World Bank and IMF

LIST OF MAPS AND ILLUSTRATIONS

Maps

Illustrations

All illustrations are in Malyn Newitt's possession unless otherwise indicated.

1. The gateway to the fort at Sena (1964)
2. Mozambique Island in the 19th century. From Lyons McLeod, *Travels in Eastern Africa*, 2 vols Hurst and Blacket (London, 1860)
3. Mount Morumbala (1964)
4. A water source provided by the colonial government on the road to Nampula (1964)
5. A *chefe de posto* consults a village headman (1964)
6. Basket making. From R.C.F. Maugham, *Zambezia*, John Murray, (London, 1910)
7. Goldsmiths at work. From R.C.F. Maugham, *Zambezia*, John Murray, (London, 1910)
8. Chair made from weapons after the Peace Accord (British Museum)
9. Malangatana: the artist of the Mozambican *povo*. (1981)

THE MOZAMBICAN ENVIRONMENT
AND ETHNOGRAPHY

The Mozambican Environment

Modern Mozambique came into existence as a result of the Anglo-Portuguese boundary treaty of 1891 when the frontiers were drawn and Mozambique was formally separated from its neighbours, Tanzania, Malawi, Zambia, Zimbabwe, Swaziland and South Africa. The country was demarcated in 1891, added to slightly in 1919, and is 309,000 square miles in extent. By way of comparison, Angola is 481,354 square miles and Portugal 35,560 square miles.

Before the 1891 partition south-eastern Africa had a geographical unity and shared a common history, which the various treaties subdivided into six crudely cut out states. In the jigsaw puzzle that resulted, Mozambique was allocated the entire coastline from Delagoa Bay to Cape Delgado, which, at 1,535 miles, is a third of the whole coast of eastern Africa. Behind this long coastline is a relatively low-lying hinterland, before a series of escarpments rise towards the intermediate plateau and the high mountains along the borders with South Africa, Zimbabwe and

Malawi. The mountains create some dramatic landscapes and the inselbergs that surround the northern city of Nampula challenge Monument Valley in the United States for their spectacular effect. The highest mountains in Mozambique are Mount Binga and Mount Namuli, both of which rise to around 8,000 feet.

From these highlands rivers flow towards the coast, cutting Mozambique into sections like the slices of a layer cake. Among the major rivers are the Rovuma which forms the northern boundary with Tanzania and the Lugenda which flows diagonally from the highlands of Malawi and joins the Rovuma before it enters the sea. The Zambesi rises in the far interior of Zambia and divides Mozambique in half, providing a narrow low-lying strip of river valley which cuts deeply into the African plateau in a series of gorges and rapids. The Zambesi is joined by a number of rivers that come down from the highlands and feed the main stream. In the history of Mozambique the most important of these have been the Shire and Luangwa entering from the north and the Luenha, the Mazoe and the Musengezi joining it from the south. In many respects the lower reaches of the Zambesi have been a kind of projection inland of the coastal zone. South of the Zambesi the Pungue, Buzi and Sabi rivers flow down from Zimbabwe and the Limpopo, Nkomati and the rivers that flow into Delagoa Bay come from South Africa. All these rivers rise in the interior but reach the sea at points along the Mozambican coast. As well as the major rivers that rise beyond Mozambique's borders, there are many smaller rivers whose course lies completely or almost completely within Mozambique itself. The region immediately north of the Zambesi in particular, is crisscrossed by rivers that rise in the Milanje or Namuli highlands and that find outlets along the coast between the Zambesi delta and Mozambique Island.

Mozambique's rivers form a framework around which the history of the country has gradually formed itself. Although most of them are not navigable more than fifty miles or so from the coast, they have nevertheless become routes for commerce and corridors for migration. The route from Lake Malawi down the Lugenda to the Rovuma, for example, is an ancient trade and migration route. Along it moved caravans bringing ivory and slaves to the coast and it was along this valley that the nineteenth-century migrations brought Yao to settle in the Shire highlands. Mozambique includes within its border the eastern shore of Lake Malawi and 5,000 square miles of the Lake itself, with the anomaly that Likoma Island, that lies within Mozambique's territorial waters but where a UMCA mission was established in the nineteenth century, belongs to Malawi—not the only incident where history was to override geography.

The Zambesi, exceptionally navigable for two hundred miles into the interior, has always been a major highway fed by its major tributaries the Shire, the Luangwa and the Kafue, river routes which for centuries have linked central Africa with the world of the Indian Ocean. Until the 1960s the Zambesi was a wild and turbulent river. Flood water descending after the rains turned it into a massive torrent which in its lower reaches spread over a bed two miles wide. Vast amounts of alluvial soil came with the floods and the river channels, and the outflows through the delta changed almost on an annual basis as banks of sand shifted and resettled in the floods. Permanent settlements on the banks were routinely endangered as the floods ate away at banks that had appeared secure only a year before. Then in 1962 the Kariba dam, built by the British, began the process of taming the river. In 1969 the Cabora Bassa dam was built in Mozambique and large stretches of the Zambesi, which at one time had raged in torrents through narrow gorges became great inland seas. The flooding on the lower river now became a distant memory but, as with so many other dam schemes elsewhere in the world, the Zambesi dams brought with them profound changes to the ecology of the valley and the lives of the inhabitants.

South of the Zambesi, between the escarpment and the coast, the rivers cross a land which is, at the best of times, relatively infertile. The soil is sandy and the vegetation consists of light woodland and dry savannah. The rivers, with their flood plains, form corridors with richer alluvial soil which are relatively better watered. It is in these areas that population density has always been highest.

Rainfall in the south is irregular and this factor, coupled with the poor soils, has resulted in much of the south being thinly populated. North of approximately latitude 24 south, the land falls under the influence of the seasonal monsoon winds (which at sea can form powerful typhoons) but even here rains are irregular and the country can be subject to droughts which may last years. These droughts were, and still are, profoundly disruptive and can bring with them famine, epidemics and locust swarms. Although rural communities have traditionally had strategies for dealing with famine, these are seldom sufficient if the drought lasts over two years. Then migration becomes the only recourse forcing people to move towards areas which are better watered. This has created a population which is used to being mobile and has led to migrations, conquests and profound political disturbance. In more recent times, droughts and famines have fed the slave trade with cohorts of the destitute and have driven rural populations towards the towns.

Drought and famine punctuate the history of Mozambique and have profoundly influenced its development, as a few examples will illustrate. The famines of the 1570s and 1580s coincided with, and possibly caused, the Maravi invasions. A hundred years later famine and disease weakened the settlements of the Portuguese on the Zimbabwe plateau prior to their expulsion in the 1690s, and the environmental crises of the 1760s severely affected the Monomotapa state and the gold trade of Zumbo. The long series of droughts, accompanied by locusts and epidemics, that began in the 1790s and continued until the 1830s, coincide with the rise of the slave trade and the Ngoni invasions. In the 1860s drought and famine, following on the Gaza war of succession, brought profound social and political change, including the beginnings of the flow of migrant labour to South Africa. W.P. Johnson describes a severe famine among the Yao in the early 1880s at a moment of crisis in their relations with their neighbours. The famine years of 1920–24 helped to swell the numbers of labourers forced from their farms into working for private employers or the government and in 1990–1 a famine contributed to ending the civil war.

There are many other years when the rains failed or partly failed and ironically many incidents also of devastating flooding. There were serious floods in the south in 1966 and 1967 and again in 1977 but the best remembered are the floods of 2000 on the lower reaches of the Nkomati and Limpopo when 700,000 people were displaced and 200,000 head of cattle were lost.

Many parts of the Mozambique lowlands are infested with tsetse fly so that it has been virtually impossible for cattle, and hence a cattle-based economy and society, to thrive. The human communities inhabiting this region have been deeply influenced by this climate. Kin groups have traditionally inhabited small villages and made a living from agriculture rather than from cattle herding. The need for an agricultural labour force has put a premium on the attachment of outsiders (clients or slaves) and, in particular, of women who were often the principal form of booty taken in local wars. At other times individuals fleeing famine or war have been assimilated into clans to help expand the labour force. As a result 'the following of one individual chief was never restricted to a single clan or extended family'.[1]

Mozambican communities in all parts of the country have been characterised by the incorporation of captives taken in war, slaves purchased from dealers or destitute outsiders displaced by war or famine. In the nineteenth century slaves were purchased in northern Mozambique to supply the labour needed for the production of cash crops. In central Mozambique a kaleidoscope of polities, some dominated by Afro-Portuguese or Indo-Portuguese warlords, supported themselves through attracting clients or purchasing slaves to form their armies or to hunt for ivory. In the south the struggle between rival lineages and state systems again benefited those who could attract clients and followers and this historic form of clientship became transmuted into the political patrimonialism that marks modern Mozambique society and politics.

Village agriculture has always been supplemented by other forms of economic activity, hunting, trade, mining and artisan crafts such as working gold and iron, the weaving of cotton cloth and, more recently, the carving of ebony. Men in these communities were often traders, hunters, river boatmen or migrant workers, which made them absentees, while female labour was static and remained focused on the agricultural sector. North of the Zambesi this commonly led to the dominance of social relations based on matrilineal descent. Village agriculture, the allocation of land, and the organisation of labour, was the responsibility of female heads of lineages, and descent systems and conflict resolution recognised the primacy of a woman's brother rather than her husband.

The small, lineage-based communities of the lowlands (the 'little society'), particularly in the north, would frequently come together to form loose confederations under some charismatic leader but they did not build large and permanent state systems. They were easily dominated by warlords who acquired an armed following, swelled its numbers with captives and created semi-militarised polities. Over the *longue durée* this low veldt region was vulnerable to invasion from cattle-based states on the high veldt which wanted access to the sea and the networks of Indian Ocean trade. The historical record, both the chronicles of the

Portuguese, the archaeological record and the oral histories of the indigenous inhabitants themselves, tell of invasions by Karanga-speaking rulers from the Zimbabwe plateau in the fifteenth century, the Maravi coming from the interior north of the Zambesi in the sixteenth, the so-called *landins* in the eighteenth century and the Ngoni moving north from South Africa in the nineteenth century.

Links with the wider Indian Ocean World

The seasonal monsoon winds blow as far south as latitude 24 south, roughly where the port of Inhambane is situated. When the winds are regular they not only bring rain but they link the communities of the Mozambique coast with the ports of the Red Sea, the Hadramaut, the Gulf and India as well as the nearby Comoro Islands and northern Madagascar. Between October and March trading dhows would visit the coast, primarily to trade for Central African gold but also taking on cargoes of exotic skins, turtle shell, ivory, mangrove poles and slaves. Here a maritime and commercial economy led to the formation of substantial urbanised settlements, some large like those situated on Mozambique Island and Angoche, which had commercial links throughout the western Indian Ocean. The port-town on Mozambique Island was visited by Vasco da Gama in 1498 on his pioneering journey to India. The chronicler who accompanied his fleet recorded that the inhabitants

> are Mohammedans, and their language is the same as that of the Moors. Their dresses are of fine linen or cotton stuffs, with variously coloured stripes, and of rich and elaborate workmanship. They all wear *toucas* with borders of silk embroidered in gold. They are merchants and have transactions with white Moors, four of whose vessels were at the time in port, laden with gold, silver, cloves, pepper, ginger and silver rings and also quantities of pearls, jewels and rubies all of which articles are used by the people of this country.[2]

Other smaller settlements were founded either on the relative safety of offshore islands or in river estuaries, wherever there was a secure anchorage for dhows. These smaller settlements were principally concerned with local rather than international trade, building boats and dealing in foodstuffs, pottery, timber, straw mats and local artisan crafts. Through intermarriage and commercial contact much of the coastal population adopted aspects of Islamic culture. South of Inhambane, however, the monsoon did not blow. The trading dhows did not venture there and Islamic coastal culture never took root.

Opposite Mozambique Island, the Mozambique Channel narrows and the coast of Madagascar is only three hundred miles away, with the four Comoro Islands lying like stepping stones to connect it to mainland Africa. Northern Madagascar, the Comoros and coastal Mozambique form a single maritime region where trade and migration have helped to create communities with a shared Islamic cultural tradition.

Although it has a very extensive coastline, Mozambique has very few ports suitable for oceanic shipping. Much of the northern part of the coast is lined with coral islands and reefs while the rivers that enter the sea bring with them alluvial sand which the strong Mozambique current stretches out into spits or deposits as sand bars. The old port of Sofala used by the Portuguese in the sixteenth century first silted up and was then swept away by the tide; access to Quelimane, for centuries the main port of entry for the Zambesi, had a notorious sand bar which made it almost inaccessible to any boats but those with the shallowest draft. Mozambique Island was suitable for ships in the age of sail, although its entrance was dangerous, but Ibo was surrounded with shallows left dry by falling tides.

Mozambique has only two major deepwater ports. Delagoa Bay in the extreme south, regularly visited by the Portuguese after 1545, was the site for short-lived Dutch and Austrian trading stations. In the nineteenth century, during the era of slaving and whaling, it grew in importance but finally came into its own as the best port for access to the South African mining areas. Nacala in the bay of Fernão Veloso lies only a few miles north of Mozambique Island. Although it was known to the Portuguese and the coastal Swahili, it appears that very little use was made of it, and the full extent of its deep and safe anchorages was only charted and made known by the British Consul, Henry O'Neill, in 1881. Even then, the Portuguese were reluctant to develop a port to rival Mozambique Island, and the growth of Nacala only began in the 1950s. In the twenty-first century Nacala has become the terminal for coal exports and the main point of growth for the economy of the north.

Mozambique and its peoples have always been participants in the economy and civilisation of the Indian Ocean, which has influenced many aspects of their economic life and has linked them to the civilisations of India, Arabia and the Gulf. Mozambique, for its part, has provided migrants (often in the form of slaves) who have helped to people the Indian Ocean islands and Madagascar, and who have contributed substantially to Indian Ocean political and cultural life. The prominent role played by India in modern Mozambique, therefore, has deep roots in the region's history.

Ethnography and the problem of ethnic identity

Historians have too often fallen into traps laid for them by anthropology and have described African society in what has been called the 'anthropological present'—depicting African social, cultural and political systems as apparently timeless and unchanging. As a result it has been common to ascribe to Africans primordial ethnic identities, even if the old idea that people were born into 'tribes' and inherited defined tribal characteristics no longer holds the sway it once did. Ethnic identities are fluid and flexible, and relating past descriptions to present realities has many pitfalls. Not least among these is the fact that any description of African society in the past has to make use of contemporary accounts written by Europeans who liked to classify the people they met but frequently had little idea what they were describing and consequently, were often guilty of gross misunderstanding or misinterpretation. To complicate matters, some distinctive markers, like body ornamentation, once used to classify ethnicities, have fallen into disuse. The Dominican priest, João dos Santos, commented in the early seventeenth century that the Makua *nação* were distinguished by cultural traits like the filing of teeth into points.[3] This practice, along with tattoos and the use of the lip ring by women were still common in the early part of the twentieth century and were the subject of a monograph published as recently as 1962, but by the end of the century this practice had almost entirely disappeared.[4]

Archaeologists, for their part, can successfully identify styles of building or pottery and can speculate about long distance trade and even local economies but ascribing these things to a specific historical ethnic group without the corroboration of written or oral evidence is very uncertain.

When the Portuguese first settled in the ports along the East African coast at the beginning of the sixteenth century, they employed names which were in use to describe the people of the region—Tonga was used to describe the inhabitants of the Zambesi valley and coastal lowlands; Karanga was used for the peoples of the high veldt south of the Zambesi; Bororo and Makua were used for the populations north of the river and the all-purpose term 'Mouros' (Moors) was used for the coastal Muslim populations.[5] It is likely that these generic terms referred to broadly perceived linguistic and cultural differences but did not pretend to any more specific identification. João dos Santos, writing in 1609 about the people living south of the Zambesi, is quite clear about this.

> All these Cafres are called Mocarangas, as all speak the Mocaranga language, and for this reason all these lands are also called Mocaranga, except parts of the kingdoms along the sea coast, where other languages are spoken, particularly the Botonga tongue, for which reason these lands are called Botonga and their inhabitants Botongas.[6]

The name Karanga described the dynasties of rulers who established a paramountcy over the Zimbabwe plateau and the region south of the Zambesi as far south as Inhambane in the late fifteenth and early sixteenth centuries. As the Portuguese used the name, it came to apply to all the people who were Shona-speakers. The term Tonga meant simply 'slave' or 'subject' and was a general term used by the Karanga and later the Maravi to describe the subject populations of the Zambesi valley and the coastal lowlands who had little in common with each other—speaking different dialects, recognising different political authorities and venerating different spirit cults. The names Tonga or Amatonga, with the same inference that they were slaves or subjects, were later used to describe the population of the extreme south round Delagoa Bay. As Patrick Harries wrote, 'the Gaza, Zulu and others employed the term to distinguish themselves from subject neighbours, and gradually the term became a synonym for inferiority and meanness'. The term Ndau, used today to describe a section of the Shona-speaking population of Zimbabwe and Mozambique, also originated as a pejorative term used by the Ngoni to describe people they had conquered.[7]

These broad classifications, on which the Portuguese relied for at least three centuries after their arrival in eastern Africa, were supplemented, after the European practice, by dividing the land and the population into identifiable polities or states. The African population was perceived as belonging to kingdoms and the Portuguese imposed conceptual order on those they met south of the Zambesi by assuming the existence of an original 'empire of Monomotapa' from which the various kingdoms had broken away but to which they were still loosely connected through tradition, the payment of tribute and the recognition of titles. Later they were to imagine the existence north of the Zambesi of an 'empire of Maravi' governed by its emperor, named Caronga and also an 'empire of Moenemugi' whose name appeared on many contemporary European maps—though this name, as Gamitto pointed out in the 1850s, was simply the honorific title born by many minor rulers of the region.[8]

Subordinate to these imagined 'empires' were kingdoms. Writing in the 1630s António Bocarro described how Mokaranga 'is divided among petty kings and other lords with fewer vassals... who are all vassals of Monomotapa'. He then lists twenty-two kingdoms each with its own name and a royal title. In many instances the name of the kingdom is used to describe the people who live in it—very much after the fashion in contemporary Europe.[9] The logic of allocating populations to kingdoms was that they could be classified as rebels and coerced if they did not accept such an allocation. The same logic could also lead to claims being made to control land and resources, and in the seventeenth century the Portuguese made generous use of this attribution of sovereignty, asserting that African kings, by signing various treaties, had transferred population, land and mineral resources to Portugal.

In the eighteenth century the Portuguese described the people of the Zimbabwe plateau as Rosvi. Like the Karanga, the Rosvi were originally a ruling elite. They were the followers of Changamira Dombo who rose to power after 1680, conquering the lands of the long-established Karanga chieftaincy of Butua, where he not only founded a new ruling dynasty, but established his kin and followers as a new aristocracy. Once the Rosvi had established their dominance over the high veldt the Portuguese started to use the name to describe all the people subject to them.[10]

ENVIRONMENT AND ETHNOGRAPHY

What the Portuguese had witnessed south of the Zambesi was repeated in the north. In the second half of the sixteenth century, the region north of the Zambesi was invaded by armed groups organised, like the Imbangala of Angola, in war camps and practising ritual cannibalism. These war bands, which appear to have originated in the central African interior, ranged further north still to Cape Delgado, Kilwa and even as far as Mombasa and Melinde. The Portuguese referred to these invaders as Zimba and Mumbos, names which have continued to be used to describe small and specific ethnic groups to the present. These migrants eventually established new states stretching from the Luangwa to the Shire and the Mozambique lowlands, the most famous of whose rulers bore the titles Lundu, Kalonga (or Karonga) and Undi. To these the Portuguese gave the collective name Maravi, from which the modern Malawi is derived.[11]

The kingdoms that were ruled by Maravi dynasties were not composed of homogeneous populations, but over time the name 'Maravi' became attached to their kingdoms and then became a generic name used to describe the populations of those kingdoms. However, as soon as the Maravi kingdoms began to fragment in the nineteenth century, the groups that broke away and established their independence assumed new names and new identities. Gamitto is very explicit about this trend.

> Formerly this region was divided into two dominions, Munhaes [south of the Zambesi] and Maraves; and today these people have taken various names. Those referred to above are properly the Marave; Bororos are those who dwell on the left bank of the Zambezi and are bordered by the territory of Quelimane and on the west by the Shire. Between these and the Lupata [gorge] are the Maganjas. And from the north to the coast at Cape Delgado are the Makwa. West of the Marave, as far as the river Luangwa, live the Cheva, and to the east of these and near the mouth of that river are the Senga and between these and the Portuguese territories of the left bank of the Zambezi are the Mogoa. East of the

Makwa, and on the shores of the river or lake Nyanja [Lake Malawi] are the Yao or Nguru. All these people today are totally independent of each other, and each is known by its own name. Nevertheless it is beyond dispute that all are of the same Marave race, having the same habits, customs, language etc.[12]

The Ngoni invasions of the nineteenth century provide further examples of invading war bands, evolving into more or less stable states with associated ethnicities. The Ngoni war parties that invaded Central Africa in the period 1820 to 1840 were probably quite small and were led by men linked to the ruling clan of the Ndwandwe in Natal. Eventually, these Ngoni warlords and their immediate followers established a series of powerful states in southern Mozambique, Malawi, northern Mozambique, Zambia and Tanzania, absorbing people from the local populations who then assumed an 'Ngoni' identity.[13] The most powerful of these Ngoni states was that of Gaza which at its height dominated the whole of southern Mozambique from the Zambesi southwards as well as a considerable part of modern Zimbabwe. Although some of the conquered populations were incorporated into the Ngoni state system with its militarised institutions, other population groups remained separate, distinguishing themselves with separate ethnic names. For example the Ndau (a Shona-speaking group), or the Chopi, while the population around the Portuguese slaving port of Inhambane clung to a Tonga identification.

This instability of population, political power and ethnic identity is especially characteristic of the Zambesi valley. In times of drought the valley, and in particular the delta area, remains relatively well-watered, attracting immigrants and refugees. At the same time the river has been an important trade route, linking Central Africa with the Indian Ocean, along which there has been a regular movement of people. Indian Ocean merchants (among whom were Portuguese) established trading fairs and river ports, around which settled dependent groups of Africans.

The long distance traders, hunters, canoe men, and artisans—people who were largely detached from the primarily agriculture-based societies of the interior—either formed their own communities or became attached to wealthy and powerful patrons. Distinct ethnic identities were acquired by those living around such coastal and riverain towns as Sena, Tete and Quelimane, which provided protection and employment to those who lived in their vicinity. The name Chuabo was given to those living near the fort (or *Chuambo*) of Quelimane; Asena became the name for those living in the vicinity of the ancient trading town of Sena, whom the Portuguese had originally described generically as Tonga; and Nyungue described those in the vicinity of Tete (Nyungue being the local name for Tete). Inhabitants of the Portuguese *prazos* (seigneurial domains) were also often known by the name of the *prazo*. For example, in the later nineteenth century the term a-Mahindo was used to describe inhabitants of the delta *prazo* of Maindo.[14]

The creation of new polities and ethnic identities

Among the people who inhabit the region north of the Zambesi, the dominant social unit of the 'little society' has been the matrilineage. Children belong to the mother's family, and a mother's brother is the dominant male figure of the family. One consequence of this has been a tendency for rich and powerful men within matrilineal societies to seek to establish their own patrilineal families through the acquisition of slave wives whose children would belong to them. This process was particularly important in the nineteenth century when Muslim Yao rulers extended their control over matrilineal populations in the interior of modern Mozambique and Malawi.[15] The rise of powerful patrilineal lineages in a predominantly matrilineal world can give rise to separate and competing centres of power, and ultimately to distinct ethnic identities.

The absence of cattle in much of the country also generated its own political and ethnic dynamic. In the cattle-owning societies of the high veldt the accumulation of cattle, by raiding or by natural increase, was a way of acquiring, storing and increasing wealth. Cattle ownership regulated social relations through bride price and underpinned political power and patronage through the loaning of cattle. Cattle ownership enabled patriarchal rulers to maintain their authority over the 'little society' and allowed kings to establish relatively centralised control over large populations and extensive territories. However, in areas where cattle cannot be kept, wealth has to be accumulated and patronage dispensed in other forms. One way of doing this was through trade and the distribution of imported goods; another was through the acquisition of male and female slaves to increase the productive and reproductive capacity of the community. In many parts of pre-colonial Africa the acquisition of slaves routinely supplemented natural population increase in communities where the agricultural labour of women was the principal source of wealth and economic security. Male slaves could be incorporated as junior kin while women became wives with an important reproductive as well as productive role in the family.

Where the disease environment prevented the maintenance of large cattle herds, raiding became a natural strategy for the survival of the community. Successful communities constantly added to their populations by incorporating captives whose assimilation was achieved by the adoption of various symbols that marked the distinctiveness of the group—dress, body ornamentation, observance of rituals, the narration of oral traditions etc.—creating in this way a new ethnicity. There are numerous references in the Portuguese documents to women being treated as the 'spoils of war'. Santos, for example, described the successful campaign of the captain of Tete against the Mumbos in 1592, in which the Portuguese were assisted by fighters recruited from the eleven chieftaincies subject to Tete, after which 'he returned with his men to Tete, taking with him as captives all the women of the enemy in the place'.[16] António Bocarro gives an account of Madeira's attack on Chombe early in the early seventeenth century. 'Reaching a village of Chombe's...our Cafres attacked and destroyed it carrying off many black women and much spoil'.[17]

In the low veldt regions of the coast and the Zambesi valley, any successful trader, hunter, warlord or bandit leader could quickly build up a following through the purchase or capture of male and female slaves and by rewarding followers with plunder or prestigious imported items. Santos describes with devastating clarity how raiding and warfare supported this system of reward and patronage.

> These Cafre vassals of Tete are very much addicted to war and, if it depended upon them, they would always be fighting, for the sake of the spoil which they obtain; and they say they would rather fight than dig, as those who die in battle end their labour and the survivors become rich with the spoils. For this reason they respond joyfully whenever the captain of Tete summons them to take part in war.[18]

Such societies often began with bands of male warriors or hunters, built primarily on the success and charisma of a powerful individual. These groups might prove ephemeral, disappearing with the death or defeat of the original founder. However, once women had been obtained and families established, they could acquire some permanence, their leaders establishing their legitimacy through adopting practices that in the region designated chiefly authority, winning over the spirit mediums of the local cults, and taking wives from influential local lineages or clans.

The rise of the Chicunda as a proud and clearly differentiated ethnic group has long been thought of as a special case in Zambesian history. They are usually described as being the descendants of the slaves of the Portuguese and, in a sense, this is true as the term 'Chicunda' was employed by the Portuguese in the eighteenth century to describe their personal slaves. However, this has led to profound misunderstanding. Portuguese slavery in Zambesia was not an institution similar to the military slavery found in North Africa, India or the Middle East or the plantation slavery of the Americas.[19] The Chicunda have to be seen as similar to other Zambesian military/hunter communities and understood in the context of the relations of patronage and clientelism that form the basis of the vast majority of African polities.

Along the coast were populations whose economic livelihood and maritime contacts created cultural affinities with the world of the western Indian Ocean and in particular with the Swahili cultures of the northern part of the East African coast and with the Comoro Islands. As mentioned above, Portuguese tended to refer to these populations generically as Mouros (Muslims) and to differentiate them by reference to the names of the sheikh-doms which ruled the coastal towns like Angoche, Sancul or Tungue. In the nineteenth century the Portuguese became more familiar with this part of the coast and better informed about conditions in the interior where, once again, they tended to differentiate populations by reference to rulers. For example, the rise of Namarulo as a powerful Makua warlord led the Portuguese to describe his followers as the Namarrais.

The Portuguese had been familiar with the Yao as ivory traders for centuries but after the migration of sections of the Yao south towards Lake Malawi, they were often referred to by the names of rulers, like Mataka, who in turn gave their names to individual Yao states. Once again the paradigm is that of a powerful ruler or warlord creating a state, which in turn created an ethnic identity for his subjects.

Linguistic Classifications and Regional Identities

In the twenty-first century, although past political allegiances still inhabit the uncertain world of historical memory, people have got used to the idea of being citizens of the colonial or post-colonial state. As a result it has become common to catego-rise a country's population in terms of the languages spoken rather than by primordial ethnic identities. However, this is a solution that results in less clarity than might at first be imag-ined. In a country whose population has experienced mobility on an unprecedented scale as fugitives from drought and famine or as refugees who fled abroad during thirty years of war and civil strife between 1960 and 1990, and which has more recently expe-rienced the migration from rural areas to the towns, common in much of Africa, language identification is far from stable or cer-tain. Most Africans speak more than one local language or dia-lect and, since children may have been born in exile or to parents from different localities, for many it is not clear to which linguis-tic group they belong. An extraordinary 34 per cent of the popu-lation cannot be classified as having a particular mother tongue. Moreover linguists do not agree how to categorise languages. Most African languages belong to language families and there is often no agreement where the boundaries between individual languages and mere dialects should be drawn. As a result opin-ions vary as to whether there are as few as 17 languages spoken in Mozambique or as many 42, though there is a kind of consen-sus around the number 22 (including Portuguese). No one lan-guage is anywhere near being dominant. Although Makua is the mother tongue of 26 per cent of the population, its speakers are concentrated in the north and its nearest rival, Shangana, sup-posedly spoken by 11 per cent, is equally concentrated in the far south. Mozambique, according to Michel Cahen 'is a country of linguistic minorities'.[20]

In the twenty-first century Mozambique is divided, for admin-istrative purposes, into ten provinces. These are not identical with the provincial divisions established by the Portuguese (there were nine provinces at the end of the colonial period), but they broadly follow the same pattern. For example, the modern provinces of Manica and Sofala correspond with the former territory of the Mozambique Company, while Niassa and Cabo Delgado correspond with the territory of the Niassa Company. These administrative divisions also broadly reflect the pattern of language distribution and the historical background, which has helped to determine certain cultural traits.

For the purpose of linguistic and cultural description Mozambique can broadly be divided into three zones—the south, from the Pungue river to Delagoa Bay, the centre, consisting of the Zambesi valley and escarpment and the land immediately to the north and south of the Zambesi delta, and the north, from approximately the borders of the Zambesia province to the Rovuma. These zones overlap. The provinces of Manica, Sofala and Zambesia clearly straddle such a divide, so there is nothing set in stone about such a division.

In the south there are nine languages commonly spoken—the most widely spoken are Shangana/Tsonga, Ronga, Tswa and Chopi. The others are Tonga, around Inhambane, and Zulu, Ngoni and Swati, spoken by minorities and clearly linked to larger groups in South Africa. Most of these languages are related, share lexical similarity and are often mutually intelligible. Within each there are numerous dialects with their own name or names. From this it can be seen that using language as a mark of ethnic identity produces a result that is extremely lacking in focus. Shangana is thought to be the most widely spoken with 1.4 million claiming it as their mother tongue. The ninth language is Ndau, widely spoken in Sofala and Manyika provinces and related to the Shona of Zimbabwe and to some of the languages of the centre group.

The centre provides a complex mosaic of dialects and languages, most of them closely related. Seventeen languages have been identified as spoken in this part of Mozambique. Chuabo, Nyungue and Sena are most widely spoken. Others include Barwe, Dema, Kunda, Manyika, Phimbi, Tawara and Tewe which are spoken by people living south of the Zambesi and are all languages that share much in common with each other and with Shona. North of the river Nsenga and Nyanja are spoken by people west of the Shire, and Kokola, Lolo, Maindo, Manyawa, Marenje and Takwane are spoken in Zambesia province and linked to languages in the northern group. The mobility of people along and around the Zambesi valley has made the cultural and linguistic history of the population a kaleidoscope, which is constantly being shaken by events both natural and man made.

There are fourteen distinct languages in the northern sector, but once again most of these are closely related and are often considered by linguists to be a cluster of dialects within a single language family. Eight of these belong to the Makua-Lomwe family. In the extreme north Makonde is a language which is also spoken by people in Tanzania. Along the coast and among the populations in the islands there are various dialects related to as Swahili including Mwani, Makwe, Nathembo. The Yao language is spoken inland and along the coast of Lake Malawi from Gurue in the south to the Rovuma.

As all these languages go by a variety of different names and, because many of them form a continuum of dialect, they are very uncertain as markers of ethnic identity. As a result, it is perhaps not surprising that ethnic loyalties have played a less important part in modern Mozambican politics than has been the case in other African countries.

The official Mozambique censuses since 1960 have not asked any question about ethnic identity and in the twenty-first century, although ethnic identities are not unimportant, regional identities often seem to count for more. These regional identities are firmly rooted in the country's history. For much of the colonial period up to 1942, Mozambique was divided into separate administrative zones, which fragmented the colony and prevented the emergence of a common system or law and administration. The location of the capital in the extreme south of the country, and the proximity of South Africa, concentrated resources and the modern sector of the economy in that region, while much of the rest of the country continued relatively unaffected by these social and economic changes. Until the 1960s there was no direct road link between the regions north and south of the Zambesi and no paved road between Beira and Lourenço Marques, the country's two major cities. Moreover patterns of human migration were always inland towards neighbouring states rather than within the country between north and south. During the war of independence the two northern provinces and Tete became a war zone, while most of the rest of the country was not affected by the war. The period of the civil war (1980–92) also helped to accentuate regional differences, as Renamo's activities were concentrated in the centre of the country, regions where it has polled strongly in recent elections.

Regional identities have therefore tended to be stronger rather than specifically ethnic identities in Mozambique. There are marked differences in population distribution. Population is heavily concentrated in the extreme south and in the central area north of the Zambesi. In contrast the Gaza and Tete provinces have notably small populations as do Niassa and Cabo Delgado in the extreme north.

Until the nineteenth century Islamic influence was largely confined to the coast, but Islam began to expand inland with the Yao migrations and with the increasingly militarised activities of coastal slave traders. Around a quarter of the Mozambican population are believed to be Muslim, with most of them located in the extreme north of the country. Islam still tends to be focused on long established brotherhoods and local centres of Islamic culture in Mozambique itself, Zanzibar or the Comoros rather than on centres in the Gulf or Saudi Arabia.

2

THE SIXTEENTH TO THE
EIGHTEENTH CENTURIES[1]

Mozambique and the carreira da India

The first Portuguese ships to reach the Indian Ocean via the Cape of Good Hope left Portugal in 1497 and reached India the following year. The Portuguese wished to trade spices in western India and after 1500, sent fleets each year to the East. However, they found it difficult to establish a position for themselves in Indian Ocean trade, partly because of their violence towards Muslim merchants and their Indian patrons, who the Portuguese suspected were deliberately trying to sabotage their trade, partly because they had to buy spices with bullion as they had no commodities which found a market in the East, and partly because of the long distances they had to travel and their lack of any secure base in the East from which to operate.

So, in 1504, they determined to establish a permanent foothold in the Indian Ocean and to claim it as a kingdom of the Portuguese Crown. They called this the Estado da India. The Estado da India was a wholly new concept in international law and practice as the Portuguese declared the sea, rather than any land, to be the sovereign realm of the Portuguese Crown. It was to be defended by a series of strategically sited bases which would be garrisoned and where ships could be repaired and provisioned. Ships belonging to all merchants crossing the ocean would have to seek the permission of the Portuguese, and pay duties on their merchandise. To overcome their uncompetitive position in eastern markets the Portuguese Crown decided to declare the trade in certain commodities to be Crown monopolies and they attempted to enforce these monopolies by a system of *cartazes* or passes which merchants would have to acquire to trade in the king of Portugal's dominions. This basic structure was underpinned by a series of alliances with rulers of maritime states around the Indian Ocean who were persuaded that friendship with the Portuguese would be in their interest. By the 1530s the Portuguese had bases on the west coast of India at Cochin, Goa (which was the capital of the Estado da India) and Diu, controlled access to the Gulf from Ormuz and to the lands beyond the Straits of Malacca from their fort at Malacca.

In two different ways Eastern Africa had also come to play a major role in the structure of this empire. The Portuguese ships arriving from Europe needed a port of call on the east African coast to revictual and carry out repairs, land the sick and take on fresh crew before catching the monsoon winds for the last stage of the journey to India. Vasco da Gama had visited the Muslim sheikh of Mozambique in 1498 and in 1506 the Portuguese established a permanent settlement on the island, which they gradually expanded into a major fortified base. Mozambique Island lay half a mile from the shore and protected a wide and deep anchorage where Portuguese Indiamen could remain in comparative safety before resuming their voyage. During the sixteenth century 131 India ships 'wintered' in Mozambique— that is they remained there, sometimes for as much as six months, waiting for a change in the monsoon winds. Mozambique also had facilities for the repair of ships and became one of the most important naval bases of the Estado da India. Tens of thousands of individual Portuguese passed through the island, which in the latter part of the sixteenth century also became a centre for the missionary work of the Jesuits, Augustinians and Dominicans.

However, there was a second reason why eastern Africa became important. The Portuguese knew that gold, mined somewhere in the interior, was traded at a number of coastal ports. They wanted to control this trade in the hope that the gold would provide them with the means to purchase spices in India. To achieve this they established fortified trading posts at two of the coast's leading commercial centres Kilwa and Sofala. Kilwa, on the coast of modern Tanzania, was soon abandoned, but Sofala, near the modern city of Beira, became the centre of their gold trading operations' and the site of a permanent garrison and commercial settlement.

Relations between Portuguese and Swahili on the coast

Portuguese relations with the people who inhabited the coastal towns of eastern Africa were fraught with problems from the start but the Portuguese gradually adapted to the patterns of trade and commercial relations which had already been established with the peoples of the interior. At first the Portuguese sought to monopolise the gold trade and did their best to force the traders of the coast to accept their right to do so. They hoped that the coastal rulers would accept an alliance with Portugal that would be mutually beneficial. However, only Melinde, on the coast of modern Kenya, among the major trading communities of the coast, welcomed this Portuguese alliance, Melinde remained Portugal's main support throughout the sixteenth century. In Kilwa and Sofala the Portuguese also tried at first to work through local rulers but relations soon broke down. When the Portuguese abandoned their fort at Kilwa, the town resumed a precarious independence under its own ruler but never recovered its position in international commerce. In Mozambique Island the Portuguese were able to establish a working relationship with the ruler. It soon became clear, however, that the tiny island was too small for the Portuguese and the Muslim population to live comfortably side by side and the sheikh therefore removed to the mainland and made the centre of his settlement at Sancul. However, a residual Muslim population remained on the island alongside the stone town of the Portuguese. Other coastal trading towns, which the Portuguese believed were hostile to their interests, were attacked. Angoche was raided in 1513 and Querimba and Mombasa were plundered in 1522 and 1524.

On the northern part of the coast (modern Tanzania and Kenya) the Portuguese belief that the Muslim coastal communities would seize any opportunity to collaborate with Portugal's enemies and undermine Portugal's commercial position led to a series of wars, raids and reprisals in the 1580s when Turkish galleys appeared on the coast and encouraged the local population to turn on the Portuguese. The Portuguese tried to strengthen their position by building a large fortress at Mombasa in 1593 and installing the sultan of Melinde there. However, in 1631 the sultan, whom the Portuguese believed was a convert to Christianity and their close ally, staged an insurrection which expelled the Portuguese from Mombasa and raised armed opposition along the whole northern part of the coast. The Portuguese returned in force but the appearance of Omani ships in the 1650s once again led to a series of wars between the Portuguese and the rulers of some of the Swahili towns. Although an Omani fleet raided Mozambique Island in 1670, these conflicts took place almost exclusively in the northern sector beyond the borders of what later became Mozambique. In 1698, after a prolonged siege, Mombasa was finally captured by the Omani and with it Portuguese influence along the northern Swahili coast came to an end. Cape Delgado became recognised as the frontier dividing a Portuguese sphere of influence to the south from one controlled by Oman to the north. The first piece in the jigsaw that eventually built modern Mozambique was put in place.

Apart from one particularly violent episode during the expedition of Francisco Barreto to the Zambesi in 1571, relations between the Portuguese and the Muslim populations of the Mozambique coast remained reasonably amicable. After the violent overthrow of the ruler of Sofala and the initial raids on Angoche and Querimba, the Portuguese and the coastal populations established a relationship built around the trade in ivory and the provisioning of the fortress at Mozambique. Ivory being a bulky commodity could not, like gold, be concentrated in the hands of a few specialist traders. Instead it was brought to many different coastal and estuarine ports along the coast and the Portuguese had to purchase the tusks through established local networks. Foodstuffs, and other locally produced items of consumption like pottery, matting, cloth and timber, also had to be purchased from the scattered coastal communities and the Portuguese established local agents in a number of the ports. Small boats, often crewed by local seamen, operated along a network of trade routes which extended to the coast of Madagascar and the Comoro Islands and which converged on the Portuguese fortresses of Mozambique and Sofala. Over the course of a century and a half individual Portuguese settled at various points along the coast, notably in the Querimba Islands where they obtained formal titles to the possession of individual islands, in the fertile Zambesi delta and the hinterland of Sofala. Although Dominican and Jesuit missionaries were active in the region, it is clear that many Portuguese 'went native' and adapted their lifestyles, religious allegiance and commercial practices to fit in with local traditions, marrying local women and participating in local trade networks.

Although the Portuguese had set out to try to create a commercial system in the western Indian Ocean which they would dominate, by the seventeenth century they had largely abandoned this experiment and became just one of a number of merchant communities adhering to the age old patterns of monsoon trade. Some changes did, take place, however, which were to have a major impact on the African peoples who participated in the Indian Ocean commercial networks. Although the gold trade remained important and was given a new impetus when the Portuguese began to work hitherto unexplored deposits of alluvial gold north of the Zambesi in the eighteenth century, it was the trade in ivory that expanded most notably after 1500. Here the Portuguese were undoubtedly influential as, from 1545 onwards, they began to buy ivory from areas south of the traditional monsoon ports, especially in Delagoa Bay.

Another development was the increased involvement of Indians in the commerce of eastern Africa. Indian merchants were already well established in east African trade when the Portuguese first arrived on the coast and mistook them for Christians. However, as the Portuguese expanded their activities inland, increasing numbers of Indians followed in their wake and by the end of the seventeenth century they were to be found in all the main trading towns and fairs both on the coast and in the interior. In the early eighteenth century it was Indians who pioneered new settlements like those of Zumbo and Inhambane, while Indian priests from Goa became important in serving the African churches. However, it was the expansion of Indian capital that was the most notable development of the late seventeenth and early eighteenth centuries. Indian merchant capital began to penetrate all areas of the western Indian Ocean and Indian trading houses came to dominate the ports of Arabia and the Gulf as well as eastern Africa. Indians gradually took over the collection of revenues and the financing of the Swahili sultanates of the coast and in the Portuguese sphere south of Cape Delgado Indian merchant capital came gradually to dominate the ivory trade, especially after the establishment of the Diu Company at the end of the seventeenth century.

The arrival of Europeans, therefore brought about radical change in the patterns of Indian Ocean commerce, but it was not as a consequence of their largely unsuccessful attempts to establish monopolies but indirectly through their role in opening the way for the expansion of Indian merchant capital.

The captain's monopoly and Portuguese institutions

During the hundred years after the Portuguese set up their forts at Sofala and Mozambique their institutions underwent some important changes. At first the fortress captains were simply salaried royal officials who commanded the garrisons and warships, while factors were appointed to administer the Crown monopolies of gold and ivory. Command on the East African coast was divided between a northern sector under the Captain of the Coast of Melinde and the southern sector under the Captain of Mozambique and Sofala. By the middle of the sixteenth century the latter had moved his headquarters from Sofala to Mozambique Island, which had become the important port of call for the ships on the *carreira da India*. At the same time the Crown gradually ceased its attempts to administer the trade monopolies directly and instead leased its monopoly rights to the captains.

By the beginning of the seventeenth century the new system was in full operation. The captaincy of Mozambique was granted to a deserving servant of the Portuguese Crown for three years and those who had been awarded this post gradually formed a lengthy waiting list. When a grantee's turn came to hold the office, he had to pay a substantial sum (40,000 *cruzados*) for the right to exercise the Crown's commercial monopolies. Having made this payment the captain then took over responsibility for maintaining the forts and garrisons of Mozambique and Sofala and appointed subordinate captains over the Zambesi settlements. In compensation for this he had the sole right to import cloth and to trade for gold and ivory in the Zambesi settlements and the region immediately to the south. A few areas of commerce, notably the direct trade from Mozambique Island to the northern coastal regions and to Madagascar, were reserved for the private traders settled on Mozambique Island.

Early in the seventeenth century Estevão de Ataide, the captain of Mozambique, had to confront two determined attempts by the Dutch to capture Mozambique Island. However, after prolonged sieges in 1607 and 1608, the Dutch were forced to abandon their plans and thereafter offered no further challenge to Portugal's position on the East African coast. This successful defence of the important way station for the Portuguese fleets appeared to justify the policy of entrusting its defence to the initiative of the captains.

The advantage of this system was that the Portuguese Crown received a substantial sum from each captain on taking office and at the same time was able to off-load the defence costs of the fortresses while maintaining some control over the captains because their tenure was so short. However, there were disadvantages as well. In order to recoup their expenditure, the captains tended to neglect the maintenance of the forts, while the existence of a monopoly administered by the captain discouraged other Portuguese from settling. Towards the end of the seventeenth century the Crown became convinced that the regime of the captain's monopoly had to be replaced and after 1672 it was discontinued. Over the next few decades the Crown experimented with different systems, first establishing a monopoly administered for the Crown by a Junta, then briefly allowing a period of free trade to merchants on payment of customs dues and finally granting a monopoly to the Indian-based Diu Company. The command of the forts and the civil government of the settlements were now once again entrusted to a captain appointed and salaried by the Crown.

The impact of the captain's monopoly on the African population and on the overall development of the region is difficult to assess. The penetration of Portuguese *sertanejos* into the African kingdoms does not appear to have been impeded by the captains and interference in the internal affairs of the Monomotapa state was more often directed by missionaries than the agents of the captains. It is possible that the restrictive practices of the captain's monopoly had the effect of diverting African long distance trade away from the areas of Portuguese settlement towards coastal regions not controlled by the Portuguese, around Kilwa to the north or Mambone and the Sabi estuary to the south, but African rulers themselves seldom allowed 'free trade' in their own dominions any more than did the Portuguese captains, and long distance caravans were taxed in one form or another in both African and Portuguese controlled regions.

Drought and the Maravi invasions

Drought is a recurring theme in Mozambique's history. A failure of the monsoon rains can have a profound effect on communities that are overwhelmingly dependent on agriculture, while droughts are often accompanied by other scourges, including epidemics and locusts, which can devastate a population weakened by starvation or malnutrition.

Two droughts are of particular significance in Mozambique's history, that of the early nineteenth century, which is considered in a later chapter, and that of the last quarter of the sixteenth century. 'There have been four chastisements or general scourges on this coast in our time', wrote Friar João dos Santos who was resident in Mozambique from 1586–97.

The first was the war with the Zimbas.... The second chastisement, which occurred in these lands at the same time, was the cruel plague of very large locusts.... Famine was the third chastisement [and] ... the fourth affliction and trouble that overtook Kaffraria was a severe outbeak of smallpox, of which a great number of people died.[2]

During the 1580s, when these scourges were affecting the region, the Portuguese chroniclers record the arrival in the lands north of the Zambesi of various armed bands made up of people they described as Mumbos, Zimbas or Cabires. The Portuguese confronted these groups and suffered some humiliating military reverses at their hands. The chroniclers in particular described the invasions of the Zimba, as these marauders moved on from the Zambesi valley to attack the coastal communities opposite the Querimba Islands and then to devastate the Swahili town of Kilwa and to attack Mombasa in 1587.

Shortly after these dramatic events, the records begin to mention new polities that had been established north of the Zambesi—the kingdoms of Lundu, Undi and Kalonga, collectively called the Maravi by the Portuguese. Early in the seventeenth century these Maravi polities controlled the whole region from the Luangwa as far as the coast opposite Mozambique Island. They effectively blocked any attempts by the Portuguese to expand north of Zambesi and controlled the main trade routes to the coast.

Based on a complex interaction with the indigenous populations and with the spirit cults, notably the Mbona rain-calling cult on the Shire, the Maravi kingdoms formed polities which dominated a large part of northern Mozambique for the best part of two centuries. As a ruling elite the Maravi remained distinct from the bulk of the population, finding their identity in belonging to one or other of the ruling clans (the Banda and the Phiri). Although the Maravi rulers established complex relationships with the spirit cults and the clans of the conquered peoples, their

paramountcy ultimately depended on reciprocal relations of tribute collection and gift-giving, these in turn necessitated the
control of trade that passed through their kingdoms. Goods
obtained through trade were dispensed as patronage, which
explains why the rulers in this region tried to control itinerant
traders and to insist that trade was either conducted directly with
themselves or at centrally controlled markets.[3]

By the end of the seventeenth century the shifting patterns of
Indian Ocean trade were weakening the position of the Maravi
elites and in the eighteenth century their states began to visibly
disintegrate. Undi increasingly allowed people from the Portuguese
controlled parts of the Zambesi valley to penetrate his area of
influence and to open up gold diggings, while Lundu's paramountcy over the Makua-speaking and Lomwe-speaking peoples
of the coast also largely disappeared and was replaced by the
rule of local warlords and confederations of lineage heads. The
great drought of the early nineteenth century, coinciding with
the Ngoni invasions, saw the last vestiges of the Maravi states
disappear.

The Portuguese and the Monomotapa Empire

The region south of the Zambesi, extending as far as the Sabi and
including the Zimbabwe plateau, was a region where gold was
mined and traded, and where a distinctive culture, or series of
related cultures, thrived. The most distinctive feature of these
cultures was the tradition of building in stone. The earliest archaeological sites date back to the ninth century and by the fifteenth
century the impressive walls and the tower of Great Zimbabwe had
been constructed. Then, in the fifteenth century, the region witnessed the establishment of a number of states ruled over by a new
elite who called themselves Karanga. The dynasties of the Karanga
were linked and, according to tradition, descended from common

ancestors. They appear to have recognised the ritual paramountcy of the Mwene Mutapa (Monomotapa) whose extensive territory included the northern part of modern Zimbabwe and the parts of the Zambesi valley known as Chedima and Dande which are mostly located in Mozambique.

When the Portuguese arrived, the Karanga elites were still expanding their control into the Mozambique lowlands between the Zambesi and the Sabi. As well as the large territory ruled by the Mwene Mutapa, separate Karanga states were already established: Sedanda, Quiteve (inland of Sofala), Manica (in the mountains on the borders of Mozambique and Zimbabwe), Barue (in the low veldt between the lower Zambesi and the Zimbabwe border) and Butua (in the south of modern Zimbabwe). Dazzled by the Castilian reports of the great empires of Central and South America, the Portuguese tried to represent the Mwene Mutapa as the ruler of just such an empire with the other Karanga rulers subject to him but, whatever may have been the case in the past, by the sixteenth century the different Karanga rulers were politically independent of any central control and the 'empire' of Mwene Mutapa was largely a myth.

The rulers of the Karanga states maintained their power through marriages with important local clans, through collaboration with local spirit cults and through control of the gold trade, which was conducted at fairs to which merchants travelled from the coast. On the high veldt their economy was based on cattle ownership rather than trade. At the centre elaborate court rituals, described in detail by Portuguese writers, helped to bind the people of the 'little society' to their rulers. The weakness of these states lay in the uncertainty of the rules of succession, which led to frequent civil wars when a ruler died and which presented opportunities for outsiders to intervene.[4]

Throughout the gold-bearing regions, fairs were established which attracted merchants from the coast and from the settlements in the Zambesi valley. These brought textiles, beads, metalware, porcelain and other commodities to exchange for gold. Once the Portuguese became established as traders on the coast they began to travel inland to the fairs. The quantity of gold traded convinced the Portuguese that there were mines in the interior, which could be captured and exploited directly. The first serious attempt to capture these mines was made between 1569 and 1575, under the command of Francisco Barreto, a former viceroy of the Estado da India. This expedition was a failure as the soldiers died of fever and there were, anyway, no large valuable mines to be discovered. The small scale washing for gold in the mountain streams was not worth a major military effort. Instead individual Portuguese began to intervene in local politics and gradually the lands along the Zambesi valley and inland from Sofala were granted to them by the Karanga rulers. By the beginning of the seventeenth century the Portuguese controlled the delta region and two towns on the Zambesi, Sena and Tete, separated by the Lupata gorge, from which they organised trade caravans to the fairs on the plateau still under the control of the Karanga.

During the seventeenth century the Portuguese became increasingly active throughout the plateau region. At the gold fairs they established a permanent presence and built fortified stockades and churches. They also started their own gold mining operations and obtained further land concessions from Karanga rulers. This increasing activity was made possible by the divisions between the Karanga ruling elites and, in particular, by disputed successions within the Mwene Mutapa ruling dynasty. The Dominican missionaries hoped that, by achieving the conversion of the Karanga rulers, they could achieve mass conversions of the population and they encouraged the Portuguese captains to support their candidates for the succession.

The Portuguese also established themselves in the Karanga states of Manica (which was rich in gold) Quiteve and Barue and there was even a Portuguese fortified settlement in Butua in the southern part of the plateau.

Towards the end of the seventeenth century the political situation south of the Zambesi underwent a radical change following the emergence of a new ruling elite in the southern state of Butua, known as the Rosvi. In a series of campaigns, Changamira, the Rosvi leader, defeated both the Portuguese and the Mwene Mutapa and expelled them from the plateau. From the beginning of the eighteenth century, the Mwene Mutapa was therefore confined to Dande and Chedima, two regions of the southern escarpment bordering on the Zambesi, thereby reducing the once large Karanga state to relative insignificance. These wars established a boundary between a region under Portuguese influence and a region controlled by the Rosvi. This boundary survived the events of the nineteenth century and formed the rationale for the frontier demarcation when the boundary between Mozambique and Southern Rhodesia was drawn in 1891.

The Rosvi, meanwhile, extended their rule throughout most of the plateau region of modern Zimbabwe and made the ruler of Manica tributary. The economy of the Rosvi rulers was largely based on cattle but the trade in gold remained important and, although they would not allow individual Portuguese to enter their dominions, they did allow them to trade gold at the fair in Manica and at a new fair established at Zumbo where the Luangwa enters the Zambesi.[5]

Portuguese expansion in the Zambesi valley and the origin of the prazos[7]

Soon after their arrival on the coast, individual Portuguese men began to travel inland and establish themselves at the gold fairs of the interior. At first their main point of departure was Sofala but sometime around 1530 they began to use the port of Quelimane on the northern arm of the Zambesi delta, which had been briefly visited by Vasco da Gama in 1498. By the second half of the century these individual Portuguese were to be found settled at the main gold fairs. Their status as a community was recognised by the Mwene Mutapa who appointed one of the Portuguese to manage relations with the local population.

In 1569, a major military expedition was sent to try to conquer the mines. This was a failure but, as a result, the Portuguese took formal possession of the river towns of Sena and Tete, expelling the Muslim that had settled there.

In the fifty years following the withdrawal of the expedition in 1575, the Portuguese in Sofala and the Zambesi towns acquired control over increasing amounts of land and population, as jurisdiction was granted to them by the Karanga rulers. In return for effective control of the population in these areas the Portuguese paid an annual tribute, called the *curva*, to the Karanga rulers. Although the Portuguese always thought of the *curva* as a gift, its regular payment became a form of tribute necessary to allow Portuguese traders free passage to the fairs.

It was common practice in India and Sri Lanka for the Portguese that obtained land concessions to seek titles for them from the Portuguese Crown and to secure these titles in Portuguese law. The titles were based on the emphyteutic tenures common in Portugal—a form of leasehold which guaranteed title for three lives after which the Crown reserved the right to grant the title elsewhere.

In the early seventeenth century a list relating to the year 1637 shows eighty-one crown lands had been granted titles—seven of these being made into religious orders for the support of the mission churches.[6] These grants became known as *prazos da coroa* and the *prazo* system was to continue, in one form or another, until 1930. A *prazo* was not generally a small estate or plantation but a large tract of land, sometimes many hundred square kilometres in extent, on which there would be numerous African villages. The holder of the *prazo* acted, in many respects, as a kind of paramount chief, or overlord, exacting tribute from the population in kind or in labour services as soldiers, boatmen, hunters and carriers. He in turn paid a quit-rent to the Crown. In time, some of the *prazo* holders assumed the ritual functions of an African ruler, performing ceremonies connected with planting and harvest, while on their death spirit mediums continued to commune with the dead *senhor*.

The holders of the largest *prazos* could become powerful feudal lords with their own armies, able to pursue private warfare against their rivals or against the independent African polities on their borders. However, all of them were involved in the gold or ivory trades and depended on the Portuguese authorities in the Zambesi towns or Sofala for the import of the cloth, which was the local currency, firearms, and other manufactures. The Portuguese authorities, for their part, depended on the *prazo senhors* for armed support to maintain their position against local African enemies.

By the end of the seventeenth century the Crown was aware that its reliance on the *prazo senhors* was a mixed blessing. It was the ambition of the Crown to turn its eastern African possessions into a new Brazil but to achieve this it needed to encourage settlement by Portuguese subjects. However, relatively few of the Portuguese who rounded the Cape of Good Hope and headed for India found their way to the Zambesi settlements and a large part of the 'Portuguese' population in eastern Africa was made up of Indians or people of mixed racial origin. In order to try to increase the settlement of European Portuguese, the Crown decreed that the titles to *prazos* would pass to the holder's daughter and would be confirmed only if these women married Portuguese men. This policy had relatively little effect in increasing the population of European origin, but it did have the unintended consequence of opening the way to a succession of powerful female figures—the Zambesi *donas*—who became a distinctive feature of Mozambican society.

During the eighteenth century, although denied access to the southern plateau regions which they had dominated in the previous century, the Portuguese of the Zambesi valley expanded their activities around the *feira* of Zumbo, situated at the confluence of the Luangwa and the Zambesi, and in the region of the north bank facing Tete where a number of gold diggings were worked and some of the land was distributed as *prazos*.

A distinctive feature of the *prazo* system was the emergence of a social group, which were the clients of the *senhor* and did not belong to the local African communities. The Portuguese often referred to these clients as their 'slaves' but they also used the term *chicunda* to distinguish them from the local population who they called *colonos*. The *chicunda* performed a variety of functions for the *prazo senhor* as hunters, fighters and traders but they might also be employed in more menial tasks in agriculture, domestic service or as boatmen or carriers. Among the *chicunda* there was a hierarchy with the highest ranking holding positions of power and responsibility in the *prazo* or being entrusted with leading the caravans which went to trade for gold and ivory in the interior. *Chicunda* clients of the Portuguese could expect to marry, have their own villages and bring up their own families. Many of them acquired slaves or clients of their own. This kind of clientelism, familiar in many African societies, helped to mould the *prazos* into African-style polities rather than European-style plantations.

By the middle of the eighteenth century the *prazo* system extended from the Ligonha river north of Quelimane as far south as Sofala. Up the Zambesi *prazos* covered the south bank as far as the Cabora Bassa rapids and on the north bank a substantial area opposite the town of Tete. The Querimba Islands off the northern part of the coast were also granted as *prazos*. In area the *prazos* covered territory very much larger than Portugal itself.

The people of this region were divided between an indigenous population—those on the south of the Zambesi being generically described as Tonga and those around Quelimane and to the north being called Lolo (or Bororo) and Makua—and a creole elite made up of some Portuguese, people of mixed race, Indians and other people of East Asian origin. The economic position of the creoles was rooted in the control of the *prazos* and in trade, while many held office in the Portuguese administration. In between them and the African population were the *chicunda*, whose position depended economically and socially on their service to the creole elites. This society was nominally Christian and was served by the Jesuit and Dominican mission churches but, although it was very dependent on trade with the Indian Ocean world, it reflected the African origin of most of the population in particular in the reciprocal relations of clientilism that held the society together.

Delagoa Bay and the ivory trade—the importance of long distance trade

From the middle of the sixteenth century Portuguese trading ships had regularly visited Delagoa Bay to buy ivory. This was a marked extension of the network of Indian Ocean trade as the region lay beyond the regime of the monsoons and had not been visited by trading dhows before the Portuguese arrived. The Portuguese did not establish a permanent settlement in the Bay but organised seasonal trading fairs on one of the islands and sent boats up the rivers that entered the Bay to buy ivory from the Africans along their banks. Occasionally Delagoa Bay was visited by Dutch or English ships but it was only in 1710 when the Dutch decided to set up a permanent trading post there. This 'factory' survived barely a decade before being forced to close due to the deteriorating relations with the local population.

Trade then reverted to the original pattern of seasonal voyages until the Trieste Company tried to establish a factory in the Bay in 1778. This also only lasted a few years but prompted the Portuguese at last to set up their own permanent post there in 1787. Over a period of two and half centuries, the ivory trade from Delagoa Bay linked the peoples of what would later become South Africa and Swaziland with the Indian Ocean trading networks, where ivory was being brought from the interior to be exchanged for cloth, beads and Asian manufactures. The importance of this trade for the polities in the interior was to become apparent in the early nineteenth century when Delagoa Bay became an important hub in the slave trade and its trade a significant factor in regional politics.

During the seventeenth century the Portuguese had sent trading ships to buy ivory at Angoche, Sangage on the northern Mozambique coast and at Inhambane south of the Sabi. Inhambane was located at the southern limit of the monsoons and its hinterland also saw the extreme southern extension of the Zimbabwe culture and of Karanga influence. The Jesuits had hopefully sent a mission there in the 1560s. However, it was only in the eighteenth century that a permanent Portuguese settlement was established. This appears to have been largely supported by Indian traders and the church staffed by Indian priests. Inhambane tapped the ivory trade coming from the central areas of southern Mozambique and, again, helped to tie the populations of its hinterland into the trade networks of the Indian Ocean.

Decline of the Estado da India

The Portuguese settlements in Mozambique had been important for the Estado da India and they had been successfully defended against the attacks of both the Dutch and the Omani. The revenues resulting from the gold and ivory traded there were of great importance to the economic survival of the Estado da India. After catastrophic losses to the Dutch in the middle years of the seventeenth century, the Estado da India, was reduced to its stations along the Indian coast north of Goa (the so-called Provincia do Norte), its valuable outpost in Bandar Kung in the Gulf and its possessions in eastern Africa. In the second half of the seventeenth century the Portuguese position recovered somewhat but in 1698 Mombasa was lost to the Omani and in the early eighteenth century Chaul and Bassein were captured by the Marathas. On the Indian sub-continent the Estado da India was now reduced to Goa and the two northern Indian ports of Diu and Damao.

In 1752 it was decided to separate the east African stations from Goa and to create a separate government in Mozambique. Ten years later the Portuguese settlements there were all upgraded and given the official status of Portuguese towns. For the first time the Portuguese settlements between Cape Delgado and Delagoa Bay all came under a single authority whose centre was on Mozambique Island—an important landmark in the evolution of the modern state of Mozambique.

After eighteen years in prison Father Thoman reflects on life on the Zambesi missions

Mauriz Thoman was a German Jesuit who was sent out to Goa in 1753 with sixteen colleagues. Later he was to write a chapter in his autobiography about Mozambique as he had known it. On the way their ship touched at Mozambique Island and Thoman gives his impressions of arriving at this strange island city.

> The Father Rector of the Jesuit College on the island sent some small boats to bring us seventeen Jesuits to the College. Each boat had twelve oars, and was manned by coal-black moors, who were naked but for some

clothing around the waist. It can well be imagined what a strong impression seven coal-black naked and fearsome people made on us, newly arrived as we were from Europe. Yet in a short time we became accustomed not only to seeing them but also to moving in their company.

The trade of the island was conducted by Portuguese and 'Asiatic heathen and Mohemmedans' but

it would be still more lucrative if the ships of other nations could also land there, but it is laid down that no ship of a foreign nation may enter the harbour.... Whenever the island suffers from a great shortage of provisions, the people pack up axes, awls, knives, scissors, mirrors and similar wares in casks, load a moderate sized vessel with them, and carry them across to the island of Madagascar opposite, where they buy the necessary cattle and other provisions.

Later he describes how a ship that ran aground trying to enter the harbour was refloated using barrels attached to the hull at low tide.

After some years in Goa, Thoman was sent back to Mozambique, sailing on the same ship as the newly appointed governor, João Manuel de Melo. Shortly after arriving the governor committed suicide by falling upon his sword and Thoman was summoned to hear the dying man's confession. He then proceeded to the 'Rivers of Senna', which he says is larger than the County of Tyrol. At Quelimane he was accommodated at the Jesuit Residence and observes that 'once and for all it should be noticed here that the word "residence" should not be taken to mean a magnificent building, but a common and often very bad house where one or more missionaries live together'. Left in charge of the church there, Thoman fell ill with fever and was treated with the 'primitive cure customary there. They sat me naked on a chair full of holes, covered my head up with many cloths and under the seat placed a large pot filled with hot water and herbs and then left me to languish and sweat'.

Eventually he made his way to Sena,

the seat of a Portuguese governor and of a vicar-general for spiritual affairs. The Dominicans have a residence and are the parish priests of the place. The Augustinians, Franciscans and Brothers of St John of God come only yearly to collect alms and to have a good time. The place has a fort, which is well made from sun-dried bricks. Its only use is to hold the kaffirs in check for these men have no firearms and this otherwise laughable fort can provide adequate defence against them.

There are so many different African languages that the Portuguese 'only learn enough of the language... to be able to trade and not be cheated by them'. Preaching also was done in Portuguese because the African languages were 'deficient in words to explain the Catholic faith'.

In May 1759 he travelled up to Tete to try to recover his health and 'found the residence there in confusion and desolation without anyone even to bake the bread.... By his excessive harshness my predecessor had driven away all the servants and slaves but they soon returned when they heard that I was of a kinder disposition'. From there he went on to Marangue where even the *mucasambo*, the overseer of the slaves had deserted. 'The residence of Marangue lies in a wilderness where not a single European is to be met with'. The Africans he found to behave very respectfully towards whites and Asiatics 'particularly towards women' and 'there is no danger of their harming a European or Asiatic, still less of their seeking their lives' though they might 'take orders from their master or mistress to get rid of some person, as happened to a missionary of the Society of Jesus... who strongly criticised the evil unchastity of some high-ranking persons'.

The Africans were easily trained as tailors, smiths, carpenters, goldsmiths and barbers. They also learned to cook very well, but the Portuguese seldom had black women as cooks 'for very good reasons'. 'A true moor does not learn to read or write.' but 'it is astonishing what beautiful work the African goldsmiths do, and

yet they only use small iron instruments worth a few *groschen*.
Usually they work sitting on the bare earth and use both hands
and feet. In this way they make the finest filigree work—in particular gold buttons...'

These people are not at all displeased if war breaks out among them.
Generally there is not much bloodshed. They rather seek to get the
better of each other by cunning. If a group sees itself outnumbered, it
at once takes to flight. The victor robs whatever he finds in the district
of the conquered; sets fire to the huts; makes slaves of the wives and
children; and remains in possession of the region until he is hunted out
by another enemy.

The Portuguese bring cloth and beads to trade for gold dust
and ivory. The cloth has to be coarse and of a dark colour. 'If one
gives a moor a white cloth, he wears it until it is quite dirty and
then colours it completely black'. The beads are also 'made from
the worst glass... They are fixed to a strong thread and bound
together in a great bunch. Such bunches are packed by the thousand into barrels.'

Elephant hunters first 'smear themselves with a certain oil or
juice, whose smell they say stupifies the elephants'. He records the
local custom that the tusk of a dead elephant that lies on the earth
belongs to the lord of the land, the other tusk to the hunter.

Everything in the region was transported by river, and Thoman
says the hippopotami often caused me the greatest anxiety when
they followed my boat'. Many things were made from the teeth of
the hippopotamus, especially 'rosaries... which are valued very
greatly because of their beautiful and enduring whiteness and
because they have the power of stopping bleeding'. Thoman was ill
for much of his time in Africa and was interested in the precau-
tions taken by locals to preserve their health: the hoof of a large
eland is good against convulsions, but it must be a left hoof and a
piece has to be carried on the left hand side of the body. A certain
type of root if carried protects against snakes. Syphillis, however,

was the great scourge, and 'it has greatly gained ground in Afica and Asia, especially, however, in areas where the Portuguese and other Europeans have settled.... For this reason...I would not advise my greatest enemy to go to this country.'

The canoes, he says, are made very quickly, the centre of the tree trunk being burnt out. The largest can have as many as eighteen rowers. The inhabitants all depend on the river for their water but the Portuguese find 'the water which comes from the river too muddy and unclean. So they store it in large earthen jars brought from Persia.... These are buried in the ground, sealed so that no impurities can fall in, and left for a considerable time until the water becomes clear, fresh and good to drink'.

Digging for gold dust is carried out by women only.

'The men do not take a hand in it. Their office is only to command the women, to keep them at their work and to protect them against attacks by hostile moors. For it so happens that some enemies cunningly fall on the women, fill their mouths with meal so that they cannot cry out and carry them off as slaves'.

He tells the story of a white ant hill that turned out to be so rich in gold that when it was dug away, there was enough gold to pay off all the debts of the Jesuit residence.

Thoman explains the nature of slavery in Zambesia.

A moor becomes the slave of another moor or of a Portuguese in the first place through a just war or through an agreement made justly and freely whereby for an agreed quantity of goods, namely cloth or glass beads, he places himself under a master; or through birth... To become a slave, particularly of a European or someone descended from one, is for a kaffir more good than bad fortune. For the master must feed and clothe him and protect him from others. A custom has also arisen there that whosoever harms my slave harms me. If a slave has the ability, he is allowed to learn a trade in which case he will be more valued by his master, better looked after and finally well-instructed in Christianity. I am sure that the servant boys and maids in Europe work ten times as hard and are worse treated than these slaves, for the latter must always be shown a certain consideration by their masters because otherwise they would run away and the master would suffer great loss.

Thoman mentions the Monomotapa, reflecting that his kingdom has been broken up due to a succession dispute between rival brothers. 'His black majesty's palace is made of strong poles and cane... It is however more roomy and finer than the other huts of the kaffirs. It is always surrounded by a decorative fence made of elephant teeth.' The Portuguese, he says, still pay him an annual tribute which consists of 'a red velvet cushion, a chair and other trifles. Over and above this they send him a company of soldiers. Everyone considers himself lucky to be sent there, and especially the captain, for they are always richly rewarded, particularly if they bring with them some favourite trifle from Europe or Asia for his black majesty.'

In September 1759, while on a visit to Tete, Thoman was arrested along with the other Jesuits and began the long and painful journey back to Portugal where, following the suppression of the Society of Jesus, he was imprisoned for eighteen years, only being released after the fall of the Marquês de Pombal.

3

THE NINETEENTH CENTURY

AFRICAN AGENCY IN THE CREATION
OF MOZAMBIQUE

Introduction

During the three hundred years from the fifteenth to the eighteenth centuries, there was a certain stability in the way the African
population of what would later become Mozambique, related to
the wider world of the Indian Ocean. Ivory and gold were traded
through Islamic middlemen in return for imported cloth, beads
and metal ware. The African societies were organised in decentralised segmentary states based on reciprocal gift-giving and on the
support of spirit mediums associated with the land, with rain calling or with the spirits of dead rulers. The arrival of the Portuguese
had not altered these relationships in any radical way and the *prazo
senhors* who came to control large sections of the lower Zambesi
valley and the coastal lowlands had largely adapted to traditional
African social and political practices.

All this was to change in the nineteenth century when most
aspects of the lives of the peoples of south-eastern Africa were
fundamentally transformed. Some of these changes occurred as a

result of the accelerating growth of the global economy, which increased the demand for labour and for African raw materials. Some also resulted from the strategic rivalry of Britain and France in the Indian Ocean and from the expansionist ambitions of the Sultans of Oman who relocated the centre of their monarchy to Zanzibar in 1840. However, the greatest motors of change came from within Africa itself and of these climatic instability, and in particular the great drought of 1823 to 1831, was the most important. Drought and famine resulted in major political conflict and in migrations, especially the migrations of the Ngoni. The long periods of drought, coming at the same time as the expansion of the slave trade, led to the emergence of a new class of warlords and slavers who were able to expand their sphere of activity among the weakened and dislocated populations of the interior. When the peoples of south-eastern Africa emerged from these decades of crisis it was to find a world radically different from that of their ancestors.

The great drought of the 1820s

The beginning of the cycle of droughts which affected south-eastern Africa from Zululand to Lake Malawi started around 1794 and lasted till 1802. A further dry phase began in 1817, reaching serious proportions in Mozambique in 1823 where it continued with relentless severity until 1831 but did not finally come to an end until 1836. Portuguese reports describe the devastating consequences for the population of drought and famine, exacerbated by the outbreak of smallpox and by the arrival in 1828 of swarms of locusts. In 1828, for example, it was reported that the *prazos* had become 'complete deserts through famine and the pestiferous smallpox which has reduced the villages of the *chicunda* and the *colonos* to mere depositories of corpses.' Later that year swarms of locusts invaded the region and 'day after day the sun was covered by the passage of clouds of these insects and they destroyed even the virgin bush'. The story was the same along the whole coast from Delagoa Bay to Cape Delgado. In 1831 it was reported that 1,000 people had perished on Ibo Island; villages were deserted and the troops too weak to stand sentry duty.[1]

Drought was a common circumstance for the peoples of south-eastern Africa but such a prolonged dry period completely destroyed the economic base of traditional society, not just on the Zambesi *prazos* but in all the neighbouring communities. Trade, gold mining and normal artisan production ceased and the gold fairs at Manica and Zumbo closed and were abandoned. The waters of the Zambesi fell to such a low level that many of the streams of the delta had no water and became overgrown with bush. The social and economic structure of the *prazos* was destroyed as agricultural production and trade ceased and the destitute inhabitants abandoned their villages. More serious even than the lack of water was the appearance of wanderings groups of armed men, bandits as the Portuguese called them. In 1829 the governor was told of

> the ruin which these insurgents have caused through the lands of the district of this town, destroying the luanes [rural estates] some of which have been reduced to ashes, and causing immense mortality among the natives... However there is no cause except the despair and hunger which incites them and leads them rather to die from arrows or at the mouth of musket than from thirst and hunger.[2]

The result was that many of the *prazo* owners left the country and retreated to Goa or Brazil, leaving a political and social vacuum throughout much of the region. Their place was taken by a few powerful families, which rented the vacant *prazos*, recruited slave armies and from fortified strongholds began to participate in the growing trade in slaves.

The slave trade: world markets and African sources of supply

The drought also fed the slave trade as large numbers of destitute people were rounded up to be sold into slavery, to satisfy a demand that had been growing since the last quarter of the eighteenth century.

For many hundreds of years slaves had been exported from the ports of eastern Africa to markets in Arabia, the Gulf and India where they were in demand as soldiers, domestic servants and sailors. From the early sixteenth century, the Portuguese, with the centre of their eastern empire in Goa, employed slaves in the same capacities as their Asian and Arab counterparts. During the 1640s, when the Dutch had temporarily occupied Angola and São Tomé, the Portuguese began to dispatch slaves round the Cape to markets in the Atlantic although this does not seem to have resulted in a major long term increase in the trade. Meanwhile, the Dutch colonies at the Cape and Mauritius bought their slaves in Indonesia and later in Madagascar, rather than on the east African coast.

In the eighteenth century, however, the demand for slaves from eastern Africa rose sharply as a result of the French occupation, after 1710, of the Mascarene and Seychelles island groups. There they began to develop plantation agriculture, producing indigo, coffee and sugar, with the accompanying demand for labour. Before 1770 the French brought most of their slaves from Madagascar, with only around 19 per cent (10,677, or an average per annum of 106.77, over the period 1670–1769) coming from eastern Africa. After 1770 the situation changed dramatically and between 1770 and 1810 approximately 100,000 African slaves were imported (constituting 60 per cent of the total). Although Britain abolished the slave trade in 1807, slaves continued to be imported into Réunion (which was restored to France in 1815) until France itself abolished slavery, in 1848. Between 1810 and

1848 it has been estimated that 75,767 slaves from eastern Africa reached the Mascarenes.[3]

The Mascarenes were not, of course, the only market for East African slaves. There were 'traditional' markets in the Red Sea and the Gulf and a small trade to south-east Asia. Imports into the Gulf region between 1830 and 1866 may have averaged between 2,700 and 3,100 per annum.[4] However, by the middle of the century Zanzibar and its dependencies had become a major importer rather than exporter of slaves as the removal of the capital of the Omani sultanate from Muscat to Zanzibar in 1840 led to a great expansion of plantation agriculture along the coast.

The seaborne slave trade was not a purely European or Arab affair. During the eighteenth century there was also a significant expansion of Indian trade, investment and settlement in the lands bordering the western Indian Ocean. The expansion of Indian commercial activity came from trading firms based in British and Portuguese controlled ports on the western coast of India such as Bombay and Damao. The general expansion of this economic activity (most strikingly seen in coffee growing in Arabia) increased the demand for labour and Indians were actively involved in financing the slave trade and providing shipping.[5]

After the end of the Napoleonic Wars, eastern Africa was drawn increasingly into the world dominated by global capitalism and this was to have a dramatic effect on the demand for slaves along that section of the coast, which was the Portuguese sphere of influence. In the early nineteenth century the demand in America for slaves from eastern Africa rose steeply until, around 1830, exports from eastern Africa were almost as great as those from western Africa. The background to this was the gradual restriction of the slave trade in West Africa. Diplomatic pressure, backed by Royal Navy patrols, had led to the trade being officially abandoned by all countries except the Portuguese. Even Portugal signed agreements stopping the trade north of the equator. However, as the slave trade was gradually squeezed in the Atlantic, demand in the Americas was rising sharply as the expanding European market for sugar and coffee revived Brazil's long-established but languishing plantation economy.

Mozambique now became the major supplier of slaves for Brazil and Cuba.[6] Between 1800 and 1850, Brazil imported around 2,460,000 slaves, most of whom came from Portuguese ports in eastern Africa, from Ibo in the north to Delagoa Bay in the south, with Quelimane briefly becoming the most important centre of the trade after 1815.

Following Palmerston's unilateral action in 1839 declaring the slave trade to be piracy, Portugal finally agreed to end the seaborne trade in slaves in 1842 and began to co-operate with the Royal Navy in taking action against the known centres of the trade. After this date the slave trade conducted by Portuguese ship owners and traders lingered for a while as a clandestine smuggling operation but slaving from the main Portuguese centres was now virtually dead.[7]

The Portuguese, from the governor downwards, had been closely involved in the trade and when the Portuguese authorities formally abolished the slave trade the economic impact on many of the coastal settlements was serious. In 1880 the British Consul, Henry O'Neill, visited Quissanga on the mainland near Ibo.

> As the terminal point of a caravan route, that in the old days brought down slaves in thousands for export to the Brazils and Cuba, it must have presented some busy scenes. But when the Brazilian and Cuban markets ceased for export from the coast, and the slaving days (for the Portuguese) in the province of Mozambique were known to be doomed, it fell away, the whites deserted it and their houses fell into ruins.[8]

It took the rise in the trade in agricultural products to revive coastal towns such as Quissanga.

Although there has been extensive research into the demand side of the slave trade, the supply side is less well known. During the period 1810 to 1850, the years when the slave trade from eastern Africa reached hitherto unprecedented levels, the expansion in the supply of slaves was almost as important as the rise in demand. Two factors in particular contributed to the rise in the numbers of slaves available for export. The first was the cycle of severe drought that hit south-eastern Africa, especially the Zambesi region, between 1823 and 1831. As starvation and marauding bands of armed men disrupted society, it was easy for slave dealers to fill the baracoons, and statistics suggest that exports of slaves reached a peak in 1828–1830 the very years when the drought was at its most severe. At the same time, and partly as a consequence of this drought, armed groups of Ngoni left southern Africa and began their conquests in the Mozambique lowlands, in Zimbabwe and across the Zambesi. As they advanced, the Ngoni took slaves for their own purposes but also became major participants in the slave trade, particularly in the southern, Portuguese-controlled ports of Inhambane and Lourenço Marques.

With supply and demand both increasing rapidly, it is no surprise that the slave trade expanded to such an extent in the first half of the century. However, although by the 1860s slave exports to Brazil and Cuba had largely ceased and British pressure was gradually reducing the slave trade that operated in and out of Zanzibar, this did not put the slavers out of business as the trade found new markets and assumed new guises.

Ngoni

Just as the great drought was reaching its climax in the late 1820s, the region south of the Zambesi was invaded by Ngoni war bands originating in the Natal region of modern South

Africa. Movement of people from the southern interior into Mozambique were not a new phenomenon. In the eighteenth century groups of Tsonga speakers had expanded northwards into the dry low veldt region north of the Limpopo, pushing the previous Tonga inhabitants towards the coast and supplanting some of the southernmost Karanga polities. Then, as a result of the dry period that began at the end of the century, there were fresh movements of peoples from the densely populated area of modern Natal. The spread of drought conditions placed great strain on the mixed agricultural economy of the Ngoni and led to increasing conflict between clans and the raiding for cattle to exchange with European traders in Delagoa Bay. Out of these conflicts emerged powerful, militarised groups who organised themselves for war in age-set regiments, and who exerted a centralised control over the cattle and human resources of the community.

In 1819, with drought placing ever greater pressure on resources, a decisive conflict took place between the Zulu and the Ndwandwe which led to the defeated Ndwandwe regiments leaving the Natal region and invading the southern areas of Mozambique. With their tight military organisation, the Ndwandwe found the Tsonga and Karanga polities easy prey. As they advanced they recruited captives into their regiments, seized the cattle of the people they encountered and turned their attention to the coastal towns where plunder was to be had. The most important of these Ngoni groups was led by Nxaba who advanced through the region between the Sabi and the Zambesi, destroying the former Karanga polities, plundering the hinterland of Sofala and from 1830 establishing a tributary state, which included Barue and the Sena *prazos*.

Other Ngoni groups invaded the Zimbabwe plateau and destroyed the already weakened Rosvi state of Changamira. Further clashes between rival groups led to the Ngoni of Zwangendaba and Maseko crossing the Zambesi where, after a few years, they proceeded further north to the shores of Lake Tanganyika. From there different Ngoni groups headed into modern Tanzania while others returned to establish states on the western side of Lake Malawi. By the middle of the nineteenth centuries there were Ngoni states established in the highlands of the country north of Tete, while the Ngoni in Tanzania had begun raiding across the Rovuma into northern Mozambique.

Meanwhile two other powerful Ngoni groups had advanced from the south. One of these was the Ndebele under Mzilikazi who entered the southern regions of modern Zimbabwe in 1840 and gradually consolidated a Ngoni state in the region that had once been dominated by the Rosvi. In the same year Soshangane had led a group north of the Limpopo where he defeated Nxaba and gradually extended his rule over the whole of the country between the Limpopo and the Zambesi. Although he was threatened by Zulus and Swazi in the extreme south—a Zulu force had raided Delagoa Bay in 1833—Soshangane gradually consolidated what was to become the largest and longest lived of all the Ngoni kingdoms.

Always known as the Gaza kingdom, Soshangane's state was based around an Ngoni core with a large subject population from which he took slaves and levied tribute. Many from this subject population of Tsonga speakers adopted aspects of Ngoni culture even though they were not fully assimilated. On the fringes of the kingdom, and particularly in the north, the peoples were simply made to pay tribute while retaining their own basic social formations. The Afro-Portuguese of the Sena *prazos*, gradually recovering some of their prosperity after the years of drought, were among those who paid tribute to Soshangane, and after 1858 to his successor Umzila, but they remained at the same time part of the Portuguese colony and subject to the Portuguese Crown. Many of the Shona speakers (later called Ndau), the Chopi and the Tonga who lived around the Portuguese port of

Inhambane were never fully incorporated into the Gaza kingdom or subjected to Ngoni cultural influence and maintained a precarious independence, while the small kingdoms immediately inland of Delagoa Bay never accepted Gaza overrule at all.

The Gaza kingdom was not as centralised as the Zulu or Swazi kingdoms and over much of its area depended on Gaza soldiers being able periodically to exact tribute. As Patrick Harries put it, 'from an Amatonga perspective, there was frequently little distinction between tax-gathering and pillage.'[9]

The Ngoni of the Gaza kingdom were not the first ruling elite to establish their hegemony in the region south of the Zambesi. The Karanga dynasties had done this before them. Never before, however, had the whole country between the Zambesi and the Limpopo been brought under the control of a single ruler. This was another important step on the historical path towards the creation of the modern state of Mozambique.

The Yao

Another consequence of the great drought and of the expansion of the slave trade was the movement of a significant number of the Yao from northern Mozambique to the Shire highlands east of Lake Malawi. The Yao had been well known to Portuguese writers (who called them Ajawa) since at least the seventeenth century, as they organised caravans to bring ivory to the East African coast and to the Portuguese towns on the Zambesi. The homeland of the Yao at that time appears to have been the region of the Rovuma/Lujenda confluence in the northern part of modern Mozambique and, like their Makua-speaking neighbours, their society was matrilineal. Then, in the early nineteenth century, the historic patterns of long distance trade were disrupted by the great drought and by the increase in the slave trade. The drought led to the invasion of the Yao lands by Makua-speaking peoples from the south who were said to have obtained guns from coastal traders. Around 1830, at the height of the drought, a number of Yao groups began to migrate along the established trade routes to the better watered and more fertile regions of the Shire Highlands. This was no mass movement of a whole people, but the gradual relocation of separate Yao groups, moving independently, while others remained in their ancestral homeland.

Coinciding with this migration, many of the Yao appeared to have adopted a form of Islam. The precise reasons for this are not known but Islamic law allowed Yao men to establish patrilineal families made up of their slaves and slave wives. This was an undoubted attraction for the Yao rulers who now established powerful states along the edge of the Shire highlands. The Yao, while not abandoning the ivory trade, now began to round up slaves in the highland region and in the Shire valley, and to organise the expansion of the trade in slaves with the coast, arming themselves with guns bought from the proceeds of slaving.

The Transformation of Mozambique in mid-century

By 1850 south-eastern Africa had recovered from the years of drought and the turmoil of the Ngoni invasions but the social and political landscape had changed in many important ways. In the north the slave trade had led to the emergence of a number of alliances or confederacies among the clans of the Makua-speaking people. By coming together under powerful military leaders the population were able to protect themselves against raids by slavers and the Ngoni from the Rovuma valley. It also enabled them to participate themselves in the slave trade. In the middle of the century the most important of these groups was the Gwangwara, who imitated the Ngoni in their organisation and tactics and were often mistaken for Ngoni, and the followers of Namarulo who raided the Islamic and Portuguese trading settlements on the coast.

The northern region of Mozambique also experienced the spread of Zanzibari influence. The 'soft power' of the Zanzibar state, exercised through the appointment of officials, the flying of the Zanzibar flag and the offer of the Sultan's protection, proved increasingly attractive to the small Islamic communities around Tungue Bay in the north near Cape Delgado and to some further south. In October 1880 Consul O'Neill described a visit to Tungue.

> Found the Zanzibar flag hoisted here and the place occupied by a Jamedar and a party of the Sultan's soldiers. Sent my servant on shore to deliver the usual notice of arrival. He returned in a short time with a message from the Jamedar, begging me not to land, unless I had letters from the Sultan [of Zanzibar], until he had consulted with the Arabs of the place. Upon receiving this I immediately went ashore and interviewed this official, whom I found seated in consultation with a number of Arabs, and asked him if he had sent a message requesting me not to land. He replied that he had, as no white man ever came here without letters from the Sultan. On my explaining from whence I came, and telling him also that I had been some years on the Zanzibar coast without ever until now receiving such a reception from the Sultan's authorities, he became very polite, and ended by offering me any assistance I might require. The behaviour of this Jamedar and the Wali at Tunghi, is only noticeable as a proof of the semblances of power held by some of these officials.[10]

Further south the ancient Islamic trading town of Angoche had started to expand its influence in the interior using guns obtained in the slave trade to recruit and arm an increasingly formidable army. Under the leadership of Mussa Quanto this army raided as far as the Shire valley and threatened the region of the Quelimane *prazos*.

Change had also come to the Zambesi valley. The society based around the *prazos* had changed radically and the region was now dominated by five powerful families whose Portuguese names disguise the fact that they were mostly of Asian origin. Deeply Africanised, they conducted their affairs in the same way as warlords who had emerged in the north. The economy of the polities ruled by these families was partly based on slave trading but increasingly on the revived and expanding trade in ivory.

The revival of the ivory trade resulted from an expanding market in Europe and was another aspect of the penetration of the region precipitated by the world demand for African resources. Before the nineteenth century ivory had been brought by Yao or Bisa caravans to be traded at the Zambesi towns, but now, as the ivory trade picked up, trading expeditions were organised by the Zambesi Portuguese themselves. The route they took was up the Zambesi to its confluence with the Luangwa and the Kafue and in 1861 an official Portuguese expedition, led by Albino Manuel Pacheco, reopened the old fair at Zumbo, abandoned since 1835.[11] As Portuguese and Afro-Portuguese ivory traders became established in the region, land concessions were negotiated with local African rulers, sometimes accompanied by a repetition of the old tactics of intervention in locally disputed successions. Titles to the land thus acquired were then sought from the Portuguese government. In this way new *prazos* were created and the old institutions of Zambesia received a new lease of life, while communities of *chicunda* elephant hunters became established deep in the interior.

In his account of the expedition to restore Zumbo Pacheco described the way in which Portuguese sovereignty over the African peoples was consolidated.

Having concluded my journey and restored my strength, which had begun to be exhausted through work and illness, I began to carry out the orders which had been expressly given to me in my instructions. I sent to inform Buruma of my arrival and the reason which had brought me to this place and, in the name of the governor of the district, I requested that he should come to hand over the territory which, by orders from above, had been placed under his administration since 1836. At the same time, and in the same way, I informed *régulos* Masombe and Mutunda that, according to ancient custom, they also were obliged to be present at these formalities. I waited for some days for my notification to have an effect for I had omitted to send a present or to pay the respects which were due to the said *régulo* since I was entirely ignorant of this formality. Once this important lacuna had been filled the aforementioned Buruma, accompanied by a numerous suite, appeared on the afternoon of 24 March, showing in his face that he expected to receive a considerable reward for his trouble. I was not mistaken.[12]

The old fair at Manica was also restored and some gold began once again to be traded. It was also the availability of ivory that attracted traders from the Zambesi. Manica, however, was in the region which was tributary to the Gaza kingdom and the Portuguese traded there on sufferance from the Gaza king.

By the 1850s the Portuguese were actively in trying to increase the effectiveness of their presence in eastern Africa. In 1842 Portugal had finally agreed to co-operate with Britain in establishing naval patrols against the slave trade. These focused on the slave trade in the northern part of the coast and the Portuguese took advantage of them to strengthen their presence and to establish firmer ties with the Islamic polities of the region. Not all the campaigns against the slavers, however, were successful and the expansion of Portugal's effective presence on the coast was slow.

The Afro-Portuguese warlords and the Zambesi Wars[13]

It was in the Zambesi valley, where Portuguese and Africans had traded and lived together since the sixteenth century and where a distinctive Afro-Portuguese creole culture had grown up, that the contradictions between traditional social and economic relations and the forces of the modern outside world led to a prolonged series of wars that ended with the virtual destruction of the old creole society.

The long drawn out and complex conflicts, together referred to as the Zambesi Wars, lasted from the 1840s into the twentieth century. During the period of the drought and the Ngoni invasions a number of powerful families, mostly of Asian origin, had established their control over the *prazos* which had been abandoned by the older generation of *prazo senhors*. Among these the most important were the Caetano Pereiras, who founded a militarised state on the north bank of the Zambesi opposite Tete, taking over the north bank *prazos* and territory which had formed part of Undi's kingdom. The polity carved out by the Caetano Pereiras was known as Macanga and the family acquired or assumed the traditional title of Chicucuru. Macanga was very much involved with the ivory trade and the *chicunda* clients of the Pereiras were active in advancing into the northern interior.

The great rivals of the Pereiras were the Da Cruz, apparently of Thai origin, who rented vacant *prazos* both north and south of the Zambesi. The Da Cruz fortified a stronghold at Massangano at the confluence of the Luenha and the Zambesi from where they could dominate river traffic moving up the Zambesi towards Tete. The third Indian family of note was the Vas dos Anjos who controlled land on the lower Shire river from their stronghold at Shamo near Mount Morumbala. From this vantage point their *chicunda* captains penetrated the upper reaches of the Shire, buying slaves from the Yao. There were other important families, also of Indian origin. The area around Sena was dominated by the Ferrão family who held a precarious position subject to the Gaza kingdom which periodically levied tribute on the Sena Portuguese. Finally, and in the end most important of all, because he became the closest ally of the Portuguese authorities, was Manuel António de Sousa, from Goa, who became a successful elephant hunter in the 1840s and gradually established a power base in Manica from where he conquered the ancient Karanga state of Barue.

The only one of these families not of Asian origin was the Alves da Silva who were Portuguese. They took over the *prazos* north of Quelimane and, when Quelimane became closed to slaving, established their own port at the mouth of the Moniga river.

These warlords were in some respects the heirs of the old *prazo senhors* and like them they attached considerable importance to land titles granted by the Portuguese authorities and the nominal ranks they held in the local militias. Like them also they depended on the Portuguese controlled ports to export their ivory and import the firearms they needed for their hunting and slave raiding activities. Moreover when they conquered and occupied new territory they always raised the Portuguese flag and received the submission of the local population in the name of Portugal.

However, in other respects they were very different. This new brand of warlord raised and maintained formidable armies of *chicunda* soldiers and built large fortified strongholds, known as *aringas*, from which they dominated the surrounding population and which proved very difficult to attack. They also immersed themselves more completely in local African customs, marrying into the families of local African elites and acquiring all the trappings of traditional African rulers. They became known by African names and titles. The Caetano Pereiras used the title of Chicucuru, the Da Cruz were known by their African sobriquets of Nhaude and Bonga and eventually used the traditional title of Motontora. The Vas dos Anjos also used the African name of Bonga and the Alves da Silva that of Mpassu. Sousa, having seized Barue and married a daughter of the Macombe, eventually assumed this venerable title himself in 1880. Although these Afro-Indian families were nominally Christian, on their death their spirits continued to speak through mediums according to the patterns of belief common among Zambesi peoples.

The *chicunda* clients of these families were no longer, in any real sense, slaves but were a military elite and their captains held considerable power and in some cases supplanted the ruling families. After the demise of the Mpassu and his brother, the *chicunda* soldiers of Maganja established what has been described as a military republic, which they ruled from the Mpassu's great *aringa*. Sousa's captains also operated as independent rulers when their master was captured by the British in Manica in 1891. By the end of the nineteenth century the *chicunda* had established a firm ethnic identity which proudly distinguished them from the other ethnic groups of the Zambesi valley, while the inhabitants of the different polities also were often referred to as though they possessed a distinct ethnicity, the followers of the Vas dos Anjos being known as Massingire and those of the Alves da Silva as Manganjas.

From the early 1850s the Portuguese authorities tried to establish some control over these warlords partly to suppress their slaving activities and face down the criticisms levelled at them by the British, and partly in pursuit of the liberal policies of the Lisbon government that wanted the colonies to enjoy free trade and to develop peaceful commerce and plantation agriculture. In trying to assert their authority the Portuguese embarked on wars, which began successfully but soon involved them in a series of spectacular military disasters.

The main problem the Portuguese faced in trying to establish their authority was the lack of an effective military force on which they could rely. From the start they had to supplement the few soldiers they had with locally recruited *chicunda*. This, in effect, meant enlisting one warlord to fight another, which was an inherently unsatisfactory position.

The first phase of the Zambesi Wars began in the late 1840s when forces raised by the government unsuccessfully tried to attack Macanga. With the establishment of the Da Cruz at Massangano in 1849, conflict soon broke out between that family and the Pereiras leading to the first attack on the Da Cruz *aringa* in 1853 and the following year to another unsuccessful government expedition raised on the lower Zambesi. The next phase of the wars took place on the lower Zambesi where *chicunda* in the service of the Vas dos Anjos were raiding the Sena *prazos* for slaves, while fighters from Angoche, under the command of Mussa Quanto, raided for slaves in the former Quelimane *prazos*. In dealing with these threats the Portuguese, making use of the services of the *chicunda* of Afro-Portuguese friendly to the government, had some success driving the Vas dos Anjos from their *aringa* at Shamo in 1858 and supporting an expedition organised by João Bonifacio Alves da Silva in 1861 which destroyed Mussa Quanto's base in Angoche. The year 1861 also witnessed the successful government expedition to reopen the fair at Zumbo.

Encouraged by these successes the government once again sought to reduce the power of the Da Cruz who controlled both banks of the Zambesi below Tete. This time some troops were sent from Portugal and Goa to support the locally raised forces. In all four expeditions were launched against Massangano between 1867 and 1869. Ill-equipped and unfamiliar with African warfare, these expeditions resulted in spectacular failure, the heads of slaughtered soldiers being displayed on the stockade that surrounded the Da Cruz *aringa*. After these defeats a lull ensued and no further attempt was made to capture Massangano until the 1880s when the international environment of the scramble for African colonies forced the Portuguese once again to seek to establish their authority within the core of their colony.

The slave trade continues

Although in the 1840s Portugal had eventually combined with Britain to suppress the seaborne slave trade and had mounted joint expeditions against some of the known centres of the trade, and although Brazil had formally ceased to import slaves in 1851, the trade in African slaves continued unabated, driven now by forces within Africa itself.

When Livingstone and his companions brought the first steam boats to the Zambesi in 1858, they found the slave trade still very much alive, but now largely serving markets inside Africa itself, supplying slave soldiers to the armies of Afro-Portuguese and Islamic warlords who were carving out domains for themselves in the Mozambique lowlands. There was also growing demand for agricultural labour as the expansion of the export of African foodstuffs—in particular grains and oil seeds—was just beginning. If this trade in slaves within Africa was flourishing, so too was the external slave trade, in spite of the efforts of the Portuguese authorities and the Royal Navy. One important market existed in the French islands of Réunion, Mayotte and Nossi Bé. As the purchase of slaves was now illegal, French planters adopted the system of contracting supposedly free labour on the African coast. The slave trading networks operating on the Mozambique coast supplied the French with this so-called *engagé* labour—a loophole in the anti-slave trade treaties that was hard to close. On average 4,250 labourers were recruited for the French islands each year between 1860 and the 1890s.

By the 1880s a large market had also opened up in Madagascar. In the eighteenth and the early part of the nineteenth centuries Madagascar had supplied slaves for the French planters in the Mascarenes but in 1820 Britain had forced a treaty on Radama, the Merina ruler, by which he agreed to put an end to this slave trade. As Madagascar stopped exporting slaves, it began to develop its own demand for slave imports. This was due to two factors, the Merina conquests in the north, resulting in a need for slaves to fill the ranks of the army, and the growth of the demand for agricultural labour. The Madagascar market continued to expand—with possibly as many as 23,000 slaves being imported annually during the 1880s and continuing to the end of the century when the establishment of French administration in 1900 finally brought it to an end.[14]

This late expansion of the seaborne slave trade was no longer conducted from the main ports of the coast and instead operated from new areas that had been virtually unknown and unexplored by the Portuguese a generation earlier. This in turn brought about changes in the routes used by the caravans coming from inland and in the *modus operandi* of the trade itself. The slave trade had become an African affair not only with regards supply but also markets. To obtain slaves, traders organised armed expeditions, which operated ever further inland. Male slaves were incorporated into newly enlarged armies, which served the interests of 'warlords' like Namarulo in northern Mozambique or the ruling elites of Angoche whose influence now extended inland towards the Shire and Lake Malawi. Other groups like the Ngoni or the Gwangwara raided the country inland from the Querimba Islands, taking captives to swell their numbers as well as to sell into the market. The Anglican missionary W.P. Johnson, established at the town of the Yao ruler Mataka in the 1880s, witnessed the assembly and departure of slave caravans—indeed he accompanied one of them heading for the coast.

> The heads of caravans made friends with the headmen...and generally left some intelligent man at the larger villages there, who would pick up a good number of slaves while they themselves... made friends with the chiefs there, principally with the Angoni. Sometimes they would help these chiefs with their guns in raiding and so have a share of the captives. At other times they would buy captives already taken by the Angoni.... Such people taken in war, furnish the principal supply of slaves, but two other classes are fairly large. First, there were people who had been sold in order to get rid of them, for instance those who had been convicted on some serious charge of witchcraft, which might

or might not mean that the man or woman was a really bad character. Anybody who was merely suspected of having caused the death of another might be sold away from his village if he was friendless.... Second, another class of slaves consisted of people sold away in times of great famine. This need not imply any cruelty on the part of their relatives, as those who were sold were often willing to go for the sake of getting food....[15]

Further south both Inhambane and Delagoa Bay became centres of the trade, the slaves coming from the inland Ngoni and Ngoni related states. In the 1860s the rising demand for labour in South Africa led to the slave trade in the south evolving into the organised export of contract labour.

The expansion of African agricultural production in the nineteenth century

One of the most important drivers of the late nineteenth century slave trade was to be found in the great expansion of African agriculture, as African growers started to produce grain, oil-bearing seeds, cashew, copra and rubber for the world market. As the areas under cultivation expanded, slaves were obtained to provide additional labour and the carriers to take products to the coast. The growth of the export trade in agricultural products, which began in the 1860s, reached a peak in the 1880s and continued into the colonial period, was significant in a number of ways. Before this, south-east Africa's trade with the outside world had been almost exclusively in ivory, gold and slaves— commodities which had not required any manufacturing process, and little value added by human labour. Even the cattle exports, which began to be important in the south towards the end of the eighteenth century, and which saw African rulers replenishing their cattle herds by raiding neighbours, a contributory factor to warfare in the region, probably required little change to traditional herding practices.

The export of rubber in the second half of the century was a new commodity and to some extent fitted the traditional pattern of extraction without value added. Rubber came from trees and vines that grew wild in the bush. African traders bled the trees but did not cultivate them in any way. Other agricultural exports, however, had to be grown or, in the case of copra, processed before export. The labour input was considerable as was the organisation of production.

The British Consul, Henry O'Neill, described this 'agricultural revolution' in detail in his reports to the British Foreign Office in February 1881.

> On passing through the Kivolani district, which may be said to extend 10 or 12 miles to the South of Mokambo Bay, I was particularly struck with its fertility and the industrious nature of its people, as evidenced by the cultivation carried on in it. Several thousands of acres are here under cultivation, chiefly with cassava root and Kaffir corn, in a great part the food supply of Mozambique, and also with a little amendoim. The latter however is chiefly grown in the higher country inland, and is brought down by the Makuas in great quantities for sale. I had not sufficient time to make a properly careful enquiry, into the nature of the labour by which all this cultivation is carried on, but, from what I saw I should say that much of it is here done by the country people themselves. On the 'shambas' of the chiefs things would be managed differently.[16]

In July of the same year O'Neill was visiting Angoche.

> I saw a considerable tract of country covered with this plant [groundnuts], now nearly full grown and ready for the collection of the crop, but here as well as in the town I was assured that the greater quantity came down from the villages of the Makua country 6 and 8 hours, and even a day's journey further inland.... The labour on the shambas of these chiefs, outside Portuguese jurisdiction, is carried on by slaves, but an immense amount of cultivation is collectively carried on by the free Makuas, each one working his plot, large or small, as it pleases him where ground costs nothing, and bringing its crop to the coast for

barter. Whilst at Angoche I saw several parties coming in, in twos and threes to sell their produce and on enquiry was always assured it was the property of the bearers, who obtained cloth in exchange.[17]

There is little doubt that the rise of the export trade in agricultural products was, in part, achieved by the purchase of slaves to increase the labour force. This was not an entirely new development as the capture of slaves, especially women, in warfare had always been a way in which communities that depended on agriculture rather than cattle herding, increased their productive (and reproductive) capacity. However, in the context of the nineteenth century this growing internal market for slaves had a special significance. As the slave trade to the Atlantic destinations was ended after the 1850s and the traditional trade to Arabia and the Gulf was curtailed after 1873, the organised networks that supplied slaves had to find new markets. Madagascar and the *engagé* trade to the French islands remained important but increasingly slave dealers turned to internal markets. After 1870 a wholly new market for labour opened up in South Africa as mining for diamonds, gold and coal rapidly expanded. The mobilisation of labour for the mines was to take the numbers of Mozambicans who went, or were sent, abroad to work, to new heights.

The nineteenth-century slave trade, therefore, transformed social and political organisation in a variety of ways. It helped the creation of larger political units, brought into being by Muslim or Afro-Portuguese warlords who equipped their 'slave' armies with firearms paid for from the profits of the trade. At the same time it encouraged the expansion of Islam as the coastal communities began to play a more active role in establishing slaving networks in the interior. Other communities found it necessary to organise into larger units more effectively to protect themselves against slavers and to acquire slaves of their own to increase agricultural output. The rise of the migrant labour phenomenon was to bring about profound social change, particularly in societies in the south and centre of the country, as migrant labourers broke free from traditional social ties and the societies themselves became increasingly monetised.

4

THE INTERVENTION OF EUROPEANS AND THE SCRAMBLE FOR AFRICA

British and French interest in south-eastern Africa

Mozambique had for centuries been part of the Indian Ocean world and had been visited by merchants from India, the Gulf and Arabia. The arrival of Europeans in the form of the Portuguese had not radically altered the relations of the indigenous population with the outside world but the Portuguese presence had deterred other Europeans—Dutch, English and French—from taking any major part in the affairs of the region. By the late eighteenth century, however, a variety of circumstances converged to increase European interest in south-eastern Africa.

As indicated in the previous chapter, French purchases of slaves brought increasing numbers of French vessels to Mozambican ports and in the early nineteenth century French planters from Réunion extended their activities to the Mozambique Channel, taking over the islands of Nossi Bé and Mayotte which, according to contemporary French propaganda, would become 'the Gibraltar of the Indian Ocean'. Wary of the strategic implications, the British, who had taken Mauritius from France in 1811, also began to extend their diplomatic and naval presence in the western Indian Ocean. This took two forms: the organisation of a hydrographic survey of the coast of eastern Africa and the gradual implementation of a policy to outlaw the seaborne slave trade.

The hydrographic survey of the East African coast was carried out by Commodore W.F.W. Owen between 1821 and 1826. As well as charting the coast, Owen used the opportunity presented by his command of British warships to try to establish a claim to Mombasa and Delagoa Bay, which he rightly appreciated were the two strategically most important points on the coast. Two accounts of the survey were published, Owen's journals in 1833 and an account by Captain Thomas Boteler in 1835. Owen's survey was gradually amended and improved as British warships paid ever more frequent visits to the coast and it prompted the Portuguese themselves to produce maps of the Mozambique coast and to carry out their own surveys. Then, during the 1880s, the British Consul in Mozambique, Henry O'Neill, a naval officer and expert in surveying, made his own careful survey of the main ports on the coast north of the Zambesi delta, enclosing his charts in his despatches to the Foreign Office and attaching detailed maps to the papers he presented to the Royal Geographical society.

Meanwhile the navy had begun to be actively involved in support of Britain's campaign against the slave trade. The campaign was underpinned by treaties made with Radama, the Merina king in Madagascar in 1820 and with the Sultan of Muscat in 1822, and subsequently by the treaty signed with Portugal in1842. After this date there were regular naval patrols in the Mozambique Channel and Britain established consulates to monitor the slave trade in Zanzibar (1840) and the Comoro Islands (1850) and finally in Mozambique itself in 1856. As a result of these activities a number of publications began to appear describing conditions on the Mozambique coast. Henry Salt published his *Voyage to Abyssinia* in 1814, which gave a colourful description of Mozambique Island. James Prior published two books in 1819 and 1820 giving an account of his cruises off the Mozambique coast and Lieutenant F.L. Barnard described a number of visits made to Quelimane and its environs in a book published in 1848. The first British Consul, Lyons McLeod, also recorded his, not very happy, experiences in a two volume work which appeared in 1860. In addition to these books, regular reports made to the British Parliament by the captains of the anti-slave trade cruisers were printed in the Parliamentary Papers.

As a result of these publications the coastal communities of Mozambique became much more widely known in the non-Portuguese world—and knowledge as always had a profound impact on attitudes and eventually on policy.

Meanwhile two other impulses, originating in Europe, were beginning to create waves in eastern Africa. The scientific exploration of Africa had begun in western Africa with expeditions to survey the Niger and the Zaire and to explore the Sahara. In eastern Africa the Portuguese had organised an expedition to the interior of Mozambique in 1798, which had, at least in part, a scientific purpose; the Portuguese officer A.C.P. Gamitto who had accompanied an official expedition to the Lunda kingdom in 1831–2 published in 1854 what is still one of the finest studies of African ethnography.[1] However, the first non-Portuguese explorer to undertake serious scientific work in Mozambique was Dr Wilhelm Peters who spent three years in Zambesia in the 1840s and eventually published seven volumes of scientific information on Mozambique between 1852 and 1882.

Missionary activity provided a second motive for Europeans to become involved in the African interior and in 1820 the London Missionary Society established its first missions in Madagascar. This was followed by the Church Missionary Society which began work in Ethiopia and sent its first missionaries to the East

African coast in 1846. These were protestant enterprises and were begun just as the victories of the liberals in Portugal were accompanied by the dissolution of the religious orders and the formal end of the Dominican mission in Mozambique.

These various strands of enterprise—scientific investigation, the campaign against the slave trade and missionary endeavour—came together in the person of David Livingstone who, directly and indirectly, was to have a major impact on the history of south-eastern Africa. Livingstone first visited south-eastern Africa in 1856 when he and his Makololo companions travelled down the Zambesi valley as the final act of his epic journey from Angola across the continent. Livingstone returned to London where the intense interest he aroused in Christian circles led to the founding of the Universities Mission to Central Africa (UMCA) in 1857. He also persuaded the British government to sponsor a major exploratory expedition to the Zambesi where, in pursuit of the campaign against the slave trade, Livingstone believed he could open a route to central Africa for the development of 'legitimate' commerce. Livingstone was accompanied by a botanist and a geologist to further the scientific objectives of the expedition.

Livingstone's Zambesi expedition lasted from 1858 to 1864. It demonstrated that the Zambesi did not provide unimpeded navigation from the sea to the interior, being blocked by the Cabora Bassa rapids, which Livingstone had not seen on his first journey. The Shire and the Rovuma rivers, which Livingstone also investigated, were also blocked by rapids or unpassable shallows. However, Livingstone did explore Lake Malawi, about which the outside world, and even the Zambesi Portuguese, had only the most uncertain information—Gamitto who travelled north of the Zambesi in the 1830s still appears to have thought it was simply a very wide river. In 1860 the first UMCA missionaries arrived, planting their church at Magomero on the Shire river just beyond the sphere of active Portuguese jurisdiction and in this way placing a rival European presence that was bound to conflict before long, not only with the Portuguese but with African polities established in the Shire Highlands.

Livingstone's expedition had other consequences. It prompted the Portuguese to become more actively involved in building a secure administration in the Zambesi valley, which resulted in Pacheco's successful reestablishment of the fair at Zumbo in 1861 but also in the disastrous wars against Massangano between 1867 and 1869. There was another, at the time wholly unforeseen, consequence of Livingstone's expedition, when some of his Makololo followers used their firearms to establish polities on the Shire river in the same manner as the Afro-Portuguese and Islamic warlords were doing at the same time. The Makololo, through their strong association with Livingstone and the British, came to be seen by the Portuguese as a fifth column in a region where they aspired to be the paramount power.

The exploration of Lake Malawi tempted Livingstone himself to return in 1866 to explore the route from the Rovuma up the Lujenda valley to the Lake, a route that was subsequently followed by missionaries from the UMCA who were based at Masasi in modern Tanzania. When Livingstone disappeared in the interior, a series of expeditions went in search of him, that led by E.D. Young travelling again through Portuguese Zambesia. After Livingstone's death in 1873 both the Church of Scotland and the Free Church of Scotland exerted themselves to found missions in the Shire Highlands and on the Lake which Livingstone had explored. These missions, which were established between 1875 and 1877, planted a Scottish community in the African interior which depended for its links with the outside world on a river passage through territory where the Portuguese had been established for four hundred years. These Scottish communities found themselves surrounded by potential enemies and their own internal divisions and some incidents of scandalous behaviour soon raised the question of where responsibility for them lay and under whose jurisdiction they came. Reluctantly the British government agreed to appoint a vice-consul in 1883, inching reluctantly towards the creation of some form of protectorate.

Probably the greatest impact that Livingstone had had, however, was to raise public awareness in Europe, and especially in Britain, of conditions in the south-eastern African interior. Livingstone's book *Narrative of an Expedition to the Zambezi and its Tributaries*, which appeared in 1866, was a masterpiece of African travel literature and inspired a generation of would be explorers. After its publication, the part of Africa that would become Mozambique, from being little known, became one of the most talked about regions of the continent.

The Boers and Delagoa Bay

Meanwhile, unmoved by any interest in science, missionary endeavour or a desire to end the slave trade, other people of European origin had begun to take an interest in the southern regions of Mozambique. By 1834 the movement into the interior of pastoralists from the Cape, which had begun soon after the British occupation of the Cape, first in 1795 and then permanently in 1806, had intensified, culminating in the mass movement of some 500 Boer families and their servants, which became known as the Great Trek.

As the trekkers moved north they founded *ad hoc* 'republics' and sought access to the sea in order to become independent of the British authorities in the Cape. One group, led by Louis Tregardt, made the thousand mile journey across the Drakensberg mountains towards Delagoa Bay which it reached in April 1838. There the party fell ill with malaria and Tregardt himself died. Crossing the low veldt in the hinterland of the Bay, the trek oxen and horses were severely affected by tse-tse fly, which made this route to the coast difficult as well as remote. Other trekkers meanwhile had tried to settle in the Natal region where they came once again into conflict with the British who annexed the area in 1842.

Since Britain's annexation of Natal barred the way, Delagoa Bay, for all its difficulty of access, became the window on the world for the new Boer republics. The commercial activity of the small Portuguese settlement in the bay gradually grew and some Portuguese and Afro-Portuguese hunters and traders made their way from the port onto the high veldt. The most important of these was João Albasini who allegedly employed hundreds of African hunters armed with rifles. Albasini married an Afrikaner woman and established close relations with some of the high veldt Afrikaner communities, founding his own settlement which he called the Colónia de São Luís. Through his African wife he also founded a family that was to become of some importance in Mozambique during the period of the Republic.

Although Delagoa Bay and the Portuguese settlement there, known as Lourenço Marques, gradually grew in importance for the Afrikaner republics, as it was the nearest seaport to the South African Republic (henceforward Transvaal) and was a port out-side direct British control, it became increasingly clear that the problems presented by the difficult route to the port would only be resolved by the building of a railway. This became a possibility once the first gold and diamonds were discovered in the interior in 1867—just four years after Livingstone departed from the Zambesi and while the Portuguese were struggling with their unsuccessful military campaigns against Massangano.

In 1869 the Transvaal and the Portuguese signed a treaty, which marked out an agreed frontier between their spheres of interest. By this agreement the Transvaal recognised Portuguese sovereignty over the Bay and over a hinterland extending to the

Lebombo mountains. It also agreed to build a road to the port. This treaty was followed in 1873 by a free trade agreement. The 1869 treaty prompted Britain to dust off the treaties that Owen had made with some African rulers in Delagoa Bay in 1823 and challenge Portugal's sovereignty in the region. The subsequent dispute over Delagoa Bay was to be the first serious conflict between Europeans over the possession of territory in south-eastern Africa. A railway to Delagoa Bay would make any port established there the principal port of southern Africa and one of the most important port-cities of the Indian Ocean. Moreover it would be a port outside British control. Surprisingly the British government agreed in 1871 to arbitration by the president of France, Marshal Macmahon. When MacMahon delivered his verdict in 1875 it confirmed Portugal's possession of the Bay, a decision that was to have profound consequences. Shortly after this announcement the Transvaal's president, Thomas François Burgers, aware that the Bay would now not be under British control, set off for Europe to try to raise money for the building of a railway. Britain's dominant strategic position in southern Africa had begun to crumble.

The events that followed can be described as a bilateral attempt by two European countries, Britain and Portugal, to settle the future of south-eastern Africa. It was largely unsuccessful and was rapidly overtaken by events in the following decade but it reveals the strategic and economic importance that Delagoa Bay had come to assume in the minds of contemporaries. Following the discovery of the Kimberley diamond mines in 1871 Britain had moved to try to bring the colonies and republics in South Africa together under one administration, as had been successfully accomplished in Canada. In 1874 Lord Carnarvon initiated his Confederation project but the Macmahon Award threatened the whole plan as it gave the Transvaal the opportunity to 'go it alone' without Britain. Britain's response was to invade the Transvaal and annex it to the Crown in 1877.

Britain's attitude to the Delagoa Bay railway now changed. It saw the building of a railway as of prime importance for the future of a united South Africa and entered into negotiations with the Portuguese for a comprehensive treaty (the Lourenço Marques Treaty) that would provide not only for the building of a railway but at the same time would resolve the difficulties that were arising over the navigation and commerce of the Zambesi.

The Lisbon Geographical Society and Portugal's forward policy in the interior

The European partition of south-eastern Africa was almost exclusively an affair of Britain and Portugal. The French, Belgians and Germans, important players in the drama that led to the creation of Angola, were, at most, 'voices off' in the wings, seldom appearing on stage. As for the African states that were already in existence in the area, they were excluded from international negotiations as Europeans did not recognise their legal personality nor their rights in international law, yet they were not unimportant when the factors shaping the outcome of negotiations are considered.

The Lourenço Marques Treaty, negotiated between the British ambassador in Lisbon and the Portuguese government and signed in May 1879 might, on paper, have resolved the main issues between the two European states. It made provision for the building of the railway from the port of Lourenço Marques to the Transvaal and declared the Zambesi an open waterway, fixing a low tariff for commerce using the river—an important consideration for the Scottish missions established in the Shire Highlands. Although this treaty, and the Congo Treaty that followed, did not draw any frontiers they would have confirmed Central Africa as a Portuguese sphere of influence, though one open to British commercial interests. It was essentially a liberal and laissez-faire solution to international rivalries avoiding the competitive nationalism that was soon to colour all African negotiations.

While the treaty negotiations were still underway, Britain and Portugal showed that collaboration rather than conflict could be beneficial. The Zulu War of 1879 raised the prospect of a coalition of African kingdoms against Britain. Henry O'Neill, the newly appointed British Consul, came south to persuade the African kings on the southern shores of the Bay not to join the Zulus while the Portuguese in Lourenço Marques on the northern arm of the bay stopped imported firearms from reaching the Zulus and allowed British troops to pass through.

The Lourenço Marques Treaty, however, foundered. It was never ratified and the political realities on which it had been built crumbled when the Transvaal Afrikaners rebelled against British rule. In 1881 Britain once again recognised Transvaal's independence. The imperial interest in building a railway that would only benefit the Transvaal now disappeared and with it the treaty, though both Britain and Portugal tried to salvage something from the wreckage by incorporating the agreements that had been reached over the navigation of the Zambesi into the new Congo treaty.

Meanwhile, the treaty had also run into problems with domestic lobbies in both Britain and Portugal. In 1875, inspired by the accounts of the African interior published by Livingstone, and by the expeditions led by Cameron and by the explorers sponsored by Leopold of the Belgians, a group of scientists and politicians in Lisbon founded the Lisbon Geographical Society. The aim of this society was to sponsor exploration in the areas inland of the coastal settlements where the Portuguese had been established for hundreds of years. However, the objectives of the Society were wider than mere exploration. They wanted Portugal to pursue a 'forward' policy in Africa and to be more active in promoting colonisation. The idea was mooted that Africa could become a second Brazil which could bring to metropolitan Portugal some of the benefits that it had previously derived from its great South American empire.[2] The interest groups involved in the Lisbon Geographical Society were extremely suspicious of the Lourenço Marques Treaty and the subsequent Congo Treaty negotiations by which Britain and Portugal tried to keep alive their mutual collaboration. As an alternative approach to African questions they decided to sponsor expeditions, which would assert Portugal's primacy in the central African interior.[3]

Reflecting on the expeditions of Livingstone and Cameron, the Marquês de Lavradio was later to write: 'Being the first with discovery, the first with occupation, the first to colonise, the first to produce geographical works, we could not be the last to undertake these new crossings [of Africa]. To our *amour propre* was added a political rationale'.[4] In 1877 an exploratory expedition led by Serpa Pinto and Brito Capelo set off from the coast of Angola. The expedition split, with Serpa Pinto exploring the headwaters of the Zambesi before travelling south east across the Kalahari to Durban, while Capelo and his companion Ivens explored the interior of what would later become Angola. These expeditions were duly celebrated in publications, with Serpa Pinto's account appearing in 1881 in English, German and French, and in 1883 in Italian—a well-organised exercise in propaganda. Portugal was asserting its presence in the African interior and the Lisbon Geographical Society duly published a map showing the whole of central Africa as Portuguese territory. In 1883 Capelo and Ivens set out on their own journey from Angola across Africa, following the trade routes of the Afro-Portuguese and reaching the Mozambique coast in June 1885. Meanwhile a third expedition had been organised to assert the Portuguese presence in the region between Ibo and Lake Malawi which had already been crossed by British missionaries and by Consul O'Neill. This expedition was led by Augusto

Cardoso and was successful, from the Portuguese point of view, in making a number of treaties with African rulers, including some of the most powerful of the Yao.

As part of this new forward policy, Lisbon began to grant mining and agricultural concessions in the hope that this would lead to investment in the African colonies and pre-empt any similar activities by foreigners. In 1878 the Lisbon government granted a large timber and mining concession to a Portuguese diplomat, Joaquim Paiva de Andrada. For the next six years Andrada unsuccessfully sought financial backing for his concessions but in 1884 he joined forces with the Zambesi warlord, Manuel António de Sousa, who had occupied the ancient independent kingdom of Barue in 1880. Sousa and Andrada now planned the occupation of Mashonaland, Sousa with the idea of establishing himself as king over all the land between the Mazoe and the sea, Andrada with the idea of floating a company to mine gold throughout a region known for its ancient mines.

In 1884 events in western Africa led to the calling of the Berlin Congress. This international conference was primarily concerned with the future of the Congo and Niger regions but when the basin of the Congo came to be defined in the 1885 protocol, the central African Lakes and much of northern Mozambique were included in the region covered by the agreements. In the event this was to have little influence beyond limiting Portugal's freedom to impose tariffs.

British explorers describe northern Mozambique

While southern and central Mozambique was entering the consciousness of the outside world, the interior of northern Mozambique remained, as it had for centuries, almost entirely unknown. Although the centre of Portuguese administration was located on Mozambique Island, Portuguese from this base seem seldom to have ventured more than a few miles inland. This lack of enterprise was often attributed to the singularly ferocious Makua-speaking people who were alleged to prevent any Europeans penetrating their domain. This explanation is highly unlikely as the few Portuguese who are known to have travelled in Makua country (for example Gaspar Bocarro in the seventeenth century or Moraes Pereira in the eighteenth) did so without any difficulty and the British explorers of the nineteenth century also found travelling throughout the region to be relatively problem free. A more convincing reason for the apparent lack of any Portuguese knowledge of the interior lies in the nature of the relations between the coastal Portuguese and the Makua-speaking peoples. The Portuguese had developed collaborative relations with the Islamic peoples of the coast who acted as middlemen in the commerce of the interior. Slaves and ivory, and later raw materials like rubber and agricultural produce, were traded via these networks of middlemen which, built up over long periods of time, would have been rudely disrupted if the Portuguese themselves had sought to travel or trade in the interior.

After Livingstone's pioneering journey up the Lujenda valley in 1866 a succession of British missionaries and explorers crossed and recrossed the northern Mozambique interior, describing the results of their journeys in papers presented to the Royal Geographical Society in London. In 1878 Joseph Thomson had accompanied an expedition organised by the Society to explore the route between Dar es Salaam and Lake Malawi. Meanwhile the UMCA had become increasingly active. After the initial failure of the mission in the Shire valley under Bishop Charles Mackenzie, the UMCA had been relocated to Zanzibar from where a station had been built in 1874 at Masasi in the south of modern Tanzania. From there a succession of missionaries opened up an overland route to Lake Malawi where a settlement and forward base was made on Likoma Island. In 1880 the

Reverend Chauncy Maples's paper 'Masasi and the Rovuma District in East Africa' was presented to the Royal Geographical Society', which was followed by 'Makua Land, between the Rivers Rovuma and Luli' in 1882. Maples also published the first study of the Makua language. In 1880 the first Anglican mission had been established among the Yao by W.P. Johnson, whose travels took him as far as Lake Malawi where he investigated the connection between the minor lakes of Amaramba and Chiuta and the river system of northern Mozambique. Although Masasi was attacked by the Gwangwara and burnt in 1882, the station was rebuilt and in 1885 another missionary, J.T. Last, travelled as far as the Namuli mountains.

While the missionaries were exploring the country along the road leading to Lake Malawi and their forward base at Likoma, two British Consuls had also been active. Frederic Elton, who had been appointed in 1875, spent two years travelling along the Mozambique coast and exploring the country around Lake Malawi, where he died of fever in 1877. His collected papers were published in 1879 under the title *Travels and Researches among the Lakes and Mountains of Eastern and Central Africa*. In 1879 Henry O'Neill was appointed his successor. Between the time of his appointment and 1885, O'Neill made some fourteen journeys in northern Mozambique. He explored and mapped the coast with its creeks, offshore islands and small trading settlements and then embarked on some pioneering journeys inland, to the very areas where local information suggested that the local populations were irredeemably hostile. O'Neill visited the Makonde of the Mueda plateau and made two journeys through Makua and Lomwe country to Lake Malawi, returning by a southern route to the coast. In his reports to the Royal Geographical Society, he described large areas of northern Mozambique, which had never before been explored by Europeans. O'Neill was a skilled surveyor and provided detailed geographical information about this region. Information obtained on his travels soon found its way into Portuguese publications and he himself wrote two papers for the Lisbon Geographical Society. As well as being a surveyor, O'Neill was a good linguist and made a careful comparison of the different dialects in the region and, unlike some other European travellers of the time, he established good relations with all the African groups he met. He appears in Rider Haggard's *King Solomon's Mines* as Captain Good. In 1885 the Royal Geographical Society awarded him its Gold Medal. O'Neill planned a two volume book about northern Mozambique. However, this was never published.[5]

In 1889 O'Neill was involved in events at the north end of Lake Malawi, which proved to be controversial. He was retired to the insignificant posts of Consul at Livorno and then Rouen. He was so forgotten that he did not earn an entry in either the old or the new *Dictionary of National Biography*.

The Rose Coloured Map

That Africa could be a 'new Brazil' had been central to the propaganda of the Lisbon Geographical Society. The Berlin Congress now made it urgent for Portugal to develop a coherent strategy for its African possessions, which had not existed before. The Congress had laid down basic rules for European countries wanting to claim sovereignty over African territory. Brushing aside the traditional Portuguese argument that prior discovery conferred rights, the Congress decided that effective occupation should be the accepted criterion and that all claims should be notified to the international community. This was to lead to a stampede on the part of adventurers, commercial interests and empire building enthusiasts to be seen to occupy territory. In central Africa Portugal had a head start. Portuguese traders had already penetrated to the headwaters of the Zambesi and to the

Luba Kingdom in the Lakes region. Trading stations and depots existed and the Portuguese flag flew from stockades. No other European country had any claim to occupation which could rival that of Portugal; the claims of the indigenous African peoples were, of course, not considered beyond the perfunctory process needed to make treaties of protection or to obtain the concession of mineral rights.

In 1885 Portugal produced a map in which its claim to territory was coloured pink (*cor-de-rosa* in Portuguese and usually rendered rose-coloured in English) and extended across Africa from Angola to the Mozambique coast. It included Barotseland, the Ndebele Kingdom and Lake Malawi. It was a bold assertion both of Portugal's intentions and the reality that this was an area where the presence of the Afro-Portuguese *sertanejos* gave Portugal an apparently unassailable precedence. Throughout 1886 and 1887 the Portuguese conducted bilateral negotiations with France and Germany settling the frontiers of Portuguese Guinea and the boundary between German and Portuguese spheres of influence on the southern borders of Angola. To each of these treaties the Portuguese attached their 'rose coloured map' hoping that this acquiescence in their clams by France and Germany would set firm into internationally recognised concrete.

Meanwhile expeditions were organised to occupy the 'rose coloured' territory. Paiva de Andrada, armed with an extensive land concession and backed by Sousa's *chicunda* soldiers set out to claim the region later known as Mashonaland. However, before he and Sousa could fulfil their ambitions, they had to face a coalition of local enemies, which linked the Da Cruz family in their stronghold of Massangano with the Shona ruler of Mtoko and the exiled aristocracy of Barue. In 1887 a Portuguese force captured the fortified *aringa* of Massangano and, elated by their victory, Andrada and Sousa went to Lisbon where the new

Mozambique Company was duly incorporated. They were six months ahead of Cecil Rhodes whose British South Africa Company was only formed in October of 1888.

During their absence the head of the Da Cruz clan reoccupied the old *aringa* at Massangano and once again raised rebellion on the middle of Zambesi. Another major expedition had to be mounted, led by the governor-general Augusto de Castilho. This time Massangano was not only captured but effectively neutralised, as a garrison of government troops was established there.[6]

Meanwhile time had been lost and Portugal's great opportunity had passed.

Cecil Rhodes, Salisbury and the Ultimatum[7]

In October 1888 Cecil Rhodes's agent Charles Rudd had obtained a concession of mining rights which covered the country that Paiva de Andrada had sought to occupy. Armed with this concession Rhodes established the British South Africa Company and in October 1889 obtained from the British government a charter which famously extended from the north of the Transvaal and to the west of Portuguese territory with no northern frontier fixed. Rhodes had no effective presence in this vast territory. Indeed he had no occupation at all but he had an overblown imperial rhetoric that talked about establishing British territory and building a railway from the Cape to Cairo. His plans cut right through Portugal's rose-coloured territory.

Portugal hastened to maintain its initiative and despatched two armed expeditions. In July 1888 Victor Cordon departed with a column to establish effective occupation along the Zambesi beyond Zumbo but was delayed by the war against Massangano. Another expedition under António Cardoso and Serpa Pinto was despatched to secure Portugal's position in the Shire valley and the highlands.

Even now, in the race between European powers to seize the territory of African people, the Portuguese were ahead of their Anglo-Saxon rivals. But it was not a race that would be won or lost in Africa itself. In January 1890, alarmed at the prospect of the Portuguese controlling the territory where Scottish missions were established, the British prime minister, Lord Salisbury, presented Portugal with an ultimatum to halt their African expeditions pending a negotiated settlement. Threatened with a naval blockade of Lisbon should they not comply, the Portuguese had to call a halt to Serpa Pinto's and Cordon's expeditions.

No such cessation of activity, however, applied to Rhodes. His Pioneer Column set out in June 1890 and in September raised the flag where later the city of Salisbury/Harare would be built. Meanwhile Alfred Sharpe proceeded on a treaty-making spree through the country that would later become Zambia. Rhodes had not only broken through Portugal's 'rose coloured' aspirations across the Zambesi to the north, he also planned to break through to the east and establish a corridor to the sea which would have cut Mozambique into two. In November 1890 troopers under the command of Major Forbes surrounded and captured Paiva da Andada and Manuel António de Sousa in Manica. Only then did Lord Salisbury issue an ultimatum to Rhodes as well to halt his land grab.

Gaza and the South

Since the 1840s southern Mozambique from the Zambesi to the Limpopo had been dominated by the kingdom of Gaza. The authority of the Gaza kings was exercised through the collection of tribute from subject populations, including the Zambesi Portuguese. Only to a limited extent were these populations incorporated into the Ngoni military and social system and when there was weakness at the centre, the peripheral regions became virtually independent. After the death of the Kingdom's founder, Soshangane, in 1858 Gaza was torn apart by a four year struggle for the succession. This was the first major civil war in Mozambique's history and it led to chaos and devastation over a wide area, just as the civil war that broke out a hundred and twenty years later was to. There was large scale loss of life, the regional economy was ruined and social life disrupted. The shock waves of the war were to send the first groups of migrants south towards the British colony of Natal to seek work on the sugar plantations. Umzila eventually triumphed and continued to rule a weakened Gaza from a capital in the Chimanimani mountains, distant from the coast and from the southern regions around the Limpopo. Although elephant hunters and ivory traders had contacts with Gaza, few Europeans attempted to travel in the kingdom. However, by the mid-1870s Gaza's isolation was under threat. To the north was the growing power of Manuel António de Sousa who was expanding his activities into the Manica region and in 1880 seized control of Barue. Meanwhile ever growing numbers of young men were making the journey to Natal and after 1871 to the diamond diggings and were returning with guns and money which was transforming traditional social relations, not least enabling them to pay bride price and escape the control of clan elders.

In 1884 Umzila died and his successor, Gungunhana, aware of the growing European interest in the region and concerned that he was losing control of the Manica and Zambesi region, entered into an agreement with the Portuguese authorities in Lourenço Marques. Gungunhana accepted a loose form of Portuguese protection and agreed to fly the Portuguese flag. He agreed that a Portuguese resident should reside at his capital and the first resident took up his position in May 1886. If Gungunhana believed that by this agreement he had secured his effective independence, the Portuguese for their part thought that this arrangement would secure their position in the aftermath of the Berlin Congress.

In June 1889 Gungunhana moved his capital from the Chimanimani mountains south to the Limpopo. This decision seems to have been made because Gaza was losing control of the populations in the south and in the hinterland of Inhambane. It was a move designed to reassert the king's control and coincided with the frenetic events of the Scramble further north. Rhodes believed that he might be able to bring Gaza within the sphere of interest of the British South Africa Company. When the treaty negotiations between Britain and Portugal stalled in the summer of 1890 Rhodes sent an emissary to sign a treaty of alliance with Gungunhana, promising him a large gift of rifles. In spite of these moves, the treaty that was eventually signed placed most of the Gaza Kingdom squarely within the frontiers of Mozambique, though as yet the Gaza Kingdom continued to maintain its independent status. The frontiers that were drawn recognised the historical reality of the existence of the Gaza Kingdom. Although some of the territory that the Gaza kings had ruled was incorporated into Rhodes's domain, the largest part of the kingdom came to form the southern part of the newly recognised Portuguese colony.

The Anglo-Portuguese treaty and the drawing of the Mozambique frontier

With Britain's ultimatum to Portugal delivered on 11 January 1890, the future shape of Mozambique ceased to be influenced by the people of the region and was now to be determined by diplomats in Europe. With many loose ends and with much potential for further conflict, Portuguese and British negotiators began their discussions in April 1890. At the same time Britain and Germany also met to settle their outstanding differences and territorial claims. Modern Africa was being born. The first set of proposals for drawing a frontier between British and Portuguese spheres of influence was completed in August 1890. It made provision for a corridor across Africa between Angola and Mozambique but allocated the high veldt of Mashonaland to Britain. The Portuguese Cortes refused to ratify the agreement and it was not until there had been further dangerous clashes between British and Portuguese forces in Africa that eventually agreement was reached in August 1891. This agreement drew the frontiers which, with only small amendment, are those of Mozambique today.

Although it is often claimed that the colonial powers drew Africa's frontiers with scant regard for local circumstances, it is worth pausing to see how Mozambique's borders reflected a historical reality. The division of the East African coast with the region between Cape Delgado and Delagoa Bay being recognised as a Portuguese sphere of interest, had been a reality since 1698 and was now consolidated in the treaty. The Rovuma river as a northern boundary left the trade routes that ran up the Lujenda Valley to Lake Malawi in Mozambique together with the commercial hinterlands of Ibo, Mozambique Island and Quelimane. The Zambesi valley as far inland as Zumbo, together with the low veldt to the north and south also reflected the history of the region as this had formed Portuguese territory since the eighteenth century and even earlier. However, the territory occupied by the *chicunda* further up the Zambesi in the nineteenth century was included in British territory. North of the Zambesi much of the land that had formed the commercial hinterland of Tete was also allocated to Mozambique. Drawing the frontiers south of the Zambesi to run along the escarpment of the high veldt and through the Manica highlands cut through the commercial hinterland of the Zambesi towns and deprived Mozambique of access to the high veldt regions, but again this represented the historical reality established in the eighteenth century when the Rosvi state had controlled the high veldt and prevented Portuguese traders from entering the country. In southern Mozambique most of the Gaza Kingdom was incorporated into Mozambique. Of the ports on the Mozambique coast, it was only Delagoa Bay, which had been allocated to Portugal by the Macmahon Award of 1875, that was cut off from its commercial hinterland—but this had already been decided in the treaty between the Portuguese and the Transvaal in 1869 and its effect had been mitigated by the free trade agreement which allowed traders from Delagoa Bay free access to the interior.

Only on the Shire was an arbitrary frontier drawn cutting across the river valley and leaving the British Protectorate as a salient thrust into Mozambican territory.

The aspirations set out with such ambition in the Rose Coloured Map had not been realised. The Portuguese felt bitterly betrayed and the Portuguese monarchy was shaken by the very public humiliation of the ultimatum. However, the colonial frontiers, as drawn in August 1891, gave Portugal a position of extraordinary influence in the development of southern Africa. By controlling the coastline with its ports and the lower reaches of the rivers that descended from the high veldt Portugal controlled British Central Africa's access to the outside world. The ports and the routes for the roads and railways needed for its economic development were all in Portuguese hands and Portugal would now have to be treated as a partner on equal terms when any aspect of the region's future was under discussion. The jigsaw-like interlocking of territory which saw Zambesia thrust as a salient into British territory and the Shire valley as a finger of British territory in Mozambique, meant that Mozambique's future was inextricably bound up with that of its neighbours. As had been the case in pre-colonial times, the peoples of Mozambique and British Central Africa would form part of a region inseparably linked as economic modernisation gradually took effect.

5

PORTUGUESE COLONIAL RULE TO 1919

Portugal and the challenge of being a colonial power

The agreement signed with Britain in 1891 drew the frontiers of modern Mozambique, with only slight modifications made after the First World War. Portugal had failed in its attempt to claim a vast territory stretching across central Africa but it had still succeeded in securing possession of very substantial areas of Africa. It was now faced with the problem of turning paper claims into some kind of effective government. Although it had had connections with Africa over a period of five centuries, Portugal was ill-equipped to become a major colonial power in the modern era. It did not have the military resources to establish control over its colonies, and faced an immediate economic crisis at home and scepticism among the international community. To make matters worse, the Portuguese political class was divided over how to proceed and what kind of regime to establish in Africa.

The extreme weakness of Portugal's position in the 1890s is the key to understanding how Mozambique developed in the years that followed the partition of Africa. Since the 1850s when the civil wars in Portugal finally came to an end, the country had experienced some economic growth. In particular the textile and wine industries had expanded and foreign investment had facilitated the building of railways and the modernisation of the country's infrastructure. However, Portugal had suffered from the economic uncertainties, deepening to full-scale recession, that had hit Europe in the 1870s. This had coincided with the spread of phylloxera and the subsequent collapse of the wine industry. In these circumstances the African market for Portuguese goods, especially textiles, had assumed greater importance and increasingly the African empire seemed to offer Portugal some economic opportunity. It was in this context that Portuguese banks began to invest in the cocoa plantations of São Tomé and seek some opportunities in eastern Africa.

However, the economic opportunities in Africa did not come soon enough to forestall the economic crisis that hit Portugal in 1892. According to Clarence-Smith, 'Portugal effectively came off the gold standard, let the currency float, unilaterally reduced interest rates and rescheduled repayments to foreign holders of government bonds.... Throughout the 1890s governments in Lisbon struggled with impending bankruptcy.'[1] The financial crisis had several consequences for the newly established African empire. It forced the Portuguese to make short-term decisions in order to establish some kind of governance in Africa at minimum cost to itself. At the same time it made them look for the quickest way of making their African colonies contribute to the economic rehabilitation of Portugal itself—in other words to make the colonies pay. All this had to take place in a threatening international environment. The financial crisis in 1892 had raised the possibility of Portugal having to sell its colonies to meet its international obligations and Britain's desire to secure control of Delagoa Bay, which grew ever more pressing as relations with the Boer Republics deteriorated, suggested that Britain would seize the first opportunity to dismember the colony of Mozambique that had only recently been established.

António Ennes, who later became High Commissioner (governor-general with extended powers) in Mozambique, described the pessimism with which the political elite viewed Mozmbique's future, in language which reflected the emotional atmosphere of the period.

> The alienation of the province of Mozambique was discussed in the press and proposed in parliament. Its future was despaired of.... It was alleged that this relic of our heroic era was as unproductive as a laurel bush.... National industry did not have enough products to sell to its people; there were not enough people to clear the land nor the capital to make it fertile nor even the energy to turn over its soil.[2]

While Portugal had sought a way of occupying and administering its African empire, it was faced by another problem, almost as serious, namely the mass emigration from Portugal to Brazil. The two crises would interact in a revealing way. During the first half of the nineteenth century there had been a steady exodus of population from Portugal and the islands. Most emigrants headed for Brazil but significant numbers went also to the Caribbean. In the last quarter of the century Brazil stepped up its recruitment efforts and after the abolition of slavery in 1888 the numbers of poor European immigrants rose steeply. Between 1890 and 1920 750,000 Portuguese headed for Brazil while another 170,000 went to the United States and about 1,000 a year to Argentina. While some politicians were alarmed at this haemorrhage of able bodied workers, others pointed to the flow of remittances on which the Portuguese economy depended to balance its payments.

Many of the emigrants who migrated to Brazil and the Caribbean went under contract to work on plantations, often with their passage paid by recruiters who determined where they would be sent. The majority were male and many were underage youths. Caroline Brettel wrote of these contract workers, 'those who went to the Brazilian *fazendas* were badly fed, treated like slaves and punished like dogs'.[3] Plantation workers might be punished by whipping or the use of the *palmatoria*. In the British Caribbean and the United States Portuguese contract workers and immigrants faced the humiliation of not being classified as 'white'. The conditions faced by Portuguese contract workers were from time to time debated in the Portuguese parliament at the very time that the Portuguese were devising regulations for the recruitment of contract workers in Africa. While some Europeans viewed African contract labour as little different from slavery, for the Portuguese it was only what generations of Portuguese had themselves suffered as plantation labour in the New World.

As for establishing an effective government in Mozambique, there was no agreement in Portugal over how to proceed. The ultimatum had been humiliating and had severely weakened the Monarchy, which was now confronted by a growing Republican movement. At the same time emigration from Portugal to Brazil was rising and, in the early twentieth century, was to reach unsustainable levels. Some voices called for direct action from Lisbon to set up a centralised colonial regime and to encourage the settlement of Portuguese emigrants in Africa, while others saw Africa essentially as an arena for investment and as a means of securing easily realised economic returns. However, there was common agreement that the African empire was in some way a national asset, which gave Portugal some standing in international affairs.

As a policy was gradually worked out, it reflected above all what was possible, given the circumstances. In 1891 Portugal's effective presence in Mozambique was very limited and in practice did not extend far beyond the coastal port towns and the historic settlements in the Zambesi valley, which were notoriously lawless. How in these circumstances would it be possible to conjure up effective occupation? The solution emerged from the experience Portugal had with the Zambesi *prazos* and from the British experiments with chartered companies in the areas of Africa where it had claims. Mozambique was to be divided into concession areas. The whole of the north, where Portugal had no presence beyond the coastal islands, was turned into a single concession to be administered by the Niassa Company. This company received a charter in 1893 which allowed it to establish an autonomous government north of the Lurio River. In the Zambesi region the *prazos* were to be leased as concessions to commercial companies which would assume the responsibility for pacifying, policing and administering them. The area south of the Zambesi, as far as latitude 22 (just south of the Sabi river) was to be granted to the Mozambique Company which had originally been formed in 1888 and was granted a governing charter in 1891. There remained three areas of the country which were not granted as concessions—north of the Zambesi the area between the *prazos* and the frontier of the Niassa Company, a small area around Tete and the region south of latitude 22. These were to be regions directly administered and exploited by the colonial state.

In this way Portugal's new East African colony was fragmented and divided into a number of semi-autonomous regions which adopted different customs regimes, and different labour and tax regulations. The area south of latitude 22 soon became a concession area also but of a rather different kind. In this region the Witwatersrand Native Labour Association (WNLA) acquired an exclusive right to recruit mine labour, becoming, in the process, a kind of parallel administration with a more effective presence in the region than the Mozambique government itself.

As these dispositions were being implemented, the Lisbon government published a new colonial tariff which established a strong preference for Portuguese goods and which was to be the keystone of Portugal's drive to make the colonies pay their way. However, this measure had little immediate effect in Mozambique because the charter companies set their own tariffs and the colony was still tied to the free trade agreement with the Transvaal. Moreover there was no means of stopping contraband goods entering the country anywhere along its extensive borders.

These measures, however, did not resolve the uncertainties over the future of the colonies and in 1898 Britain and Germany reached an agreement for the future partition of Portugal's empire if, and when, Portugal was forced to turn to the international community for financial assistance.

Pacification

Meanwhile some kind of settlement had to be reached with the African inhabitants of the various concession areas. The Niassa Company had few resources and took possession of its huge concession slowly and uncertainly. The Portuguese expedition under the command of Augusto Cardoso had obtained a series of treaties from African rulers in 1885 but these remained little more than pieces of paper and the Makua and Yao communities in the interior remained for all intents and purposes independent, while the Makonde living on the Mueda Plateau were not only independent but their country remained virtually unvisited and unexplored. By 1901 the only achievement of the Niassa Company had been to open a route to the lake with a telegraph and a series of military posts. It had also begun to survey the route for a railway. It was not until 1908 that the Company began systematically to occupy the interior of its concession by sending military expeditions to secure the submission of the Yao and Makua rulers and to enforce the collection of tax. Even so it was not until 1912 that the last independent Yao ruler, Mataka, was defeated and his people brought under company control.

PORTUGUESE COLONIAL RULE TO 1919

The country to the south of the Niassa chartered territory was the hinterland of Mozambique Island and Angoche. The region was dominated by the leaders of the Makua confederations and by the Islamic warlords, Marave and Farelay, who were linked indirectly with the ruling elites of the ancient Islamic polity of Angoche and who continued to operate a clandestine slave trade. An unsuccessful expedition was sent against the Namarral Makua in 1896 led by none other than Mouzinho de Albuquerque, the general who had defeated Gungunhana, but the Portuguese were unable to deal with the twin enemies of the climate and the guerrilla tactics of their opponents. It was not until 1910 that Portuguese expeditions were finally able to overcome the resistance and to bring this region under direct government control.

Although there had been a Portuguese presence on the Zambesi since the sixteenth century the region remained as lawless as ever. The collapse of Sousa's authority after his capture by the British South Africa Company forces in 1890 had left a power vacuum. Barue regained its independence and the Gorongosa region remained under the control of Sousa's former captains. The power of the Da Cruz on the middle reaches of the river had been broken but Macanga north of Tete remained independent as did the former territories of the Alves da Silva in Maganja da Costa. Between Tete and Zumbo other Afro-Portuguese warlords continued to dominate the river from their fortified strongholds.

The way ahead for the colonial government had been sketched by a committee set up in 1888 to make recommendations about the future of the *prazos*. It was decided to lease the *prazos* to concessionaires who would assume the responsibility for pacification. However, this was no real solution as few concessionaires had the resources to undertake this task and the government had to take responsibility for pacification. A series of expeditions were sent against Maganja, Sousa's captains and eventually in

1902 against Barue and Macanga. These followed the traditions of Zambesia and were made up of hired *chicunda* fighters or Ngoni who were rewarded with being allowed to plunder the conquered territory. Such campaigns eventually opened the way for the concessionaires to establish their presence on the lower reaches of the river, and for labour recruiters to round up contract workers for the mines and farms of South Africa and Southern Rhodesia.

South of the Zambesi the Mozambique Company, the creation of Paiva de Andrada, had been granted a charter in 1891. By the terms of this charter it undertook 'to settle 1,000 colonists within five years; to establish schools and missions; and to construct a port, dock works, a railway, roads, and a telegraph system'.[4] Although better organised than the Niassa Company, it also lacked the resources to pacify and administer the area of its concession. It found an immediate solution in coming to an agreement with Gungunhana, the Gaza king, for joint control and the sharing of the tax revenue of the region, an arrangement which, in effect, left the independence of the Gaza Kingdom unchallenged.

However, by 1895 relations between Gaza and the Portuguese had begun to break down. The continued existence of a powerful and independent African state weakened Portuguese authority *vis à vis* the African population in the south and cast doubts on Portugal's ability to control its colony in the opinion of the watchful British and Germans. Moreover, the Portuguese wanted to open up the area of the Gaza Kingdom for labour recruitment. Early in 1895 the new High Commissioner, António Ennes, decided to force a showdown with Gungunhana. A large expedition was sent from Portugal supported by gunboats, cavalry and machine guns and in a rapid and decisive military campaign Gungunhana's regiments were defeated and the king himself captured. A rebellion mounted two years later by one of

Gungunhana's generals was also suppressed. These spectacular military successes, wholly unprecedented in the record of Portuguese military interventions in Africa, were achieved by the deployment of modern weapons against the traditional regimental formations of the Ngoni who were unable to adapt to fighting successful guerrilla campaigns in the way that the Afro-Portuguese warlords on the Zambesi or the Islamic and Makua rulers of northern Mozambique were able to do. The victories were celebrated by the Portuguese as evidence that Portugal could compete with the British, Germans and French in establishing itself as a colonial power. In Africa the victories boosted Portuguese prestige and enabled the colonial authorities to put in place arrangements for turning southern Mozambique into a labour recruitment area.

Railways and labour recruitment

Already before 1891 Portuguese politicians had begun to appreciate that Mozambique's greatest assets were its control of the south-east African coastline and the existence of the large population that lived in its hinterland. The Macmahon Award, which gave Portugal control of Delagoa Bay, had been followed by prolonged negotiations with first the British and then the Boer authorities in the Transvaal and finally with various concession holders for the building of a railway to connect the mining areas of the high veldt with Lourenço Marques, their nearest and best available seaport. Although the longest part of the railway's route would lie within the Transvaal an all important fifty mile stretch passed through Portuguese territory. The complexity of the issues surrounding the building of the railway were not resolved and the railway completed until the first day of January 1895 when a line was finally opened linking the Rand to Delagoa Bay.

The railway transformed the politics of southern Africa and the outlook for Portugal's future as a colonial power. First and foremost, however, it made the Transvaal effectively independent of British control, enabling it to import arms as well as industrial machinery. Over the next few years this increased the political tensions within southern Africa, and with it Britain's desire to secure control of the Bay, a threat Portugal could not ignore.

The second major consequence was that the income Portugal derived from the port and the railway pointed the way to making their African empire profitable. The flow of passengers and freight using the port and railway increased dramatically so that in 1900 it accounted for half of all the commercial activity of Mozambique. By 1909 126,000 passengers were using the railway and 638,000 tonnes of freight were being carried. The foreign exchange earned by these services were invaluable for a Portugal with a massive balance of payments problem and was to remain a key factor in determining policy until the end of the colonial era.

The third change, which resulted from the opening of the railway, was greatly to facilitate the flow of migrant labourers from Mozambique to the mines. Africans from the southern regions of Mozambique had been making the long and dangerous journey to Natal ever since the 1860s and to the mines following the major discovery of gold and diamonds at the end of that decade. The major incentive had been the possibility of purchasing guns but migrant labour had also resulted in the flow of money to societies that were still largely non-monetarised. Over the succeeding twenty years mine labour began to transform African society. Young men could obtain access to bride wealth by going to the mines rather than remaining subservient to clan elders who now found their authority increasingly undermined. Mine workers also bought consumer goods or invested their savings in such things as ploughs. As labour recruiters became increasingly active within African society and were willing to pay bounties on the migrants recruited, many elders themselves sought to cash in on the opportunity and to coerce young men to enlist. A flow of labour that had at one time been voluntary became increasingly forced and unfree.

Attempts to regulate the flow of migrant labour, and at the same time tax it, began in the 1870s and this presented the Portuguese authorities with opportunities which, after the defeat of the Gaza kingdom, they were not slow to take. In an attempt to deal with the chaotic situation created by competitive recruitment practices in a country that was still largely without any effective administration, the Portuguese introduced detailed regulations in 1897 to govern the licensing and conduct of labour recruiters: the Portuguese would receive a per capita payment on the labourers recruited and a *curador* in Johannesburg would supervise the work contracts.

The outbreak of the Boer War in October 1899 interfered with mining operations and the flow of labour—though not the operation of the railway, which was now used by British military authorities to supply their campaigns. However, in 1900 British forces occupied the Rand and mining operations could begin once again. To renew the flow of migrant labour was essential and in December 1901 Britain and Portugal signed an agreement, which became known as the *modus vivendi* as it was thought to be an interim measure to be replaced at the end of the war. By this agreement the recruitment of labour in Mozambique resumed with a per capita fee paid on each labourer recruited. A further provision gave the WNLA, which had been established in 1896 by the mining companies, the sole right to recruit labour, while civilian traffic on the railway was to be resumed.

The *modus vivendi* provided the formula, which would govern all future agreements between Mozambique and South Africa, though further details would be negotiated in subsequent years. The agreement was renewed in the Mozambique-Transvaal Convention in 1909, which in turn was renewed in another Convention signed in 1928. The Portuguese pressed for the withholding of wages to be paid to miners on their return home and for the deduction of tax from wages at source. They also demanded, unsuccessfully, that Portuguese wine should be served to miners on the Rand. The 1909 Convention also guaranteed that between 50 and 55 per cent of Rand traffic would use the port of Lourenço Marques. Meanwhile the free trade agreement, which had originally been signed with the South African Republic in 1873, was confirmed bringing huge advantages to Mozambique in its relations with its rapidly industrialising neighbour, not least for its burgeoning sugar industry.

The numbers of Mozambican miners working in the Transvaal mines rose from around 52,000 in 1904 and climbed to a peak of 97,000 in 1911 before settling down to between 70,000 and 80,000 in the following decade. Most of these were on eighteen month contracts and many miners returned for more than one contract. As well as those recruited by WNLA there was a significant number of clandestine migrants who made their own way to the Rand hoping to be able to choose the mining company for which to work.

WNLA was able to treat the whole of Mozambique south of latitude 22 as a labour reserve, and mine labour and the wages earned on the mines came to define the lives of those who lived in the southern quarter of the country. WNLA was not able to recruit in the territory of the Mozambique Company nor in the region where the *prazo* concessions were in force as the concessionaires wanted to control local labour resources themselves. However, WNLA did sign an agreement with the Niassa Company, which in 1908 was taken over by Lewis and Marks, a South African company with industrial, mining and agricultural interests, who planned to turn it into another labour reserve. Eventually the high death rate of African miners from tropical regions led to the mines closing this northern recruitment operation in 1913 and the Niassa Company shares were sold to a German consortium.

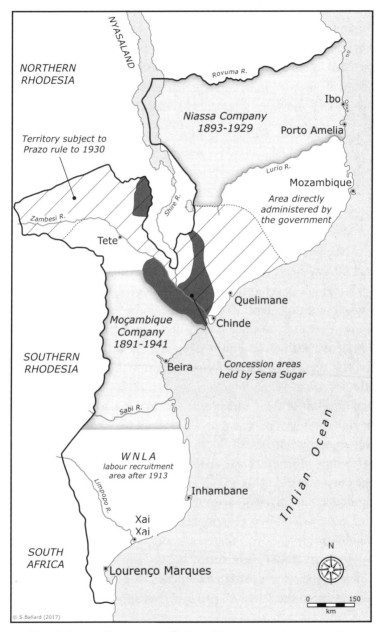

Map 1. Areas of operation of Mozambique concession companies

Meanwhile Beira in the Mozambique Company territory had begun to develop as a port for Southern Rhodesia. In 1898 a narrow gauge railway had been rapidly completed from Rhodesia to the coast. According to the British Consul, R.C.F. Maugham, the loss of life involved in its construction 'resulted in a death for every sleeper laid' and when a passenger travelled in the open trucks,

> the showers of sparks which issued from the smoke stack required constant watchfulness, and not seldom, on arrival at his journey's end, his clothing presented the appearance, by reason of the number of small holes visible therein, of having been stored away over a prolonged period in some receptacle infested by some phenomenally hungry race of destructive moths.[5]

Although this line had to be largely rebuilt after 1900, traffic had already begun to flow along it from the coast to the high veldt regions, passing through the Manica highlands where some European settlers tried to grow maize and where there were still hopes that gold mining would prove profitable. In 1910 the Rhodesian authorities signed an agreement with the Portuguese for the regular supply of labourers from the Tete district for Rhodesian farms and mines.

The result of these agreements was that much of Mozambique became a labour reserve supplying migrant labour to the developing economies of British South and Central Africa while at the same time providing these territories with the transport links to the outside world. This was an arrangement which proved highly profitable for Portugal, enabled Mozambique to pay its way and tied the Mozambican economy, and the country's whole future development, closely to that of the British colonies.

However, labour recruitment and railway traffic were not the whole of the story as, after a number of false starts, Mozambique also began to grow its own productive economy.

The Rise of the Plantation Economy

Parts of Mozambique, in particular the lowland regions of the Zambesi and Limpopo valleys, but also areas along the northern rivers, are fertile and well watered. In the second half of the nineteenth century a great expansion of African agriculture had taken place. This may in part have been the result of a general improvement in the climate after the disastrous decades of drought but it seems also to have been connected to the growth of export markets. Exports of peanuts, rice, grains (especially sesame) and wild rubber grew rapidly and in 1881 the British Consul, Henry O'Neill, described seeing 'many parties of Makua proceeding to the coast from districts as far inland as Mohemela, a distance of over 250 miles, each man carrying a small bag, containing generally rice and sometimes a little India rubber, with which to purchase a few yards of calico'.[6] Indian trading houses had, for a long time, been established in many of the northern ports but with this boom in agricultural exports they were now joined by German, Dutch, French and British concerns.

In a report to the Foreign Office in 1883, O'Neill speculated on the nature of this agricultural revolution, which clearly indicated the considerable productive potential of the region.

'The cultivation of *amendoim* and *gergelim* ... are the only established agricultural industries of this coast, it is a remarkable fact that their culture is entirely in the hands of natives. They get no assistance, no scientific aid whatever from the whites on the coast. There is no one really skilled in the cultivation of this produce to advise and direct them. Their own instincts and experience, if it can be so called, that has had the growth of only a few years, are their sole guides; ...The hundreds and thousands of acres that are utilized in the cultivation of these seeds are cleared in great part with an axe that is actually of native make, of tomahawk shape, and with an edge hardly 2 inches in length—a tool that a backwoodsman would laugh at—and yet I have seen large trees being felled by it, presumably only for want of a better.

... With both *amendoim* and *gergelim*, the seeds are then packed in baskets of native manufacture, and carried on the heads of blacks, in some cases a distance of 50 or 60 miles, to the house of the coast trader, there to be bartered for cloth, beads, powder, etc.'[7]

Although Livingstone had always believed that 'legitimate' commerce would help put an end to the slave trade, it seems that this increase in agricultural production was partly due to the increased use of slave labour.

In 1874 a company was formed to grow opium in the Zambesi valley, the first major investment in capital-intensive plantation agriculture. This enterprise, however, suffered from the lawlessness still endemic in the Zambesi region and saw its plantations destroyed in the Massingire war of 1884. The idea of promoting plantation agriculture, however, was soon revived by the committee that looked into the future of the Zambesi *prazos* in 1888. The committee proposed that the *prazos* should be leased to individuals or companies with the objective of attracting investment. The lessees would have the obligation to police and administer their concession in return for which they could collect the head tax (*mussoco*) from the inhabitants, half of which would be paid in the form of labour. In this way it was hoped the concessionaires would have an immediate supply of labour and the opportunity to develop the concession in whatever way was most profitable. The concessions were leased for twenty-five years. In practice each *prazo* became a chartered company in miniature.

The success of this scheme depended on the pacification of the notoriously disturbed Zambesi valley and it took a decade before this was achieved on the upper reaches around Tete. However, on the lower river, in the delta and around Quelimane and in the region south towards Beira, the *prazo* concessions were leased to commercial companies, most of them foreign owned. The most important of these companies were Madal, Luabo, Lugela, Boror, the Zambesia Company (which also leased a large number of *prazos* on the upper river), and, most important of all, the Mozambique Sugar Company that later became famous as Sena Sugar.

These companies began to experiment with various crops including cotton, coffee and eventually tea, but sugar, sisal and copra were the most immediately successful. Sugar was produced in the coastal lowlands, while tea was eventually grown successfully in the highlands inland of Quelimane. Copra became the product of choice along the coast where between 1900 and 1902, 325,000 coconut trees were planted.

Plantation agriculture required a regular and reliable supply of workers and the major concern of the plantation companies was focused on the recruitment and employment of labour. *Prazos* were also leased by São Tomé cocoa producers so that they could obtain a supply of labour to be shipped to the cocoa *roças* on São Tomé island. The whole region soon became subject to a forced labour regime, which was almost entirely unsupervised by the colonial administration.

The British Consul, R.C.F. Maugham, described the *prazo* plantations in 1910.

> The average prazo-holder...covenants to cultivate annually a given area, to open up roads, erect buildings, and, in some cases I understand, to take steps towards educating the natives over whom he exerts authority. These latter portions of his lease, although nowadays more faithfully carried out than they were, at one time gave the proprietor no sort of uneasiness. He carried them out only in so far as he was compelled, and at times, in the remoter regions where *surveillance* never came, his position and general mode of life were not dissimilar from those of the old time prazo-holder of the early seventeenth century.[8]

The success of sugar growing at first depended on access for both sugar and rum to the Transvaal market through the free trade agreement, but by the early twentieth century sugar was also being exported to Portugal. The most successful of the sugar companies was Sena Sugar, owned and operated by the Hornung family, the centre of whose operations was on the south bank of the Zambesi below Sena. As sugar production increased Sena Sugar leased other *prazos* in order to have access to their labour resources, eventually controlling 14,000 square miles of territory. The company also invested in infrastructure, building its own canal system, railways, power plants and port facilities, and operating river steamers. In many respects it became a state within a state, self-contained, Anglophone and relying little on the colonial administration. In 1919 Sena Sugar was producing 27,000 tonnes of sugar and ten years later this had risen to 70,000 tonnes.

Sugar exports from Mozambique grew rapidly and along with copra became a major factor in the colonial economy. By 1926 together they accounted for over 48 per cent of the country's exports.

Forced labour

In the early days of colonial rule the supply of labour was seen as Mozambique's most important asset. It was highly profitable to tax the movement of labourers to the South African mines, while the plantation companies came to depend on the labour recruited on their *prazos*. But labour was also required by the growing number of settler enterprises and by the government, which needed it for the building of infrastructure (roads, railways, port facilities etc.), for police and for the provision of carriers where these were needed for transport purposes. In 1899 the Portuguese government published a labour law, which imposed on all adult male Africans the obligation to work. This obligation had to be met by formally contracting with a private employer or with the government. The regulation did not apply in the territories of the Chartered Companies (although these adopted similar regulations) or on the *prazos* and its general effect was to encourage workers to submit to recruitment by WNLA, since wages paid on the Rand far exceeded those paid in Mozambique. As a result of this haemorrhage of labour to South Africa and Southern Rhodesia, the government had to meet its labour requirements by resorting to a system of forced labour known as *chibalo*. *Chibalo* labour was either unpaid or paid at very low rates and those guilty of some offence, which might be non-payment of taxes or being dressed in an inappropriate manner in a town, could be sentenced to penal labour or even sent abroad to work in the cocoa plantations of São Tomé. *Chibalo* labour continued in one form or another until the 1960s and weighed most heavily on the poorest sections of the community. It involved women as well as men and the employment of women in road gangs was a common sight. Recruitment into the police, who were known as *cipais*, was also by compulsion, with press gang raids being carried out on villages to fill the quotas.

The only redress the inhabitants of Mozambique had from the attentions of the *cipais* sent to round them up for contract or *chibalo* labour was to emigrate and in the early years of the twentieth century large numbers began to move into the neighbouring British Protectorate of Nyasaland where they were known as Anguru or to Southern Rhodesia where they were allowed to settle on white owned farms in exchange for undertaking agricultural work.

Beginnings of a modern state

Even though the Portuguese colonial administration had direct responsibility for only a relatively small and fragmented part of Mozambique, it began to put in place some of the basic structures that would later be expanded to form the administrative framework of a new state. First, and for a long time most important, was the 1899 Labour Law which mapped the legal status of the population, dividing it into two categories *indígenas* (natives) and *não-indígenas*. The vast majority of the population were to become *indígenas* and were not only liable to the work obligations set out in the law but were held to be subject to tribal law and to be directly under the rule of chiefs, or *régulos*. This arrangement was to last with few changes until 1961. The rest of the population—the *não-indígenas*—which included *mestizos*, Indians and a few privileged Africans, as well as Portuguese and other Europeans, came under Portuguese law. In 1901 a land law declared all unoccupied land to become state owned. Provision was made for establishing African reserves but this was never implemented in any systematic way.

In 1907 a secretariat for native affairs was established. On paper this had a wide remit covering everything to do with the lives of the *indígenas* but for a long time it was understaffed and concerned itself mostly with the recruitment of labour. The country was formally divided into five provinces (later expanded to nine when the territories of the Charter Companies were absorbed by the state). These in turn were divided into circumscriptions and *concelhos* (the *concelhos* being the urban areas). At the local level the country was divided into *postos militares* though these eventually ceased to be military posts and were staffed by a civilian *chefe de posto* and a few police. At the head of this administration was a governor-general (at times this post was enhanced with the appointment of High Commissioners) who was advised by a *Concelho do Governo* made up of department heads and some representatives of local chambers of commerce. This rudimentary colonial civil service was staffed by Portuguese from Lisbon. The Republican regime which established itself in Lisbon in 1910 promised greater independence for the colonies and an Organic Law was prepared which granted local law making and financial autonomy to the colony—though not any kind of local democracy. However, the law was not promulgated until after the First World War. Local settlers and the Afro-Portuguese had no role in running the country, though they were able to elect deputies to the Cortes in Lisbon. The Portuguese settler community never acquired any hold on power or any administrative experience and had to content itself with the frustrations of pressure group politics.

The administrative capital had been moved from remote Mozambique Island to Lourenço Marques in 1898, reflecting the shift in the economic and political importance that city had acquired. This city grew rapidly as the principal port for the Rand and the terminus of the railway. The coastal swamps were filled in and the town was laid out as a modern European city. However, its location in the far south, almost an enclave in South Africa, was to have profound consequences for the future of the country. The city remained in many respects an adjunct of South Africa, dependent on its powerful neighbour for its economic livelihood and even for its power supply. It was far removed from the rest of the country and isolated from the concerns of the population. It would be a long time before voices from the north would be heard in the capital.

Beira also grew as a port and railways terminus, linked to Southern Rhodesia and developed with British capital. Here British influence was dominant and it was not until the end of the Mozambique Company's charter in 1942 that Beira ceased to be essentially an outpost of the British empire.

The First World War and the Barue Rebellion

During the first decade of the twentieth century Mozambique achieved a measure of stability as the interior was gradually occupied and a rudimentary administrative structure was introduced. Moreover the agreements with South Africa appeared to secure the future of relations with the British Empire. However, the growing international concern over labour conditions in the Portuguese cocoa-producing islands of São Tomé and Príncipe, and over labour recruitment practices in Angola and Mozambique raised the prospect once again of international action against the Portuguese empire. In 1913 Britain and Germany renewed their agreement over a future partition of the Portuguese colonies should this become necessary and the same year a German consortium took control of the Niassa Company and with it the whole northern sector of Mozambique. German control lasted only a short time and with the outbreak of the First World War the British Union Castle Company took control of the Niassa Company.

In 1910 the Monarchy in Portugal had been replaced by a Republic and it was widely anticipated that the Republicans would reconfigure the relationship of the mother country with the empire. However, no steps had been taken by the time that the First World War broke out. Portugal was at first neutral but the northern frontier of Mozambique faced German East Africa across the Rovuma river and fighting soon broke out between the Germans and a British expeditionary force which had been sent to German East Africa in 1914. The Republican regime in Lisbon was strongly pro-Ally and sought an opportunity to join the war in the belief that this would strengthen Republican support in the country and would help secure the colonies in any postwar repartition of Africa. However, it was not until March 1916 that Britain agreed to accept Portugal's entry into the war as an ally. Portugal sent two expeditionary forces to Africa and attempted an invasion of the German colony. It occupied the so-called Kionga triangle, which was a small area of the German colony located south of the Rovuma, but otherwise the invasion was a demoralising disaster.

One immediate effect of the war was to intensify the recruitment of carriers and the exaction of *chibalo* labour. This provided the grievances that early in 1917 were exploited by members of the former Barue ruling house, exiled since 1902, and by some of the spirit mediums to raise a rebellion. The rising began in March 1917 and soon attracted widespread support among the populations along the Zambesi as far as Zumbo. Remnants of the old Afro-Portuguese families and of the *chicunda* captains also joined the rising, which began to resemble the kind of coalition of interests that had marked the Zambesi wars of the previous century. The leaders of the rising tried to gain support from the British in Southern Rhodesia but otherwise had no clear long-term strategy. The Portuguese response was to send a gunboat to the Zambesi, to recruit local forces and to call on the Ngoni for assistance. By the end of 1917 the main rebel forces had been defeated but guerrilla warfare along the borders with Southern Rhodesia continued and was not finally brought to an end until 1920.

The rising among the people along the Zambesi encouraged the Germans in East Africa to attack Mozambique. Early in 1917 a German officer, von Stümer, led a raid into northern Mozambique receiving an enthusiastic reception among the newly subdued Yao east of Lake Malawi who saw this as an opportunity to throw off Portuguese control. Von Stümer's raid was followed in November 1917 by the invasion of northern Mozambique by a powerful German force commanded by General von Lettow Vorbeck who was retreating from German East Africa before the advance of a large Allied army. The Germans advanced long the Lujenda valley and then fanned out through northern Mozambique, attacking Portuguese military installations and supplying themselves from food and ammunition dumps. They were followed by the British who landed troops at positions along the coast to make sure the Germans did not secure possession of northern Mozambique.

In June 1918 the Germans invaded Zambesia coming close to the major port-town of Quelimane. However, at this point they turned back, recrossing the Rovuma and entering Northern Rhodesia where they were still undefeated when the armistice signed in November brought an end to the war.

The Germans had apparently made little attempt to link up with the Barue rebels but they had encouraged revolt among the Yao and Makua and they left behind a country where most vestiges of Portuguese authority had been destroyed. The South African and British military, who had pursued the Germans through northern Mozambique, had seen how the north of Mozambique was utterly neglected and undeveloped. As Marco Arrifes puts it, 'the whole vast space under the administration of this Company [the Niassa Company] was a complete desert in terms of administrative organisation and material development. In reality the activity of the Company was limited to collecting the hut tax and paying its employees'.[9] As a result of this experience, during negotiations that preceded the Versailles Treaty General Smuts, the South African prime minister, pressed for the mandate system, under which the former German colonies were to be governed, to include the Portuguese colonies as well. Portugal was fortunate to escape with its colonial empire intact and Mozambique's frontiers were even adjusted to include the Kionga triangle. The Niassa Company did not entirely escape retribution, however, and when its charter expired in 1929 it was not renewed.

6

COLONIAL MOZAMBIQUE 1919 TO 1975[1]

Postwar Mozambique

The end of the First World War left Mozambique in much the same state as at the beginning. The country was still fragmented, divided between the Charter Company territories, the *prazo* concessions and the areas under direct government administration, which had increasingly become labour reserves providing contract workers for South Africa and Southern Rhodesia.

The rule of the Niassa Company in the north had come under a lot of criticism during the war but any suggestion of ending the charter and bringing it under direct government control was complicated by the fact that the Company was now British owned. The Mozambique Company was also controlled by British and South African capital and the largest and most successful of the *prazo* concessions, Sena Sugar, was also a British-owned company. Given that the South African and Rhodesian mines and farms that recruited their labour in Mozambique were largely controlled by British capital and that the railways were also British owned, it might seem that Mozambique had become

119

to a very large extent an adjunct of the British Empire in Africa—almost itself a British colony.

The Republican administration in Lisbon, deeply indebted to Britain after the war, had little space in which to manoeuvre and few ideas about reconfiguring colonial policy. The government did, however, hold out against General Smuts who had wanted to bring the port and railway of Lourenço Marques under South African control in 1922 in exchange for the renewal of the labour convention. Some measures were also taken to try to eliminate the worst abuses of the labour recruiting system, particularly after the League of Nations established the Temporary Slavery Commission in 1924 and then asked the ILO to produce a Convention on Forced Labour. This Convention was produced in 1930 but not signed by Portugal until 1956.

During the period of the Republic Portugal's trade with its colonies declined until it only accounted for 10 per cent of the total. At the same time colonial debt rose and had to be covered by funds from Portugal. Relations between the small white settler community and the government deteriorated, and there were a succession of strikes by white workers in the port and railway of Lourenço Marques.

The only significant change brought about by the Republicans was to appoint High Commissioners with increased powers in both Angola and Mozambique—in this way fulfilling the pre-war ambition of making the colonies to a large extent autonomous. The High Commissioner appointed to Mozambique, Manuel de Brito Camacho, is principally remembered for the agreement he signed with Sena Sugar in 1921 to supply the company annually with 3,000 'contracted' labourers from government controlled territory in exchange for financial assistance in raising a loan.

In 1926 the Republic was overthrown by a military coup. This was followed by two years of instability before a new regime,

1. The gateway to the fort at Sena (1964)

2. *Mozambique Island in the 19th century. From Lyons McLeod, Travels in Eastern Africa, 2 vols Hurst and Blacket (London, 1860)*

3. Mount Morumbala (1964)

5. A *chefe de posto* consults a village headman (1964)

4. A water source provided by the colonial government on the road to Nampula (1964)

6. Basket making. From R.C.F. Maugham, *Zambezia*, John Murray, (London, 1910)

7. Goldsmiths at work. From R.C.F. Maugham, *Zambezia*, John Murray, (London, 1910)

8. Chair made from weapons after the Peace Accord (British Museum)

9. Malangatana: the artist of the Mozambican *povo*. (1981)

which came to be known as the New State, dominated by António Salazar, established itself in Lisbon. In the meantime the military junta had appointed João Belo as minister for the colonies and he had begun a major overhaul of colonial policy—not least the labour practices, which had been so widely criticised—before his sudden death in 1928. The port town of Xai Xai was named after him until the end of the colonial period.

The New State in Africa

Once Salazar was securely in control in Lisbon he began a major overhaul of colonial policy and administration. In 1930 the Colonial Act, the brainchild of Armindo Monteiro, established a new framework for colonial policy. Portugal and the colonies were declared to be a single state and colonial budgets and administration were centralised on a ministry in Lisbon. The colonial budgets were expected to balance and there would be no subventions from Lisbon. The experiment with autonomous colonies run by High Commissioners had proved short lived. All the inhabitants of the colonies were to be Portuguese citizens but full citizenship rights were only accorded to the inhabitants of the Indian Colonies, the Cape Verde Islands and São Tomé and Príncipe. In Guinea, Angola and Mozambique most of the inhabitants retained the classification of *indígenas*—natives—who had to earn full citizen status through the process of assimilation. However, full assimilation for the whole population was to be the ultimate objective of colonial policy and in the propaganda of the New State, Salazar made free use of the idea of Portugal's civilising mission in Africa. According to Marcello Caetano, Salazar's closest associate and eventually his successor as prime minister, 'Africa is for us a moral justification and a raison d'être as a power. Without it we would be a small nation, with it we are a great country'.[2] The provisions of the Colonial Act were confirmed in the new Constitution of Portugal, which was promulgated in 1933.

If the Colonial Act provided a new framework, which constituted the 'principles of action' which were so important to Salazar, it was two factors external to Portuguese politics which brought about the most radical change in the evolution of Mozambique. In 1929 the term set for the charter of the Niassa Company expired and, in spite of representations from Britain, the charter was not renewed. The whole of the north of Mozambique now came under direct state administration. In 1930 the term of the *prazo* concessions also expired. The Companies that held these concessions now lost their administrative responsibilities, which were assumed by the state. Only the Mozambique Company remained as a state within a state until its charter also expired in 1942. The end of the Niassa Company Charter and of the *prazo* concessions was fortuitous. It enabled a new colonial administration and a radical new colonial policy to be put in place without any serious confrontation with Britain or with corporate concession holders.

The second major factor, which helped to bring about profound change, was the Great Depression. Hitting the American economy first in 1929, its effects were soon felt throughout the industrialised world and in Africa where prices for raw materials collapsed and colonial economies were threatened with ruin. The apparent collapse of liberal capitalism played into Salazar's hands and confirmed him in his economic and fiscal policies. In his report on the budget for 1931 Salazar spelt out the significance of the depression for Portugal.

> The world's financial and economic situation sets us, fatally, painful and difficult conditions, which are, however, suitable for the development of a national and colonial economy, negotiated and integrated, covering the greatest number of foodstuffs, raw materials, and industrial products of first importance. Portugal will be obliged to turn

inwards, making the most of its population, its capital, its production and consumption.[3]

Out of this crisis was to emerge the doctrine of autarky—the belief that the economy of greater Portugal (Portugal and its African and Asian provinces) could become largely self-sufficient and insulate itself from the worst effects of global depression. One of the principal tenets of Salazarism was that budgets should balance (though this balancing act was not always all that it seemed) and together a series of protectionist measures were imposed and exchange controls, alongside this fiscal straitjacket, designed to steer the colonies in a mercantilist direction—with the objective that the colonies would buy from and sell to Portugal rather than other countries.

During the 1930s these two factors precipitated a major change for Mozambique and pointed the way to the country's future. The end of the rule of the concession companies necessitated the overhaul of the colonial administration. Salazar now created a professional colonial civil service, the members of which received training in Lisbon. A regular system of supervision, inspection and reporting was established to make sure that what was happening on the ground was in accordance with Lisbon policy. Understaffed and underfunded, it took some time for this colonial service to begin to work effectively but for the first time Mozambique had a single administrative framework operated by a civil service of sorts.

The effect of the depression and Salazar's fiscal conservatism was felt first of all in the tightening of colonial budgets and the end of subsidised emigration from Portugal, but by the middle of the decade a comprehensive new economic policy had been formulated in which the colonies were to play a major part. This policy has been described a neo-mercantilist, a term which adequately describes Salazar's mindset and his main objectives. The African provinces were to meet Portugal's requirements for tropi-

123

cal foodstuffs and raw materials and in their turn were to import manufactured goods from Portugal. This policy was to be accompanied by restrictions on foreign investment, designed to 'renationalise' the economy. The continuation of the labour contracts with South Africa, the income from ports and railways and the export of agricultural surpluses would ensure that the economy would continue to earn foreign exchange.

The system was operated through the establishment of quotas for colonial produce with guaranteed prices fixed in Lisbon. This was intended to provide stability for colonial producers and cushion them from the effects of world price fluctuations. Mozambique fitted into this scheme with quotas for sugar, tea, cotton and rice. Whereas sugar and tea were produced by long established companies like Sena Sugar and the Zambesia Company, a different regime had to be established for the production of rice and cotton.

The country was divided into rice and cotton growing concession areas. In these areas African villagers were forced to produce specified quantities of cotton or rice. A service department (the Junta de Exportação do Algodão Colonial) was established in 1938 to provide seed and technical advice for the cotton growers and a huge administrative machine was created to oversee African production throughout a swathe of central and northern Mozambique. The collection and marketing of the product was entrusted to twelve private concession companies. In this way the essence of the old *prazo* system, where commercial companies controlled the administration, labour resources and tax collection in their concession areas, was partly restored.

With the shift in emphasis of economic policy to the employment of African labour to produce crops on village-owned land, the New State gradually limited the role of colonial officials in the recruitment of labour for private companies. Companies that were large employers of labour now had to compete for labour in a relatively open market with Southern Rhodesian farmers and South African mine owners.

The effects of the quota system on Mozambique were varied. Sena Sugar found that it was allotted a quota below its production capacity and had to find additional markets for its sugar as well as having to compete for labour. It tried to find a solution by taking out cotton concessions so that it had some control over African labour in its concession areas. The rice and cotton concessions had the effect of greatly increasing production of these commodities so that by 1942, the African colonies were providing Portuguese industry with 81 per cent of its raw cotton, a figure which rose to 97 percent in 1954. Three quarters of this cotton came from Mozambique. But against these achievements, critics pointed out that African production of cotton and rice led to a decrease in other peasant grown crops, including food, that the cotton produced was of poor quality and was often grown in unsuitable land and that the whole scheme was deeply unpopular and led to widespread resistance. At its height in 1944 the cotton growing system employed 800,000 peasants in central and northern Mozambique, though the number declined after the war to around 500,000. As the system evolved, the less suitable areas were dropped from the scheme and the numbers employed decreased. Meanwhile a minority of African farmers began to prosper and to form a class of peasant farmers growing successfully for the market and forming co-operatives to protect their interests.

Although contract labour on plantations, *chibalo* and the forced growing of crops were all to different degrees unpopular and interfered with traditional patterns of village agriculture, and although there was large scale emigration from border areas to British colonies, the numbers of the African population grew during the twenty years after the First World War. This was a common pattern in most parts of Africa and was the result of the ending of the constant warfare that had preceded the establish-

ment of colonial rule and the subsequent colonial wars of conquest and pacification. There was also some success in controlling major epidemics, such as sleeping sickness.

C.F. Spence describes the cotton and rice concessions
in northern Mozambique in 1943[4]

In 1943 Charles Spence, the director of a trading company
located in Lourenço Marques, set off in his van to make a tour
of Mozambique. He was conscious of the 'almost complete igno-
rance about it that exists, not only in overseas countries, but just
across its borders in neighbouring territories'[5] and he intended to
write a book on economic conditions in the colony. This tour
was a 'fact finding' visit and he kept a diary during his journey.
On his return he 'wrote, and published privately, a small booklet
on the subject.' This venture into publishing was enlarged into a
book entitled *The Portuguese Colony of Moçambique*, which was
published in 1951. This in turn was revised and relaunched in
1963 as *Moçambique East African Province of Portugal.*[6]

Arriving at Angoche (recently renamed António Ennes)
Spence commented at length on the rice-growing scheme. 'The
system is for the natives to do the growing, whilst hulling and
cleaning the rice is in the hands of the concessionaires.' Each
concession has a monopoly in its district, 'the natives not being
permitted to sell to anyone else. Prices to the natives for unhulled
rice, to the traders for ready milled rice and again retail to the
natives by the traders are all controlled by the Portuguese government through the price controller.' He comments that a lot
of money has been sunk in this business, which was controlled
by four Lourenço Marques businessmen. In the conditions created by the war, the prices were three times above 'pre-war rice
imported from Burma' but he doubted if Mozambican rice would
be competitive in 'normal times.'[7]

The great advantage of rice growing, he pointed out, was that it was a food crop, and this provided Africans with an incentive for its production. A large proportion of the rice never reached the concessionaires as it was locally consumed. He concluded that 'the only possibility of increasing native rice production radically for sale to the mills is by official pressure', but later he wrote that 'incentive to the native is to be preferred with an edible crop like rice'.[8]

If rice-growing campaigns were in their infancy in 1943, cotton growing was well established. Stopping at Nametil 'a small "poste" and native trading centre', Spence discussed trading conditions with the local Indian traders. 'Their complaint—and it turned out to be the general complaint throughout the province of Niassa and the North of the colony generally—was that trade in native products had more or less come to a standstill on account of the emphasis imposed by the government on cotton growing.' He went on to explain that African farmers only grow enough cotton (often in unsuitable soil) to pay their hut tax, with a corresponding decline in the growing of other marketable crops. 'The result is a heavy accumulation of relatively poor staple cotton in the collection centres and ginneries of the cotton concession company, and the decreasing quantity of other native products in the stores of the traders.'[9] There were serious knock-on effects. Transport difficulties, due in part to the war, meant that priority was given to transporting cotton and such food crops as were produced could not be moved. 'The result is famine in both maize and groundnuts in the main consuming centres such as Lourenço Marques.'

The Lower Zambesi Bridge

As Mozambique, from its inception, had been a colony fragmented into separate concession areas, there had been no central planning of its infrastructure. There were no roads or railways that linked the north of the country to the south and no bridge crossed the Zambesi, which effectively divided the country into two unconnected regions. Just as Mozambique's rivers for the most part flowed from the high veldt to the sea, slicing the country into sections, so this pattern was repeated by the railway and road networks which were designed to link the hinterland of British Africa with the nearest port on the Mozambique coast. As late as the 1960s, road traffic from southern Mozambique to the north had to use a ferry at Tete and then pass through Nyasaland in order to enter the north of the country.

In the 1920s, however, the Mozambique Company, which had acquired mineral rights in the Tete region, planned a railway to link this area of the country to the port of Beira and between 1920 and 1922 the Trans Zambesia railway was built. The original plan had been to build two railways, one each side of the Zambesi at Sena with goods crossing by ferry as at Tete. Then in 1929, with the British steel industry, not to mention the economies of British Central Africa, in the grip of the recession, the British government was persuaded to underwrite the bridging of the Zambesi to connect Nyasaland with the port of Beira, the cost to be born by the tax payer in the Nyasaland Protectorate. Mozambique now saw the construction of one of the greatest works of engineering undertaken anywhere in the world—the bridging of the Zambesi with a two and a quarter mile long bridge of steel girders—at the time the longest railway bridge in Africa and the second longest in the world. A branch line to the Moatize coalfields in Tete was completed ten years later. This vast structure, which was completed in 1935, was to serve the diminutive market of Nyasaland and the largely unproductive hinterland of the Mozambique Company's concession, but for the first time there was now a tangible link between the northern and southern parts of the country.

COLONIAL MOZAMBIQUE 1919 TO 1975

The Second World War

Portugal remained neutral throughout the Second World War with Salazar keeping both the Axis and the Allies in play as each bid for Portugal's co-operation. Salazar was concerned that, if the Germans were to invade Portugal or if he moved too far in the Axis direction, Mozambique would be invaded from South Africa. He was mindful of the possibility of a South African take over of Delagoa Bay, which Smuts had consistently advocated after 1910—and in 1939 Smuts was once again South Africa's prime minister.

However, Mozambique came through the war unscathed. During the war prices for tropical raw materials like rice, sugar, tea and rubber, for so long depressed during the 1930s, rose steeply, as supplies from Asia were interrupted. Mozambique was in a good position to profit from the high prices and, to aid the expansion of production, the government once again made the recruitment of labour a responsibility of the administration. Labour conditions in Mozambique now reverted some way to the position that had prevailed earlier in the century when the administration had forced labour contracts on the inhabitants.

The other major change, linked also to wartime conditions, was the government's relaxation of restrictions on industrial investment in Africa. After visits from the Minister for the Colonies, the government began to encourage large corporate businesses to invest in the establishment of certain processing and consumer industries. Mozambique had begun to move out of its earlier role in the mercantilist model of the New State and, in spite of the protests of metropolitan Portuguese manufacturers, had started on the road towards a limited industrialisation.

1942 saw the end of the Mozambique Company's Charter and, although little changed immediately and the company maintained its dominant position in central Mozambique, now for the first time all parts of the country came under a single administration and were governed by a single set of laws and regulations.

During the war, with the budgets of the colonies swollen by the high prices paid for their products, the first steps were taken towards creating a network of health and education facilities. The Concordat with the Papacy in 1940 had given the Catholic church a privileged position in creating a network of schools and, although progress was slow, the bare outlines of an educational system began to emerge.

Post-War Planning

The immediate post-war period saw Britain and France embark on ambitious, centrally planned development policies in their African colonies. Portugal, so often considered to be fundamentally out of step with its colonial partners, embarked on a similar policy of intervention and sought actively to develop the economies of its African colonies. Central to this objective was the preparation and implementation of three development plans (*Planos de Fomento*). A draft plan had been produced before the outbreak of the war but in the event the first five year plan was only published in 1953. This plan allocated investment to a range of infrastructure projects, which included the development of the port of Nacala, the construction of a railway to link that port to the borders of Nyasaland, and the building of a railway from Southern Rhodesia to the port of Lourenço Marques. These infrastructure projects were all to be financed by the Mozambique government supported by metropolitan loans and with private capital being invested in developing consumer industries. The plan also provided for the building of the Limpopo barrage, which was intended both to control the flooding of the Limpopo and to enable extensive irrigation of the fertile lands along the river. To accompany these infrastructure projects, the government began to promote the emigration of Portuguese to Africa and to build the *colonatos*, which were highly subsidised rural settlements intended to encourage white settlers. The first of these opened in 1954.

The Second Development Plan was to run from 1959 to 1963. Further large infrastructure projects were outlined and for the first time significant sums were allocated for education and health. In the decade that followed nominal primary school attendance increased rapidly, though the extent and quality of this education was doubtful. Some of the plan was to be financed by grants from Portugal. After the second plan, there was a transitional plan covering the years 1963 to 1968 when a third five year plan was published.

The experience of black Mozambicans during the late colonial period

Until the very end of the colonial period the vast majority of the Mozambican population were rural agriculturalists. They had been required to pay taxes to the state and had been subject to various forms of forced labour. They were directly subject to *régulos*, chiefs appointed by the government who were responsible for levying tax and recruiting labour. Africans had to carry a *cadernete*, a form of pass, which recorded their place of origin and their labour and tax obligations. Their movement both inside the country and outside was, in theory, closely controlled, although in practice large numbers routinely evaded supervision in their search for employment and better living conditions. Studies of the region of Manica and Sofala, the former territory of the Mozambique Company, show the extreme lengths to which colonial authorities went to try to control the population but also the losing battle they fought against passive resistance and the determination of the local population to evade the network of colonial regulations.[10]

A SHORT HISTORY OF MOZAMBIQUE

During the first half of the twentieth century the growth of the Mozambican economy and changes to the administration resulted in a growing diversity of experience. The structures of the rural economy and society changed and distinct regional variations appeared which had become deeply embedded at the time of independence. Although almost all rural families could be classified as subsistence farmers, dependent on their own production for their survival, in practice most of them participated to a greater or lesser extent in the modern sector of the economy. Ever since the late nineteenth century African farmers had grown or harvested crops for sale and this continued through the colonial period. While during the 1930s and 1940s large numbers were caught up in forced cultivation of cotton and rice for the market, others farmed coconut and cashew trees, which provided a significant part of the family income. Migrant labour, both the high profile movement of migrants to South Africa and Southern Rhodesia but also internal migration and seasonal labour also provided an important element in family income.

As a result of the growing penetration of the money economy, two clear trends had developed—an increasing diversification of status among the peasant population and growing disparities between different regions of the country. The agricultural census conducted in 1970 at the very end of the colonial period brought these trends into focus. Although 75 per cent of rural holdings were two hectares or less there was a significant group of farmers, amounting to 5 per cent of the total, who were farming four hectares or more. Production for the market had enabled a class of wealthier peasants to consolidate itself. With government encouragement these had formed co-operatives, had begun to invest their profits and had become employers of labour.

The regional disparities were of even greater significance. In the region south of the Sabi, most of which was poor agricultural land, earnings from migrant labour were very important for families, although in the late colonial period this was supplemented by a great expansion of cashew production which both provided a farm income and increasingly employment opportunities in the processing factories.[11] The coastal cities apart, the region was relatively thinly populated. According to a succession of census returns since 1928, the two central provinces (Zambezia and Mozambique), a region that is predominantly inhabited by people speaking Makua and Lomwe, contained half or just under half the total population of Mozambique. This is the part of the country where plantation agriculture had been long established and where cotton and rice cultivation had been enforced. By the end of the colonial period, however, most cotton was grown voluntarily as a commercial crop and the plantations had to rely on wage labour. The two northern provinces were thinly populated but were also an area of cotton and cashew production with peasants marketing the surpluses of their food crops. According to Merle Bowen, the government

> established agricultural extension and credit programmes for both Portuguese and Mozambican farmers ... [and] a tiny stratum of peasant farmers established themselves as specialized producers of cotton, often hiring tractors and regularly using insecticides. At the same time, they increased their marketing of groundnuts, cassava, and cashew nuts.[12]

Because of the history of cross border migration, the populations of these regions had close cultural ties with the populations in neighbouring countries. These regional disparities run like geological strata through the history of Mozambique, visible in demographic and human development statistics, in the narratives of the wars that started in 1964 and in the political development of the country since 1992.

The Portuguese in Mozambique

At the time of the First World War there may have been around 10,000 Europeans in Mozambique. This number included many who were not Portuguese, as well as administrators, soldiers and some convicts. The number of Portuguese settling on a permanent basis in Mozambique was very small. By 1945, by which time regular censuses were being taken, the number had increased to just over 31,000, in part reflecting the great expansion of the administration during the 1930s and 1940s.[13]

From 1947 onwards Mozambique experienced substantial net immigration, reaching its peak in the years 1958–60 when over 8,000 immigrants arrived each year. In total between 1943 and the end of colonial rule in 1975 164,000 Portuguese arrived in Mozambique and, in spite of large numbers returning or moving on to South Africa, this was the total of the white population recorded in the 1970 census.[14] Of these immigrants 53 per cent arrived on government assisted schemes. However, the principal factor that attracted migrants was the expanding economy, which offered immigrants good job opportunities. Most of these jobs were in the cities and relatively few Portuguese settled as farmers in the planned agricultural settlements. In 1970 only 5,128 were described as working in agriculture, though it was possible to see Portuguese market women with vegetable stalls in the Lourenço Marques municipal market. In 1970 half of all the white population lived in the capital and 70 per cent in one or other of the two main cities (Beira and Lourenço Marques). In her analysis of white Portuguese immigration Claudia Castello concluded that almost all the white Portuguese who were employed worked in the commercial or service sectors of the economy.

In addition to immigrants from mainland Portugal, some Cape Verdians also arrived, as the relatively well-educated islanders were recruited to fill vacancies in the colonial service as teachers or junior administrators. The growing Portuguese population also provided a market for the expansion of consumer industries and by 1960 Mozambique's manufacturing sector included food processing, textiles, cement, fertilizer and steel, to which were now added the production of glass, ceramics, bricks and tiles, candles, paper, cardboard, matches, tyres and electrical equipment.

The growing number of immigrants from Portugal alerted the authorities to the possibility that these new arrivals would become politically active in the less repressive atmosphere of the colonies. During the Second World War groups of dissidents had published a manifesto demanding changes in government policy. After the war some dissidents from Portugal had been exiled to the colonies, among them António de Figueiredo who eventually became a distinguished journalist commenting on Portuguese affairs for the Guardian. In 1953 a branch of the political police (PIDE) had been established, initially to maintain surveillance over the Portuguese population but eventually extending its role to cover the emerging African nationalist movements.

In 1958 the Portuguese presidential elections, which were usually carefully managed by the regime, were enlivened by the candidature of General Humberto Delgado who openly challenged the regime on a number of fronts. Delgado attracted a lot of attention in the colonies as he seemed to articulate the feelings of the Portuguese immigrant population that they had no voice and that their concerns were not listened to by Lisbon. Delgado was thought to have polled very strongly among voters in Africa. Wary of the settler population, the Portuguese government kept them at arms length until the very last years of the regime. One consequence of this was that, unlike their counterparts in Southern Rhodesia, the white settlers in Mozambique had no institutions or armed forces under their own control with which to resist either Lisbon or the nationalists once Lisbon decided to withdraw.

Mestizos, assimilados and the rise of nationalism

In Mozambique's towns there was a significant population of *mestizos* and *assimilados* living alongside the Portuguese immigrants. In the 1970 census the mestizo population was counted as 50,189. Many of the mestizos belonged to creole families whose ancestry went back a number of generations. In the time of the Republic they had founded newspapers and political organisations and had become the mouthpiece for political opposition to the colonial government. Like their counterparts in Angola they had suffered a decline in status as immigrants from Portugal increasingly took jobs in business and the administration. However, as a group they were never as influential as the creoles of Angola and the reason for this lies in the history of the country. Until the end of the nineteenth century the colonial capital was located in the north, on Mozambique Island. The removal of the capital to Lourenço Marques in 1898 meant that Mozambique Island rapidly became an insignificant backwater. The other historical centre of Afro-Portuguese power and influence had been in Zambesia but the wars at the end of the nineteenth century and the rise of company plantations had largely destroyed their economic and political power base. The mestizo families of Lourenço Marques and Beira, therefore, did not have the deep historical roots in the community that made the creoles of Luanda so important.

During the 1930s most of the newspapers and organisations that had represented the views of educated Africans and mestizos had either been closed down or had ceased to have any political orientation. The 1930s and 40s were decades of silence when the voices of the Mozambican population were seldom heard and remarkably little information about what was happening in the colony reached the outside world. Educational opportunities in Mozambique were limited and this was to be a crucial factor in the development of nationalist movements. The protestant missions, particularly the Swiss mission in Mozambique, offered schooling for its converts and there was some limited access to secondary education in the main cities for the children of mestizos and *assimilados*. However, very few Mozambicans went through the difficult process of acquiring the legal status of *assimilado* and those who did were usually closely connected to the regime. Nevertheless, by the 1950s there were a number of writers and intellectuals who had begun to describe their experiences and to articulate a narrative that was very different from the official ideology of the regime.

Africans looking for higher education had to travel to Lisbon or to neighbouring African countries—like South Africa, Southern Rhodesia or Nyasaland. In Lisbon students from the colonies met each other, formed networks and exchanged ideas with opponents of the regime who were linked to MUD or the PCP (the Portuguese Communist Party). They also experienced directly the ferment of ideas that was emanating from Paris, in particular the radical leftist ideologies of Franz Fanon and the Cuban and Vietnamese revolutionaries. However, while students from the colonies were able to assimilate the left wing ideologies current in Europe, they were largely cut off from their own country of origin and had only the most tenuous links with the traditional leaders within African society and the values and aspirations of the African population.

Those Africans who crossed into neighbouring countries also found themselves largely cut off from what was happening in their own country of origin. They were surrounded by the political turmoil that accompanied the independence movements in the Belgian, French and British colonies and came under the influence of the nationalist politics of their hosts.

The various anti-colonial independence movements that suddenly blossomed in the late 1950s, therefore, originated for the most part among exiles in Europe or in neighbouring African colonies, and did not grow directly out of indigenous movements rooted among the *povo* of the colonies themselves.

Although these early nationalist movements clearly owed much to the independence politics in French and British Africa, they were also a response to the sense of uncertainty, and even crisis, that affected the Portuguese regime itself after 1958, when Humberto Delgado was briefly able to unite opposition groups in Portugal and the colonies against Salazarism. Among the Mozambicans who went to Lisbon was, Eduardo Mondlane, who had been educated at the Swiss mission and had been involved in student politics in Lourenço Marques. He obtained a scholarship to study in the United States where he obtained a doctorate, was employed by the United Nations and eventually took up an appointment at Syracuse University.

Although there was some political activity among Mozambican students in Lisbon and Paris in the 1950s, the first modern movements seeking independence for Mozambique were organised among exiles living in Tanzania, Malawi and Rhodesia. According to the official narrative of Frelimo that became accepted after independence, now being increasingly challenged by a new generation of historians, these had no real pretension to represent the people of Mozambique as a whole. They seem to have been relatively small and with little organisation within Mozambique itself where the watchful eyes of the political police made this impossible.

Crisis for the Regime

Between 1958 and 1962 the Salazar regime went through a period of crisis when its very existence and that of its Asian and African empire seemed to be at stake. The crisis had begun when Humberto Delgado, a former regime stalwart, had stood in the election for the presidency against Admiral Thomáz, Salazar's nominee. Delgado's very public challenge united a wide range of opinion against Salazarism, bringing out into the open the extent of opposition both within the ranks of the regime and in various clandestine organisations. Delgado was defeated and hounded into exile, where he was eventually assassinated by PIDE agents in 1965. In January 1961 a revolt occurred in Luanda and another regime dissident, Henrique Galvão, attracted worldwide attention by hijacking a cruise liner and sailing around the south Atlantic declaring that the ship was part of free Portugal. In March of that year a violent insurrection broke out in northern Angola and in November India seized control of Goa, Damao and Diu, the Portuguese territories on the Indian sub-continent. Britain, Portugal's oldest ally, pointedly did not intervene and come to its rescue. Early in 1962 a group of generals and regime insiders tried unsuccessfully to remove Salazar from power.

The loss of Goa was hugely symbolic. In 1960 the regime had celebrated the quincentenary of the death of Henry the Navigator with a great festival designed to reassert that the regime's ideology was rooted in Portugal's unique mission embodied in its overseas expansion. The capture of Goa by Albuquerque in 1510 had been the crowning achievement of the early phases of this expansion and Goans had been seen to be the embodiment of the Luso-tropical idea, that the Portuguese had a unique affinity with non-European peoples.

Salazar's reaction to this crisis was characteristic of someone who was a master politician. Publicly he reasserted the regime's ideology, that the African colonies were an integral part of Portugal, that Portugal had a civilising mission and was uniquely qualified by history to build a multiracial society, that the UN had no business to investigate the internal affairs of one of its members. India's occupation of Goa was not recognised. A substantial military force was sent to Angola to crush the rebellion and the military in the other colonies were reinforced.

At the same time important changes were made to the structure of the regime in Africa, changes which recognised the need to respond to criticisms that had been voiced by regime insiders as well as opponents. The most important of these changes was the official abolition of the *indigenato* and with it the end of compulsory contract labour, which had characterised Portuguese colonial rule since the beginning of the century. The regime also intensified the moves towards industrial development and the encouragement of immigration from Portugal.

Frelimo and the outbreak of war in Mozambique

From 1957 when Ghana became independent, the decolonisation of Africa had proceeded at breakneck speed. In 1960 Belgium withdrew from the Congo and in 1961 De Gaulle granted independence to all the French African colonies. A number of nationalist movements had already been formed in exile to press for the independence of Guinea and Angola. It seemed that Mozambique was slow to get off the mark. In June 1962 cooperation between the various groups of Mozambican exiles was achieved when all three somewhat reluctantly buried their differences and agreed to form Frelimo, a front for the liberation of Mozambique. Instrumental in the formation of Frelimo was President Nyerere of Tanzania who became the regional patron of the new movement. However, it seems that the United States also played a major role and it was with the encouragement of the Kennedy administration that Eduardo Mondlane left his job at Syracuse University in New York to become Frelimo's first president. Hall and Young in their book *Confronting Leviathan* limit themselves to saying that Mondlane managed 'to avoid alienating American goodwill'[15] but there was more to it than that and there were suspicions that there was CIA involvement not only in the foundation of Frelimo but in the actual organisation and running of the party. Mondlane's contacts with senior US politicians and the funding they provided to enable him to establish his control of the party have been extensively researched by João Cabrita.[16]

Although Mondlane had originally opposed an armed uprising, by 1964 he had become convinced of the impossibility of a negotiated independence and had embarked on a guerrilla campaign in northern Mozambique, designed to overthrow, or at any rate achieve the withdrawal, of the Portuguese regime. Once Mondlane became fully committed to organising a guerrilla campaign, he had to reconcile discordant pressures coming from his socialist and leftist allies in Tanzania and from the independence movements in Guinea and Angola, from the United States and from local ethnic elements within Mozambique itself. A fundamental tension grew up between those who saw the anti-colonial movement in Africanist terms, envisaging a new regime with a traditional African leadership, reflecting traditional African values, and those who wanted the movement to adopt a universal nationalist, left-leaning ideology, modernist in outlook and intent on building a new nation that was not based on ethnic loyalties or traditional African hierarchies. In the official Frelimo version, the different factions were characterised, with some exaggeration, as modernis-ers, 'young men' who were 'defenders of the interests of the masses' as opposed to 'reactionaries ... who sought to get rid of Portuguese colonialism in order to replace it as the exploiters of the people.'[17] Similar tensions had existed in Guinea and Angola but in Frelimo the problems were also organisational as the military and civilian branches of the party's structure were controlled by forceful indi-viduals with radically different ideas about the direction in which the party should be moving.

Mondlane may have been a left-leaning liberal but he was no Marxist and, according to one anonymous but admiring biogra-pher, 'did not think that the time was ripe to launch a peasants' and workers' party committed to socialism'. He tried to manage the tensions in Frelimo by formulating the front's objectives in a manner broad enough to include all shades of opinion. At the First Party Congress in September 1962, Frelimo's aim was stated to be simply to 'promote the efficient organization of the struggle of the Mozambican people for national liberation'.[18] In a message to the Central Committee in 1967, a somewhat bolder vision was articulated—'the purpose of our struggle is ... first and foremost aimed at building a new Mozambique, where there will be no hunger and where all men will be free and equal'—but again this is a formula to which all factions could readily subscribe.[19]

The initial efforts at guerrilla warfare were not very successful. Frelimo had to operate from bases in Tanzania and was only able to carry out operations in the extreme north and along the shore of Lake Malawi. This was an area thinly populated, with few settlements and no towns of importance. The support of the Makonde-speaking population, which had been the last ethnic group to be fully incorporated into the colonial state and which had branches across the Rovuma in Tanzania, was of crucial importance.

While the military campaign was not going well, tensions among Frelimo supporters in exile in Dar es Salaam had spilled over into violent confrontations. It was only at the Second Party Congress, held inside Mozambique in 1968, that the struggle within Frelimo was partly resolved. The self-styled 'modernisers', led by Samora Machel who had been the principal guerrilla commander since 1966, secured a victory over the leading 'traditionalist', Lazaro Nkavandame, who was subsequently expelled from the party in January 1969. Some of the defeated 'Africanist' elements took refuge in a rival movement called COREMO, which was based in Zambia, or defected to the Portuguese but, although defeated in 1968 and consigned to the dustbin of history in the official Frelimo narrative, they were to re-emerge during the civil war that tore Mozambique apart in the 1980s.

Mondlane was killed by a parcel bomb in February 1969 and the prolonged leadership struggle that followed meant that it was not until the middle of 1970 that Samora Machel succeeded to the presidency. He started to mark Frelimo with his own distinctive imprint and for the first time began to mount an effective military campaign against the Portuguese. The story of Frelimo's first ten years, therefore, is of a movement that gradually evolved from a small, faction-ridden group with little military capacity in 1964 into a cohesive and effective guerrilla force that was eventually able to present a serious military challenge to the Portuguese in northern Mozambique. After the 1968 Congress, Frelimo adopted an uncompromising modernist agenda and, like the PAIGC, aspired not just to win independence from Portugal but to transform Mozambican society along non-tribal, non-racial, non-capitalist lines. Frelimo gradually formulated a vision of a modern society, which rejected most aspects of traditional rural culture in favour of a modern, secular society which prioritised equality, education and collectivist ideals.

Portugal's reaction

Portugal's reaction to the formation of Frelimo and the beginnings of insurgency in the north had both a military and a political dimension. The political response has to be seen in the context of the domestic political crisis in Portugal in 1961–2, which the Salazar regime had successfully survived. As the challenge to Salazarism in Portugal had temporarily subsided, the regime saw no reason to compromise. On the international front it began to co-operate with the white regimes in South Africa and Rhodesia and to seek support from within the NATO alliance. Within Mozambique, while some reform of colonial laws were implemented and the political police successfully clamped down on internal supporters of Frelimo, the government pushed ahead with its policy of encouraging economic development. While the needs of the military led to increased expenditure on infrastructure (roads, airfields etc), the government relaxed still further the restrictions on foreign capital investment.

Central to its plans was the building of the giant Cabora Bassa dam on the Zambesi—an enterprise which involved extensive foreign investment and which, it was hoped, would strengthen international support for the regime. In spite of a high profile 'dam busters' campaign mounted by Frelimo, the construction went ahead and the dam was finished in 1969.

The government also tried to build support for itself within the country and made attempts to gain the support of the Islamic population in the north which were partly successful.

The military campaign followed counterinsurgency strategies, which had previously been pursued by the British and Americans. The most important of these was the creation of protected villages (*aldeamentos*) into which eventually a million of the population were moved, and the Africanising of the armed forces through the creation of special forces (GE, GEP and Flechas). The counterinsurgency campaign culminated in 1970 in a massive sweep by 10,000 troops to clear Frelimo bases from the whole northern sector.

As late as 1970 it appeared that Portugal was winning the war in both Mozambique and Angola. The nationalist forces were split and their operations were largely confined to thinly populated border regions. There had been no significant threat to the cities or the main lines of communication and the nationalists had not been able to infiltrate the population in the most populous regions of the centre.

The Portuguese Revolution

In 1968 Salazar was incapacitated by a stroke and was succeeded by Marcello Caetano. Caetano wanted to liberalise the regime at home and find some political solution to the wars in Africa but he moved cautiously, his hands tied by the conservative elements at the centre of the regime and in the army. He made tentative movements to allow Mozambique greater autonomy, introducing a new constitution, which allowed for elections to an assembly and devolution of much of the cost of the war to the colonial budget.

None of this had much impact on the war because in 1971 Frelimo had been successful in opening a new front in Tete Province. Although this was, once again, a frontier region far removed from the centres of population and economic activity, it greatly extended the military resources of the government and in 1973 Frelimo was able to launch its first attacks south of the Zambesi. Moreover the much publicised meeting of the nationalist leaders with the Pope in 1971 was symbolic of the weakening of Portugal's global position.

By 1973 discontent within the Portuguese army had led to the formation of the Movimento das Forças Armardos (MFA) in Portugal and early in 1974 a leading general and former governor of Guinea, António de Spinola, broke ranks and published a book, *Portugal e o Futuro*, which was widely seen as a manifesto for the ending of the African wars. In April 1974 a military coup in Lisbon overthrew the regime. It was led by junior officers of the MFA and central to their motivation was a determination to end the wars in Africa at all costs. The guerrilla forces of Frelimo had won, not by achieving military victory, nor even, as it proved, by the mass the mobilisation of the population in their cause, but by wearing down the Portuguese military and convincing the officers that a war that could not be won was ultimately pointless.

Conclusion—The Legacy of the War

The war of independence ended when revolution occurred in Portugal and when the Portuguese armed forces unilaterally withdrew from combat. Although it had been ten years since the beginning of the fighting, the conflict had had little impact on the population or on the economy of the country. Fighting had been confined to the two northern provinces and to Tete Province. There had been no popular insurrection and the most populous parts of the country (the provinces of Zambesia and

Mozambique) had seen little fighting. Frelimo had not tried, and had certainly not succeeded, to mobilise the population or to establish itself in any of the main towns. Nor had the fighting had any serious effect on the economy, which had continued to grow during the war.

Although Frelimo was able to claim victory and to take over the reins of power, it was to some extent a phoney victory as the colonial regime had capitulated before suffering any significant defeat. However, the end of the war in 1974 was to prove only a lull in a much longer drawn-out conflict which had regional as well as internal dimensions. By the end of the decade war had started again and the fragility of Frelimo's victory and its lack of an effective presence in much of the country soon became apparent.

7

INDEPENDENCE AND CIVIL WAR

Mozambique at the end of the Colonial Era

To understand the special characteristics of modern Mozambique, it is useful to pause to look at the country the Portuguese left behind them when they withdrew in 1975. The frontiers of Mozambique had been drawn in 1891, but the whole country had only come under a single administration in 1942. Until 1942 different parts of the country had been administered in different ways and the regional separateness that this created still persisted. From the pre-colonial period onwards, the coastal port-towns had always, provided the peoples of the south-east African interior with access to the world of the Indian Ocean and the coming of the Portuguese had not changed this geographically determined reality. These port-towns had handled the trade coming from the interior—gold, ivory and slaves primarily. With colonisation of the interior by the British and Afrikaners in the nineteenth century, the Mozambique ports had continued to perform their historic role providing access for the inland communities to the sea. In 1975 Mozambique's main railways

147

and roads were still those that linked South Africa, Southern Rhodesia and Nyasaland to the Mozambique coastal ports.

The historic relationship between the coast and the interior was also reflected in patterns of internal and external migration. Migrants, both permanent and temporary, went from southern Mozambique to South Africa, from the central regions to Northern and Southern Rhodesia and from the north to Nyasaland and Tanzania. These migration patterns had cultural and even political significance as they linked the Mozambican populations closely to their neighbours in former British Africa.

An internal network of roads linking the north of the country with the south was slow to be built and even as late as 1966 there was no paved road linking the country's two major cities. As a result internal migratory movements were much less developed than external, but they did exist. The situation of the capital in the far south inevitably drew people from further north seeking urban employment, while the bridging of the Zambesi at Tete in 1973 finally opened up a direct road route linking the north and south of the country. However, in 1975 Mozambique was still a country where regional divisions were very marked and a sense of national unity poorly developed.

Uncertain figures suggest that around 1920 the population of Mozambique was around three and a half million and that at independence it was about six and a half million, by far the most populous areas being the Zambesia and Mozambique provinces in the centre of the country. In 1975 80 per cent or more of the population could still be categorised as traditional farmers living in rural villages where educational and health services were rudimentary. In rural areas the only education offered were the so-called *escolas da adaptação* which can at best, be described as pre-primary schools. At independence the vast majority of the population were classified as illiterate.

The other 20 per cent lived in the towns, most in the coastal cities with high concentrations in Lourenço Marques and Beira.

Migration of rural people to the cities was already underway, as illustrated by the growth of the cashew factories where women coming from rural areas formed the largest group of factory workers. In the cities the structures of a modern state and society had taken root. Health services, education up to tertiary level and urban networks of transport, commerce and industry were all available for the settler population and the *assimilados*.

One notable feature of Mozambique's social development was the comparative absence of marked ethnic conflict. Such conflicts had occurred in the past, notably when Ngoni were recruited by the Portuguese to help put down the Barue rebellion and when Makua-speaking soldiers were used in the conquest of the Makonde areas in the far north. Moreover during the war of independence against the Portuguese, Frelimo, which had been based among the Makonde in the north, was unable to make any serious advances among the Makua and Lomwe or the peoples of the central region, partly because of the dominance of southerners in the Frelimo hierarchy and Makonde among the rank and file. Nevertheless, Mozambique became independent, apparently without the complications of pronounced ethnic conflicts and these did not immediately become a major issue in post-independence politics. Instead Mozambican politics split along the regional lines which reflected the history of the different regions but which were not specifically ethnic in character.

By the end of the colonial period Mozambique's economy had a strong plantation sector, producing sugar and tea, and a wide range of consumer industries largely created to supply the city populations. Although the rural economy was principally based on family subsistence farming, most families obtained some of their income by producing cash crops for the market, especially cotton, copra and cashew. At independence cashew products, mostly grown by rural farmers, had become Mozambique's most valuable export. The growth of cash crop production, which had its origins in the boom in rubber and peanut production in the nineteenth century, had led gradually to important changes in rural society, which in the south was matched by the accumulation of capital through the wages of returning miners. In most areas of the country there had developed a small but important class of relatively well off farmers who invested in such things as ploughs and agricultural machinery and hired their own labour.

At the strategic level, the government had implemented three development plans which focused on infrastructure and which had bequeathed a bureaucratic predilection for centralised economic planning. Among the major infrastructure developments were two dams. The Cabora Bassa dam on the Zambesi, was principally intended to provide electricity for South Africa and had the potential to bring Mozambique considerable foreign exchange earnings. The Limpopo barrage had been built to provide irrigation to farms along the Limpopo valley.

The retail and commercial sector of the economy was largely controlled by people of Asian origin—especially in the rural areas where *cantinas* provided a network through which consumer goods were distributed and cash crops collected for marketing.

The economy of Mozambique in 1975 can be described as healthily diversified. There was coal mining in the Tete district, an oil refinery in Lourenço Marques and three cement factories. There was a vehicle assembly plant and a growing sector of consumer industries, a range of agricultural export crops, some of them like tea, sugar and cashew receiving primary processing in the country, and a service sector with strong earnings from railways, ports and hydroelectricity. At independence 30 per cent of foreign exchange earnings came from the ports and railways. There were, in addition, large remittances from migrant workers and a growing tourist industry. The public debt was not large and the balance of payments, though not the balance of trade, was frequently in surplus. The country's main trading partner was

Portugal, which accounted for around a third of both imports and exports.

Most of the modern sector of the government and the economy had been organised and run by European immigrants or people of immigrant origin. No priority had been given to creating facilities to train local people in the range of professional and technical skills needed by a modern economy. When, after independence, most (possibly 90 per cent) of the population of European origin as well as many skilled Africans and Asians left the country, the result was a severe skills shortage in all areas.

Portugal withdraws

The coup staged in Lisbon by middle-ranking officers in April 1974 may have been staged largely as a protest against the continuation of the war but the new interim government that emerged was deeply split over what to do about the African territories. General Spínola, who became president, and his followers, wanted to organise a democratic transition, after the model of British decolonisation. During this period there would be freedom for political parties to be created and to campaign for different 'solutions' to Africa's future. After two years there would be a vote on the constitutional future of the country. Spínola certainly hoped that during this time middle of the road politics would triumph with a possible outcome being the continuation of some kind of federal Portuguese state.

Such a strategy, sensible enough on paper, could only have had a chance if the Portuguese army had been willing to keep the peace in Africa. However, the army was dominated by the MFA, which had made the revolution. The MFA had no clear idea of what to do in Africa, except that the army would no longer fight. The soldiers withdrew to their barracks and camps. Many fraternised with the guerrillas and made clear their sup-

port for a quick return to Portugal, regardless of the consequences for Africa. Seeing the unwillingness of the army to
maintain the colonial regime, the guerrillas adopted an uncompromising stance. They demanded a rapid Portuguese withdrawal and a hand over of power to the guerrilla forces. In this
they were aided by events in Portugal. In July the right of the
colonies to independence was recognised in Constitutional Law
7/74, and the Portuguese arranged to withdraw from Guinea. By
September Spínola was forced to acknowledge defeat and
resigned. He was succeeded by another General, Francisco da
Costa Gomes, who headed a radical left wing government. The
new government recognised that it had only at best a six month
window of opportunity during which to disentangle itself from
Africa before elections to a Constituent Assembly, scheduled for
March 1975. Talks in Lusaka with Frelimo led to an agreement
to grant full independence in July 1975—a nine-month transition. This was followed by agreements to grant independence to
Cape Verde and São Tomé, and in January 1975 the Alvor
Agreement fixed a date in November 1975 for the independence
of Angola. In Mozambique there was not to be any election,
merely a hand over of power. In Cape Verde and São Tomé elections were to be held to endorse the independence agreement,
with only the dominant party putting up candidates. In Angola
the agreement made provision for three parties to share the
transition with elections prior to Portugal's departure, but these
elections were never held and the country slipped into civil war
before the Portuguese had even left.

In Mozambique the transition to independence was to be
organised by a government made up jointly of Portuguese and
Frelimo members. The nine-month transition gave no opportunity to train new administrative cadres or make all the detailed
arrangements for independence. Indeed no Portuguese politicians
seemed to have any clear idea what a transition to independence

entailed. In the event Mozambique became independent with no settlement of debt, with no guarantees for property or pensions rights for public employees. There was no agreement over the future of the African soldiers who had fought in the Portuguese army and who were more numerous than those in the guerrilla forces, and no consideration given to the future of migrant workers. Nor was there any provision made for economic aid to help the new country get onto its feet, while relations with its immediate neighbours were not established on any firm basis.

Part of the reason for this unorganised, rather than disorganised, departure was the fact that Frelimo leaders deeply distrusted the Portuguese and did not want their hands tied by any agreement. They continued to suspect that the Portuguese might try to organise opposition to Frelimo in the three-quarters of the country where Frelimo had had no organised presence and among the seven-eighths of the population which had not been directly affected by the war. When in 1974–5 Frelimo claimed the right to succeed the Portuguese government without undergoing the legitimising process of election by the 'masses', it was doing so because it had no effective organisation in the most populous regions of the centre, in the southern half of the country, in the major urban centres, or even, it seems, among the tens of thousands of miners working in South Africa. In order to overcome the contradiction inherent in its claim to be a movement based on mass support, it refused to negotiate Mozambique's independence and adopted a strategy of taking power first and seeking legitimisation afterwards.

Understandable as this may have been, Frelimo was to pay a high price for not having its rule legitimised by an election and for failing to make adequate provision for the immediate post-independence survival of the country. In 1992, when the ensuing civil war was finally brought to an end, some of these lessons were learnt and the Peace Agreement which was signed tried to tie up all those ends that had been left loose in 1975 when the Portuguese had brought the independence phase of the war to a close.

The transition to socialism

Mozambique became independent on 25 June 1975 with Samora Machel as the country's first president. The government was faced almost immediately by a crippling crisis caused by the mass exodus of population. Within a year of independence probably as much as 90 per cent of the white Portuguese population left, along with a large but unknown number of people of African and Asian descent. This exodus had been prompted by fears for the future of property, businesses and the social services like health and education. The white and Asian population rightly assumed that preserving their relatively privileged position would not be a priority for the new government, while many Africans associated with the Portuguese regime feared reprisals, such as had taken place in Guinea where thousands had been rounded up and killed after independence. Frelimo, for its part, did little to prevent the exodus or persuade the Europeans and Asians to stay.

The result was an immediate crisis caused by the departure of professional people and skilled workers. Government offices, factories, businesses and social services lost their skilled personnel and the economy threatened to come to a virtual halt. At the same time the recruitment of Mozambican miners for the South African mines was drastically curtailed. Miners ending their contracts now began to return in large numbers, threatening the flow of hard currency on which Mozambique had depended for so long, as well as the livelihoods of thousands of families that depended on mine wages.

The position of the government was made worse by the fact that in large parts of the country Frelimo had never attracted much support. Although Frelimo had always stated unequivocally that it stood for national unity against tribalism, racism and regionalism, it had in fact become, and was seen to have become, a party led by southerners.

The response of the government to these problems was threefold. First it began to nationalise businesses that had been abandoned and to take over control of the private sector in housing, medicine and education. Then it turned to its allies in the Eastern Bloc seeking technical support to replace the departing Portuguese. Numbers of so-called *cooperantes* soon began to arrive to provide staff for schools and hospitals. Finally it organised cadres of party loyalists, which were called *Grupos Dinamizadores* (GDs), to go into factories, offices and local government in order to galvanise these into activity and to prevent 'sabotage' by dissident elements.

Machel's Plans for a new Mozambique[1]

Although the new government had to make a number of *ad hoc* decisions in order to survive the immediate emergency, the party, or at least its leader Samora Machel, had far reaching plans for the country. Machel, who was an *assimilado* and had been a professional nurse, was highly articulate and his numerous addresses to different audiences give a good idea of his thinking.

Like the leaders of the other nationalist movements in the Portuguese African colonies, Machel stated that 'our final aim in the struggle is not just to hoist a flag different from the Portuguese ... or to put a black president into the Ponta Vermelha palace in Lourenço Marques'. Instead the aim must be to end not only the exploitation of colonial rule but the exploitation implicit in the structures of traditional society where 'the brutal reality of oppression by feudal lords is cloaked in myth and superstition'. Machel was very well aware that this was dangerous ground on which to tread and in 1973 he had described with remarkable prescience how the whole modernisation project might fall apart 'When we launch this ... fight to acquire a new mentality and behaviour, we are opening the doors to serious contradictions in our midst.... The successes achieved militarily... will hasten the process of discontent among a handful of elements.... In this way a breach is made in our ranks through which the colonialist and imperialist enemy will penetrate'. This is indeed what happened with the creation of Renamo but unfortunately the discontented were not just a 'handful'.[2]

Machel indulged himself by delivering long, sometimes hours long, speeches and discourses to all sorts of audiences. While a great deal of his rhetoric echoes Amílcar Cabral's analysis of the anti-colonial movement, its tone is markedly different. Machel's speeches read like evangelical sermons, representing Mozambique's quest for independence as a moral crusade as well as a political revolution. In 1972 Machel had addressed a meeting of Frelimo activists at the party's Centre for Political and Military Training. 'Our watchword', he told them, 'is Production, Study and Combat'. New recruits must learn to accept Frelimo's values. 'The first battle is to instil national consciousness and the importance of unity and of wiping out tribalism. Closely related to the battle for unity is the struggle to wipe out the spirit of individualism and to foster a collective spirit ... the struggle against tribalism, racism, false religious and family loyalty... is essential if the barrel of our gun is always to be trained on the correct target.' Personal conduct was crucial and 'the struggle against stealing, waste and unthriftiness is a part of developing a collective spirit.' Recruits 'must not go about in tatters.... In order to help our comrades we should ... distribute needles and thread'. Moreover 'there is also a need to fight reactionary prejudices among both men and women about women's abilities and their role in the revolution, in society and in the home.' To achieve all this, 'study combined with practice is a fundamental weapon with which to heighten our political consciousness.... It also gives us ammunition for wiping out superstition.'[3]

Such moral, somewhat puritanical, exhortation was far removed from Cabral's realistic recognition that 'the people are not fighting for ideas, for things in anyone's heads.... They are fighting to win material benefits.'[4] An attentive listener to these homilies would certainly conclude that independence would mean sacrifice, study and hard work with the material benefits of freedom receding into an undefined and indefinite future.

The first year of independence brought home the stark realisation that the newly independent nation was facing massive economic problems and Machel's previous analysis that the fight was 'against the enemy in our own minds—the capitalist ideology imposed by colonialism and the feudal ideology inherited from tradition...'[5] now began to be replaced by symptoms of increasing political paranoia. Everywhere Machel saw sabotage, which he countered with ever more vehement exhortations to Mozambicans to work harder and to change their ways. The peasantry, who formed 80 per cent or more of the population, incurred some of his strongest denunciations. 'In the peasant society it is not the family's concern that the children should bath regularly, that the children's hair be combed, their teeth cleaned, that they have a handkerchief to wipe their nose....' Worse, the peasant was economically inefficient. Things were little better in the city where 'traditional superstition [is] supplemented by cinematic myths from karate films and the models of the foreign bourgeoisie'. In the factories production had collapsed 'because in enterprises there is poor time-keeping, absenteeism, liberalism, a lack of respect for institutions, confusion, power-seeking, rumour mongering, stealing and racism. In short widespread indiscipline and corruption'.[6]

Independence needed the creation of the 'new man'. The answer was education. 'We are engaged in a Revolution whose development depends on the creation of a new man with a new mentality.'[7] The teacher had to be a role model—'the lamp that leads us out of the darkness, obscurantism, prejudices and complexes of social origin'. The 'new man' was to reject traditional culture and practice and adopt 'modern' scientific and secular ideas and ways of thinking. Teachers might even have to 'show someone used to easing himself in the bush how to use a latrine or a closet'.[8]

As Machel led the drive against corruption, traditionalism and neo-colonial sabotage, and became ever more obsessed with ordering the minutiae of daily life, Frelimo became ever more authoritarian. In the process a large part of the Mozambican population came to be identified as enemies of the new Mozambique—not just the peasant society, but religious organisations, former employees of the colonial regime and workers who went on strike, while war was waged on almost every aspect of traditional social culture. The hope for national unity forged in the independence war had tragically collapsed.

All the radical independence movements in the former Portuguese colonies had as their central idea the need to build a united nation on a non-racial, non-tribal basis. However, this rhetoric of the educated leadership did not necessarily resonate across the population. For many people still rooted in a rural society, ethnic affiliations and traditional institutions provided a necessary support mechanism through which to ensure security and survival. The nation-building rhetoric of Frelimo did not prevent it being seen by some as a 'Makonde' party and its leaders as 'southerners' who did not represent the views of the majority of the population.

Gradually new laws and new institutions were put in place to underpin the party's modernising aspiration. They were modelled on Eastern bloc practice with official state run organisations for youth and women and official trades unions. These institutions were operated by the party and excluded any dissentient voice. In 1977 a new constitution was introduced. This was an avowedly Marxist-Leninist constitution according to which the country would be ruled by a vanguard revolutionary party. Elections were to be held for provincial, district and national assemblies but only those vetted by the party could stand for election. Although there was universal adult suffrage anyone associated with the previous regime was denied the vote and many were rounded up and sent to 're-education camps'. There do not appear to have been killings and reprisals on the scale of Guinea or of Angola after the 1977 Nito Alves coup attempt, but a number of prominent figures who had been opposed to Frelimo were executed including Uria Simango, Lazaro Nkavandame and Joanna Simião.

Economic Planning

In 1979 a national economic plan was produced. Here the bureaucratic traditions of the New State met and merged with the belief in economic planning dear to the eastern European advisers of the regime. The plan allocated resources among various sectors of the economy. The priorities were to favour industrialisation and the creation of state farms. Next came the creation of communal villages to be run as co-operatives and third, and a long way behind, came the development of village agriculture.

Ironically, the plan followed closely the priorities of the New State. Investment in agriculture was to be directed to the newly established state collective farms, the most important of which was CAIL in the Limpopo Valley. This took over Salazar's *colonato* which had been established at great expense on land irrigated by the Limpopo barrage. CAIL was similar to the *colonato* in that it prevented the return of peasants who had been evicted from their land and consumed a disproportionate amount of the agricultural budget. In 1977 CAIL alone consumed 50 per cent of the investment in agriculture. The other priority was to allocate increasingly scarce foreign exchange to industry, another echo of late colonial policy.

The creation of communal villages was another policy that had its roots in colonial times. During the war the Portuguese had built fortified villages (*aldeamentos*) in areas threatened by Frelimo. These were first and foremost designed as counterinsurgency measures but they also enabled the government to provide health, education and other services to the population. After independence many of these were continued by the Frelimo government, as a way of providing services but also to facilitate the replacement of traditional local leaders with party appointees.

Alongside these economic policies, a considerable effort was put into a literacy campaign and into primary health care to eliminate the threat of smallpox and other transmissible diseases.

Whether the economic policies of the Frelimo government would have been successful in the long term cannot be known as the country soon slipped into a singularly violent and destructive civil war. In some sectors production, but not productivity, had nearly reached pre-independence levels by 1981 but the peasant economy which had produced valuable cash crops like cashew, peanuts and copra (cashew products had been Mozambique's most valuable export in 1974) had suffered badly, not least from the shortage of consumer goods and the disappearance of many of the *cantinas* run by Indians that had bought the peasant grown crops.

Origins of the Civil War

The civil war, which was to devastate Mozambique, lasted until the signing of the Peace Accord in 1992. Over a period of more than a decade the nature of the conflict evolved, which makes generalisations about its causes unusually precarious. Soon after independence the Frelimo government announced its solidarity with ZANU, which was fighting the white settler government in Rhodesia, and with the ANC in South Africa. Both ZANU and the ANC had many refugees in Mozambique where ZANU had established armed camps for its soldiers. Moreover Frelimo took action to support economic sanctions against the Rhodesian regime and closed the oil pipeline and the railway that ran from Beira to Rhodesia. The effect of these policies was to court the hostility of its neighbours in the south with whom the economy of the country was intimately connected and on whom Mozambique depended for its very economic survival.

Soon after Mozambique's independence, South Africa embarked on a war in Angola to try to topple the MPLA regime which had been a close ally of Frelimo. The South African invasion was a failure but it precipitated what soon became a struggle that engulfed the whole of southern Africa, including the newly independent Mozambique.

The first sign that Mozambique would be sucked into this armed conflict was the formation by the Rhodesian intelligence service of an armed guerrilla force to carry out sabotage inside Mozambique, while Rhodesian forces carried out major raids on the ZANU camps. The guerrillas were at first known as the MNR and their first leader was Andre Matsangaissa. The guerrilla force was recruited from Frelimo dissidents and former members of the Portuguese army who had fled Mozambique. As well as carrying out sabotage, it was equipped to make broadcasts inside Mozambique. In October 1979 Matsangaissa was killed in a raid and, after a violent succession struggle, Afonso Dhlakama emerged as the new leader.

The Rhodesian attacks inside Mozambique did not, in any way, constitute a Mozambican civil war and would probably have ceased once the conflict in Rhodesia was brought to an end by the Lancaster House agreement in 1979. However, South Africa decided to take over the MNR units and had them airlifted to the Transvaal where their numbers were increased and they were trained by the South African military to wage war inside Mozambique.

For two years after 1981 the guerrillas, now known more generally as Renamo, caused devastation in the south of Mozambique, attacking schools, hospitals and factories, killing government officials and targeting economic infrastructure. It is not clear that the Renamo leaders and their South African backers actually wanted to achieve the overthrow of the Frelimo regime. The South African government was notoriously divided between those who wanted to make the independent African countries in southern Africa economically and politically dependant on South Africa and the more hard line military figures who wanted to use South Africa's military muscle to destabilise the neighbouring countries. The two groups differed more in tactics than in their final objectives, which were to destroy ANC and SWAPO through weakening their allies and destroying their ability to mount attacks inside South Africa or Namibia.

Frelimo tried to counter Renamo's violent destabilisation tactics by taking military action and by trying to mobilise the kind of international support that had helped it during the war against Portugal. However, its military response to Renamo did not do much to limit the attacks, while Renamo achieved some success on the international front by establishing a presence in Portugal and Germany and by enlisting political support in Britain and the United States by representing the struggle in Cold War terms as a battle of the free world against Communism. Renamo was also to gain some backing from radical Christian groups opposed to the avowed anti-religious policies of the Frelimo government.

The Nkomati Accord and the Death of Machel

In 1984 Machel was persuaded to meet the South African president Botha to discuss an end to the conflict. After days of discussions Machel and Botha signed what became known as the Nkomati Accord. The main thrust of the Accord was that both sides undertook to stop supporting subversive guerrilla movements. Machel agreed to expel the ANC while Botha undertook to stop support for Renamo.

At the time the Nkomati Accord was dismissed as a clear indication of the weakness of Frelimo's position and Machel was much criticised. In retrospect it can be seen as the first serious step on the way to ending the conflict and the international community now became seriously involved behind the scenes in trying to bring about a settlement.

However, the Accord had no immediate effect on the fighting and the war continued unabated, spreading into the centre and north of Mozambique. The Lower Zambesi Bridge was blown and the plantation economies of Zambesia were systematically targeted. Frelimo meanwhile chalked up some successes, including the capture of Renamo's Gorongosa headquarters where a cache of documents incriminating South Africa were found. Whatever may have been the intentions of the South African government, the military continued and even increased its support for Renamo. Meanwhile, in Angola South Africa actively supported UNITA in its guerrilla warfare against the MPLA and its Cuban backers.

Frelimo was gradually able to put together an international coalition to fight Renamo and Zimbabwe and Tanzania sent troops to guard installations. Pressure was also put on Malawi, an ally of South Africa, to close down the Renamo bases on its soil. In October 1986, after attending a meeting in Zambia, Machel was returning to Maputo in a plane with Russian pilots when the aircraft hit the side of a mountain on the approach to the airport. Machel and thirty-three passengers were killed. There were strong suspicions that the crash was not due to pilot error but that the South African military engineered the crash by activating a decoy beacon. Since then conspiracy theories, such as surround the violent death of any head of state, have multiplied and have focused on those who had had something to gain from Machel's disappearance, including the Soviet KGB.

South Africa may have hoped that Machel's death would further destabilise Mozambique, but the leadership of Frelimo and the presidency of the country passed seamlessly to the Prime Minister, Joaquim Chissano, and the sympathetic response of the international community, if anything, strengthened Frelimo's position. Machel's death probably made it easier for Frelimo to make the political changes necessary to bring the war to a close six years later, as Chissano was, in some respects, more pragmatic than his predecessor.

The Final Stages of the War

From 1986 to 1989 the war dragged on inconclusively. Frelimo held all the towns (as the Portuguese had done during the war of independence two decades earlier), but the government's army became increasingly disorganised, ill-disciplined, ineffective and indistinguishable in its *modus operandi* from its opponents. Renamo was able to move freely in the rural areas and controlled large parts of central and northern Mozambique. It was kept supplied by the South African military, which was able to use runways in the Comoros Islands for airdrops in the north. Hundreds of thousands of people were killed or displaced either taking refuge in the towns or crossing the borders into neighbouring African countries.

Since the start of the fighting Renamo had had to change. After its expulsion from Malawi it was no longer able to remain simply a guerrilla army. It now had to occupy territory and work out ways of maintaining itself inside Mozambique. Renamo appointed officials, many of them forcibly recruited, to compel rural communities to provide supplies and forced labour. In this it had some success. Gradually the rudiments of an administration began to appear and the days of living by plunder alone receded. At the same time Renamo began to create the structures of a political movement, adopting a political programme, which emphasised the free market and a multi-party system of government.

The response of the rural community to Renamo and its activities has been hotly debated in the scholarly literature. Renamo certainly achieved the acquiescence, if not the active support, of sections of the rural population. It posed as a party which respected religion, both Christian and traditional, and, perhaps more important, it claimed to support the traditional social hierarchies. Aiding Renamo was the fact that Frelimo had become very unpopular in some rural communities, which, since independence, had experienced great economic hardship and had received little government support. People resented being moved into communal villages when, as happened in many cases, this involved the loss of access to ancestral lands, while in the central areas of the country there was a generalised perception that the people had been excluded from enjoying the fruits of independence. It is significant that the issues outlined above were all ones that Frelimo set out to address after the signing of the Peace Accord.

As Carrie Manning summarised the situation,

the coincidence of pre-existing regional disparities in economic development, Frelimo's tendency to place government officials in positions away from their home areas (and especially to put southerners in positions of authority in the centre and north), along with the disastrous social and economic consequences of the combination of instantaneous decolonisation and transformative socioeconomic policy, made for a readily mobilizeable constituency with common problems that displaced former Frelimo leaders could link to ethno-regional ties.[9]

Whatever the truth of these claims, Renamo later polled strongly in areas where it had been most active, in spite of the kidnappings and violence against civilians which had marked its behaviour during the war. During the fighting Renamo employed methods that were at that time relatively uncommon. Children were kidnapped to become soldiers and were forced to carry out killings. Rape and the mutilation of civilian captives was widely practised and people were also enslaved to provide Renamo with a work force. Such methods were to become all too common in wars throughout Africa in the following decades but some writers have seen in this behaviour a continuity with the pre-colonial past where much of Mozambique had been subject to warlords and their violent enslavement and exploitation of the population.[10]

Frelimo also began to change. At the fourth party congress in 1983 it had begun the process of dismantling the one-party Marxist-Leninist State and the command economy. This process was completed at the next party congress in 1989 when Frelimo trumped Renamo by adopting the principles of the free market and a multi-party constitution. The constitutional changes were enacted in 1990. Frelimo had been greatly strengthened by the publication in the United States in 1988 of the Gersony Report which catalogued the violence employed by Renamo and ended any possibility of the US backing Renamo to the extent that it backed UNITA in Angola. As Stephen Chan and Moisés Venâncio put it, 'Renamo must have been the only so-called anti-communist guerrilla force which Washington did not actively support'.[11]

The final stages of the war witnessed the emergence of a popular movement opposed to both of the warring parties. In 1990 a charismatic leader, known simply as Manuel António, emerged in the Nampula area and rapidly gained a large following, this became known as Naparama (or Nacrama). The Naparama forces claimed to have medicine that made them immune to bullets and they were armed with traditional weapons rather than guns. They successfully drove Renamo out of large areas that had been occupied. Naparama was a strong reassertion of the power of traditional culture and in that respect it provided a challenge both to the violence of Renamo and the modernising secularism of Frelimo. The movement, however, stalled when Manuel António was killed fighting Renamo in 1991.

Peace

Ever since the Nkomati Accord, growing international pressure had been exerted on both Frelimo and Renamo to bring a halt to the war, which neither side seemed likely to win. Frelimo had limited itself to offering an amnesty to Renamo fighters and had insisted on a ceasefire before any negotiations could take place. Renamo, for its part, had demanded to be recognised as an equal negotiating partner and insisted that the one party constitution of the country be abandoned. It seems that the two sides came near to a preliminary agreement in October 1984 when the so-called Pretoria Declaration was drawn up, but Renamo backed away.

Frelimo had a diplomatic network of allies in the region and in the wider world and these continued to put pressure on the party to make important changes to its ideology and its policies. Renamo had fewer allies and the channels of communication to its leadership, which was dangerously divided between Dhlakama in Mozambique and the Lisbon office headed by Evo Fernandes, were not always easy. Mediation was attempted by Kenya, the churches and by certain business leaders but there were few people or institutions that Renamo would trust. In the end the deadlock was broken, rather unexpectedly, by the Catholic Sant' Egidio community which had long standing links with Mozambique and offered a forum in Rome for both sides to meet without preconditions.

Without acceding to Renamo's demands, Frelimo began to make important changes to the nature of its regime. The move away from a socialist command economy, which had been heralded at the fourth party Congress in 1983, was accelerated and in 1987 an economic reform plan was agreed with the IMF. Major constitutional changes were then agreed at the fifth party Congress in 1989 and in 1990 a new constitution was introduced which made provision for multiparty elections.

1989 also saw Renamo take a crucial step from being a guerrilla movement to being a political party. A party congress was held and a series of policies were adopted. Even so, more than two years were to elapse before a Peace Accord was eventually signed. These two years were taken up with prolonged negotiations held in Rome—eleven formal rounds of talks with Chissano and Dhlakama only meeting face to face in August 1992. During these two years Frelimo gradually acceded to most of Renamo's demands, recognising it as a legitimate political movement, and accommodating its demands that Zimbabwean forces should be confined in their combat role and that formal recognition should be accorded to foreign mediators and eventually to the UN. But Frelimo secured the all important recognition that it was the legitimate government of Mozambique—and it resisted all the pressures to accept the idea of a government of national unity to follow the elections.

The transformation of Renamo from a guerrilla movement into a legitimate political movement was no easy task for the mediators. As Roberto Morozzo della Rocca and Luca Riccardi put it in an article on Sant' Egidio's role in the peace process.

There were no magical emotional solutions.... The reason is simple: RENAMO would lay down its arms only when it had sufficient guarantees of the post-war period; guarantees of free political life, guarantees of a minimum of material means to get organized, guarantees of being able to compete democratically for power. RENAMO moved with a high degree of mistrust not only towards its adversary, the FRELIMO government, but towards everyone. It was convinced that much of the world was allied with FRELIMO, that everyone was its enemy.[12]

Richard Synge commented that 'the principal achievement [of the General Peace Accord] was the conversion of Renamo from an almost entirely military force and the instrument of destruction into a credible political organisation.'[13]

During the twenty-seven months of negotiation the international situation and conditions inside Mozambique changed in a number of important respects and it is possible that without these changes the civil war would have dragged on. The end of the Soviet Union brought with it the end of the Cold War and in 1990 the release of Nelson Mandela heralded the end of the apartheid regime in South Africa. Peace talks in Angola led to a linked withdrawal of the Cuban forces from Angola and the South Africans from Namibia, with promises of elections in both countries. Inside Mozambique the rise of Naparama had drastically weakened Renamo while severe drought had brought the country close to catastrophe and had undermined the morale of a government army already close to collapse.

There is some truth in the contention that the Peace Accord was eventually signed because neither side had the capacity to continue the war any longer. As Richard Synge wrote, 'in Mozambique the United Nations role was made considerably simpler by the genuine desire of both sides to halt the fighting'.[14] However, just as Portugal's withdrawal from Africa in 1975 left the wars of independence unfinished and the deeper conflicts unresolved, so too the Peace Accord signed in 1992 left the struggle between Frelimo and its enemies unfinished. Renamo has often been accused of being obstructive and of employing political brinksmanship and blackmail, threatening a continuation of war if it did not get its way. These were tactics that brought it some success in negotiations and it was tactics it continued to apply in the twenty-five years following the Peace Accord. Nor did the role of international mediators in forging compromises cease with the formal end of the war. Although the fighting came to an end in 1992, the wounds caused by the hatred and distrust between the two sides did not heal with time. The significance of this is discussed in the two final chapters.

The United Nations and the Transition to Peace

The signing of the Peace Accord was only the beginning of a two year transition period before elections for a new government were held in October 1994. During this period the United Nations assumed responsibility for the implementation of the terms agreed in Rome. Mindful of the constructive role that Italy had played in bringing the war to a close, the UN appointed the Italian diplomat, Aldo Ajello, as its Special Representative.

The UN had also been involved in the peace process in Angola but its role had been limited to monitoring the elections, the full implementation of the peace agreement being left to the combatants themselves. The Angola experience had ended in disaster as neither side disarmed and the results of the elections were rejected by UNITA. Determined that the peace process in Mozambique would not founder in the same way, the UN mounted what at the time was the biggest operation it had ever undertaken. The operation was known as ONUMOZ and under this overarching organisation the UN took responsibility for demobilisation of the rival armed forces, the resettlement of refugees, the coordination of humanitarian relief, the beginning of the de-mining process and the organisation and monitoring of the elections. Working closely with a team of international donors, the UN became, in effect, the government of the country including taking responsibility for security.

The UN was determined that its commitment to peace in the region would not fail and provided resources on a generous scale.

Over 7,000 peace-keeping military were deployed and 1,100 police; the entire operation was estimated to have cost one million dollars a day. The UN did not have the experience of running a massive operation on this scale. Mistakes were made, there was confusion in some of its activities and delays contributed to spinning out the process a year beyond the deadlines that had originally been set. The UN was determined that the disbanding of the two armies would take place before elections, so that the option of returning to war was not available. This was largely achieved, though it later became clear that although Renamo had demobilised, it had not been effectively disarmed.

Although it is difficult to imagine the Peace Accord being successful without the UN mission, it is also true that the end of the war was in large part brought about by the Mozambican people themselves:

> Millions of displaced Mozambicans showed their faith in the [peace] process by returning spontaneously to their homes as soon as they felt it safe to do so, Ultimately 5 million of a population of 16 million took advantage of the return of peace to reclaim land and property.[15]

There was not only a mass movement of people returning to their homes which was not organised by the UN but many soldiers took matters into their own hands deserting when attempts were made to incorporate them into the new national army. Although there was no 'peace and reconciliation' process as occurred in South Africa, many Mozambican communities adopted their own rituals for adopting boy soldiers back into their communities and the elites on both sides agreed to maintain future silence about the events of the war.

Although the Peace Accord, the subsequent elections and the rebuilding of the country were no mean achievement, the full consequences of the Peace Accord only became visible in the subsequent decades of 'peace' which are discussed in the last two chapters.

8

MOZAMBIQUE AFTER THE CIVIL WAR

The Difficulty of Understanding Modern Mozambique

The twenty-five years after 1992 saw the establishment of peaceful conditions in Mozambique, even if at times this peace came near to breaking down. At the same time it saw the outbreak of a new kind of war among the unusually numerous tribe of scholars, economists and commentators who turned their attention to what was happening in the country. Events in Mozambique became the subject of intense study, debate and disagreement and in particular four problems proved irritatingly intractable. The first of these related to the origins, nature and conduct of the civil war and have been discussed in the previous chapter. The second, arising out of the first, related to Renamo: how was it that a guerrilla movement, responsible for appalling atrocities and destruction, was able to turn itself into a political party that polled strongly in subsequent elections and whose leader, ultimately responsible for those atrocities, came close to winning the presidential elections in 1999? The third question, which, in spite of intense detailed study apparently defies any simple answer, concerns the peasantry. Why was improvement to the economic condition of the rural population so difficult to achieve?

The fourth debate swung to and fro around the prescriptions of the international donor community for achieving sustained economic development. The second of these questions will be further examined in this chapter; the third and fourth will be dealt with in chapter nine.

One reason why no consensus has been possible over these issues is that the interpretation of the past is hotly contested in contemporary politics. Although the makers of the Peace Accord agreed that there would be an amnesty for past crimes and silence over the events that had taken place since independence, and that there would be no Mozambican Peace and Reconciliation Commission as had been set up in South Africa, the past has not been forgotten and the silence is periodically broken. Who owns the narrative of the past, what is the default interpretation of recent history? As Daviz Simango, the leader of Movimento Democrático de Moçambique (MDM), has said, 'Frelimo acts as though it owns the narrative'. Mozambican politicians and intellectuals are left in an impossible position—all subscribe to the idea of 'silence' but this leaves one version of events, the Frelimo version, as unchallenged.[1]

The international community of scholars (and some Mozambican scholars), meanwhile, took no such vow of silence and continually raked over the embers of the past. However, this community did not always view the past with the dispassionate objectivity that might be expected from academics. Many of its members proved to be deeply, in many cases ideologically, committed. There has been a blurring of the roles of scholar, political advocate and development economist. For them also ownership of the narrative of the past is something to be fought for.

Post-civil war Mozambique. The Challenge

After the signing of the Peace Accord in 1992 there was a two year transition period during which a great dealt was done to

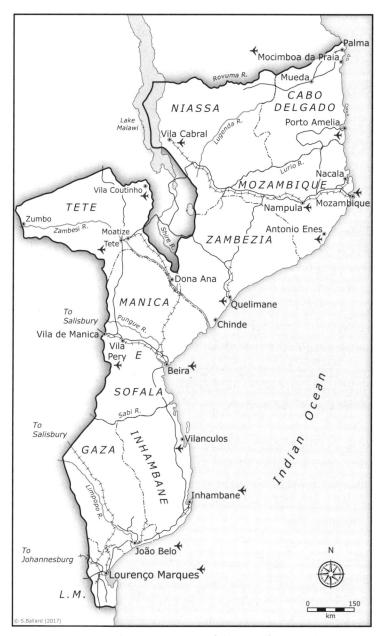

Map 2. Mozambique on the eve of the war of independence

stabilise conditions in the country before elections were held for the office of president and for a new Assembly. In retrospect one cannot help imagining how things would have been different had the decolonisation process in 1975 followed the same pattern of transition.

The challenge which now faced the new Mozambique government was immense. The country's economy and infrastructure, the legacy of the colonial era, had been largely destroyed and the institutional and cultural innovations of Frelimo's early years had proved bankrupt and had to be abandoned. Almost every aspect of the state and the nation had to be reinvented—new liberal democratic institutions and a large element of decentralisation had been promised, the economy had to be rebuilt and a new cultural identity respectful of the country's traditions had to be nurtured.

The new government was not presented with a *tabula rasa*. There were strong elements of continuity to be found, among which were many inheritances from the colonial era including the geographical constraints that resulted from the position of the capital in the extreme south, isolated from the rest of the country and embedded in South Africa, and the infrastructure which bound areas of the country to their inland neighbours rather than to each other. Important also was the way that Mozambique's history had created deep divisions between the north, the central Zambesi valley, and the south. Nor could the new government escape the vagaries of the climate that continued to deliver drought and flood with a careless hand and seemingly at random.

One major advantage that the country did have was the goodwill and active support of the international community. The scale of the political investment that had been made to bring peace to Mozambique meant that this experiment in peacemaking was too important to be allowed to fail. Aid of various kinds and from various sources flowed in to support the national budget and a wide variety of humanitarian relief and development projects. Twenty-five years after the Peace Accord the government still depended on outside aid for fifty per cent of its funding. The international donor community, therefore, remained an important partner in Mozambique's post-conflict development, what Carrie Manning described as a sort of 'external constituency', its 'soft power' and influence undoubtedly helping to shape almost every aspect of the country's future.[2] To a large extent the developments of the twenty-five years after the war can be seen as the Frelimo government trying to accommodate itself to the changing fashions of donor concerns.

Although Mozambique experienced ten years of bitter civil war and since then has staged regular elections which have entrenched the patrimonial relationships of the elites, it is remarkable that ethnic conflict has, on the whole, not characterised the country's politics and ethnic identities have not become a pronounced feature of the political scene. Renamo and Frelimo certainly have regions of the country where they are strongly entrenched but regional identity has not, on the whole, translated into ethnic identity. It is to the credit of political leaders on all sides that politicians have seldom tried to play the 'ethnic card'. Nevertheless ethnic and regional tensions lie near the surface. Frelimo has constantly been accused of being a southern party with a southern leadership and the party was slow to realise that it was to its advantage to be seen to appoint governors and senior administrators from a region's own population. This relative lack of ethnic conflict can be traced to factors in Mozambique's history—the multiplicity of languages, the political traditions that saw states built by invading military elites (Ngoni, Karanga, Afro-Portuguese, coastal Muslim) who attracted clients and tribute paying subjects rather than relying on strong ethnic loyalties, and the diminutive scale of the political units of the 'small society'. None of this history made the absence of ethnic conflict in the late twentieth and early twenty-first centuries inevitable but it helps to understand why Mozambique is not like Rwanda or the South Sudan. The political divisions of the country have remained firmly regional rather than ethnic in character.

Elections and the Problematic Establishment of Liberal Democracy

The Peace Accord had been signed by two sides in the civil war, which had been cajoled into accepting the peaceful processes of liberal democracy. The first national elections, paid for and overseen by the United Nations, were held in 1994. As provided for in the new constitution there have since been national elections, held on a regular five yearly cycle, in 1994, 1999, 2004, 2009 and 2014. The results are shown in the tables below.

Table 1: Seats won in Assembly elections

Party	1994	1999	2004	2009	2014
Frelimo	129	133	160	191	144
Renamo	112	117	90	51	89
UD	9	–	–	–	–
MDM	–	–	–	8	17

Table 2: Percentage of the vote won in presidential elections

	1994	1999	2004	2009	2014
Chissano (Fr)	53.30	52.3	–	–	–
Guebuza (Fr)	–		63.7	75.1	–
Nyusi (Fr)	–	–		–	57.3
Dhlakama (Ren)	33.73	47.7	31.7	16.41	36.61
Simango (MDM)	–	–	–	8.59	6.36

These results show fluctuations in support for each of the parties but an overall clear and consistent pattern. Frelimo was able to command a majority overall and dominated in the capital, the south and the extreme north. Renamo remained strong in the centre and north.

Five elections, passing off relatively peacefully, may seem to indicate that western-style liberal democracy has taken root. However, this conclusion needs some serious qualification. Democratisation is not just an end result but is an on-going process and the nature of this democratic process in Mozambique needs to be understood. First, all the elections were monitored by outside observers who have recorded significant irregularities, ranging from malpractice in the actual recording and counting of votes (which have been carried out in secret) to interference with the nomination of candidates and the general administration of the elections. These have led to protests not only by Renamo but also by the international observers, and to considerable violence in parts of the country following the announcement of the results. The election outcomes have been contested and demands made for modifications in the way future elections are organised.

Second, Frelimo has benefited, at the expense of its rivals, from control of the media and access to transport. After Frelimo's victory in the 2009 elections, which the Economist Intelligence Unit described as 'crushing but highly flawed', it concluded, 'there are growing concerns that public confidence and trust, the basis for the country's remarkable post-war recovery, have been seriously eroded'.[3] After the 2014 election the European Union Election Observation Mission reported that 'the advantage of the ruling party over its adversaries through the use of material and human resources of the state resulted in an uneven playing field'.[4] These irregularities continued in election after election. By 2016 the US funded Freedom House no longer ranked Mozambique as a democracy and the *Economist* funded Democracy Index described it as a 'hybrid' democracy. By 2014 the losing party (Renamo) was ceasing to believe in the electoral process and was challenging the basic principles that underpinned it. This led it to boycott some of the municipal elections. Liberal democracy, instead of becoming firmly rooted, may now be visibly withering away.

Frelimo and Renamo both have a mass following but they are organisations headed by a narrow elite. Their relations have been, from the start, essentially a process of elite bargaining. This bargaining process continues after each election, the international community involved and in some ways acting as a Third Party, with the result, according to one commentator, that 'this triad of Renamo, Frelimo and the international community ... permits the continued exclusion of the population'.[5]

Apart from elections, other aspects of a liberal democratic society have precariously survived. There are opposition newspapers which are generally free to express opinions, although there have been assassinations of journalists who have become too independent in their investigations of the government, notably the killing of Carlos Cardoso in November 2002. The weekly *Magazine Independente*, for example, which is a bilingual publication in Portuguese and English, was able to run a story in March 2016 alleging that Joaquim Chissano, who succeeded Samora Machel as president, was a KGB agent and was directly implicated in the plot that resulted in Machel's death in a plane crash in 1986.[6]

The government, again with the encouragement of international donors, has involved civil society in various consultative exercises, but most observers believe that the legislature and the judiciary are very subservient to the government, in this way transgressing the fundamental principles of the separation of powers, which is the foundation of western-style liberal democracy. Some degree of transparency has been maintained in political and economic matters (largely at the insistence of the international community), for example in the reporting on mineral and hydrocarbon production under the international Extractive Industries Transparency Initiative. Donors have provided funds to support legal aid and the access to the courts for rural populations and the government has created an office (*gabinete*) charged with fighting corruption. Perhaps most important of all, there have been notable concessions to diversity of interest and opinion in the ordering of rural society which are discussed below. All these aspects of democracy reflect donor concerns and are the price that the Frelimo government has had to be pay for continuing donor support.

The first signs that the liberal democratic 'consensus' was in trouble occurred in 2000, following the 1999 elections, when violent incidents connected to Renamo were recorded throughout the country. Although these died down, there was a resurgence of violence in 2010 and in 2014 leading to armed clashes in certain areas and a return to a kind of low level guerrilla warfare with road blocks, the burning of vehicles, and attacks on government installations. In 2016 there were reports of refugees fleeing from Tete Province to neighbouring countries. These outbreaks of violence have been accompanied by radical demands from Renamo for a significant revision of the constitution—and, much to the surprise of most commentators, by a marked revival of support for Renamo at the ballot box.

The reasons why liberal democracy is in danger are many, but any understanding of the problem has to begin with the constitution that was agreed in 1992. Although this conformed to western ideas of what a democratic constitution should be, it has proved to be seriously maladjusted to the realities of African politics. The constitution declared Mozambique to be a unitary state with no formal provision for any form of power sharing. National elections were to be a game in which with the winner took all. In western democracies this is not seen as a major problem as it is assumed that no party will hold power indefinitely, but in Africa the realities are rather different. It has also become increasingly apparent that the peace process had another fatal flaw—it did not secure the effective disarmament of Renamo.

The constitution, as was first devised, envisaged a significant element of decentralisation and local democracy. The plan was to divide the whole country, rural areas as well as urban, into 128 municipalities, which would then be controlled by an elected mayor and municipal assembly. However, soon after the elections of 1994, this idea was watered down so that only 33 municipalities were established in urban areas. This had the effect of excluding 75 per cent of the population from having a direct say in their local government. In this way, it has been suggested, the divide between the urban and rural populations, enshrined in law during colonial times in the *indigenato*, has been perpetuated. The urban population can vote for their representatives as citizens while the rural population are identified as belonging to 'traditional' communities represented by community authorities. The main political reason for this was undoubtedly to weaken Renamo's influence as far as local government was concerned and to make sure that control of the natural resources of the country remained in the hands of the central, Frelimo-controlled government. Renamo, and the other smaller parties, reacted by boycotting the municipal elections in 1998 with the result that only 14.5 per cent of the electorate voted. By 2013 the number of municipalities had been increased to 53, but still less than half the number originally planned.

Frelimo

Politics in Mozambique, as in so many other parts of Africa, are distinctly patrimonial in nature. Although Frelimo went through a phase immediately after independence of being ideologically driven in a Marxist direction and was subject to the disciplines imposed on it by Machel, this gave way after his death to a more familiar pattern of patrimonialism in which a political elite, through its control of state resources (including foreign aid), was able to reward its immediate followers, largely to the exclusion of the rest of the population. As in other African countries, one way in which patrimonialism works is through the control of appointments within the bureaucracy (even though party and state are supposed to be quite separate) and control of parastatals which can provide jobs for the elite's clients and access for the elites to soft loans. In Mozambique the most notorious case was the write-off of 'bad debts' by the Banco Commercial de Moçambique. Privatisations, insisted on by the donors, have also proved a lucrative way of rewarding regime insiders who have acquired shares and positions on the boards of privatised companies. A more sinister development has been the recent spate of political assassinations of opposition figures and the rise of criminal activity, including kidnappings, with the allegation that the police (and those in charge of the police) are among the beneficiaries and probably the perpetrators.

The new constitution adopted at the end of the civil war made clear the separation between party and state but many in Frelimo found it difficult to adjust to the new world where state and party were not one and the same and where account had to be taken of other political players. The party could not now automatically do what it liked and 'the tension between the rule of law and the deeply ingrained pull of party interest' became palpable.[7]

Although the character of this patrimonial form of politics is familiar throughout much of Africa, it is probably true that its excesses have been more muted in Mozambique than in many other parts of the continent, partly because, within Frelimo, there survives some of the idealism that had marked the independence struggle and the belief that Frelimo should be a modernising and uniting force within the country. In many respects Mozambique remains more orderly, more transparent, more abiding by the rule of law and less authoritarian than many African regimes.

Among ordinary people in the south support for Frelimo has become almost a determinant of communal identity. According to research carried out by Simona Montanari in a rural area of Gaza province in 2009, it is Frelimo, not Renamo, that is widely accredited with having introduced democracy—and indeed is thought of as being synonymous with 'democracy'. 'I can't say when democracy first came', said one interviewee, 'for I never went to school and I was never taught properly, but I remember that previously women used to sit and eat on their own, aside from men. Frelimo gave women freedom of speech, too'. And another commented: 'Now my wife can eat with me and I must not beat her'. 'Frelimo banned traditional ceremonies, maybe because it didn't want people to get drunk with our home-made beer and get killed by Renamo bands. But recently, ceremonies have been authorised again, in a manner that everything seems now back as it used to be.' Montanari sums up the widely accepted view of this Frelimo inspired democracy. 'It is fair to say that one behaves democratically, when he/she lives a life free from excesses, one where a wife is not beaten by the husband and can sit and talk in his presence, and where the possibility of perpetuating old habits, such as polygamy, has been reintegrated'. Democracy, therefore, is understood not in terms of elections but as having transformed social relations, as the Frelimo ideology of the Machel era had proclaimed.[8]

As a ruling party Frelimo is guided by the single determining principle that it will not, under any circumstances, relinquish power, ever. This determination holds the party together in spite of internal rivalries and disagreements which can become extremely bitter. Unlike so many other regimes in Africa,

Frelimo has not tried to establish perpetual rule by a single leader. The constitution provides for a president holding office for only two terms and this has been adhered to. Chissano gave way to Guebuza in 2004 and, in turn, he rather reluctantly stepped down in 2014 in favour of Filipe Nyusi, a younger man who originated from the north. Although the Economist Intelligence Unit concluded in 2010 that Guebuza's 'centralisation of power in the presidency and micromanagement have all but extinguished the tradition of internal debate and discussion inside Frelimo',[9] the accession of Nyusi allowed Frelimo to continue to reflect different strands of opinion, the ideas of different generations and even, to some extent, different regional interests, though the party is still seen by many people as essentially a southern party. Although there have been notable rivalries within the party elite, rivalries that have increased with the election of Nyusi, Frelimo has remained remarkably cohesive and its support among the middle classes fairly solid. As a political machine it has successfully won elections and secured its control over the state's resources. Party and state remain very close, almost as close as in the days when it wore its Marxist clothing, and in many respects they are still one and the same.

Given that retaining power is the basic objective that underlies all Frelimo's policies and actions, the elite have only limited room for manoeuvre in dealing with Renamo. It is not clear what strategy Frelimo can adopt to secure its avowed aim, which it has held since its foundation, of achieving a non-racial, non-ethnic, non-regional national unity. With Renamo having resumed a limited armed struggle, the dilemmas have grown: make concessions to Renamo and be seen to give way to force; allow greater devolved powers to the provinces and Renamo will be the main beneficiary; maintain strong central government control over regional budgets and resources and Frelimo will remain unpopular in the centre and north; step up security measures and see the resulting headlines denouncing the violence of government troops against civilians. To some extent Frelimo's strategy seems limited to growing the economy and hoping that this will bring benefits that will of themselves, build support. However, the growing insecurity resulting from Renamo's activities has the potential for slowing down or even halting altogether the inflow of foreign investment which for twenty years has been a major cause of this growth. Faced by these dilemmas there is a strong faction within Frelimo that look only for an Angolan-style solution—the death of the leader of the opposition.

In March 2016 the government showed that it was open to the idea of mediation between itself and Renamo, and a mediating mission headed by Mario Raffaelli was appointed, but the weekly *Zambeze*, which is generally opposed to the government, was sceptical of the genuineness of Frelimo's desire to end the stand-off with Renamo by negotiation, which, it claimed, was the result of a careful calculation of political forces.

> If these are favourable it will profit by the opportunities it offers. If they are unfavourable they will use the negotiations as a tactical manoeuvre to gain time to alter the balance of forces in its favour or to create an impression of calm and goodwill before launching an energetic offensive on another front of the conflict.[10]

It is perhaps inevitable to make a comparison between Mozambique and Angola. In Angola, José Edaurdo dos Santos has established total control over his party and has, in effect, turned the office of president into a dictatorship. He has been able to do this because his forces emphatically won the civil war against UNITA and killed its leader. In addition Angola's wealth in oil and diamonds, much of it diverted into funds directly controlled by the president, has enabled him to withstand pressure from international donors, secure allies interested in Angola's oil and use his wealth to co-opt leading members of civil society and even the opposition parties. The wealth he controls also allows him to dominate the media and to maintain a large and effective army. Having established this degree of control over the wealth and institutions of the country, Santos retains a façade of legitimacy by holding elections, which he and his party win easily. Meanwhile, in spite of the country's wealth, Angola still ranks very low in the Human Development Index. It is clear that Frelimo has not been as successful as the MPLA in Angola in co-opting important members of the opposition. In contrast to the MPLA, Frelimo remains dependent on international donors, does not have a very effective army and is unable to deploy sovereign wealth funds on the scale of Angola. Moreover its victories in elections, even with the flagrant manipulation of results, is too close for comfort.

However, the comparison with Angola does raise some important questions. Santos in Angola has been very systematic, and largely successful, in co-opting potential opposition forces and incorporating them into the patrimonial networks that run Angola. It is not clear why Frelimo, in contrast, has been only spasmodically successful in winning over members of the opposition elites and why it does not make greater efforts to win popular support in the centre and north of the country. Whatever its strategy may have been, there is no doubt that Frelimo has not succeeded in replacing its image as a party of southerners, ruling in the interests of the south.

Renamo

The political leaders of Renamo are also essentially patrimonial in their outlook. In order to secure Dhlakama's participation in the elections the international community made sure that substantial funding went to Renamo to pay the costs of its campaign. Richard Synge referred to the trust fund set up for Renamo as 'an effective insurance policy against failure'.[11] This enabled Dhlakama to reward his immediate followers with salaried positions and other benefits like houses in the capital. However, although Renamo polls strongly in up to half the provinces, as a party it has few resources to distribute. This presents Renamo with a dilemma, which cannot be met satisfactorily in a unitary state where politics is a zero-sum game.

Renamo has proved maladroit at operating within a liberal democratic framework—holding the government to account, influencing opinion and building networks in civil society—and Dhlakama has a poor reputation as a negotiator. In part this can be explained by the relatively low level of education of Renamo deputies. As a result it has increasingly sought to influence events through an orchestrated return to violence or the threat of violence rather than through 'democratic' channels. After the 1999 elections Renamo called for countrywide protests, which resulted in violence, including many deaths at the hands of the security forces. Further violence occurred after the elections in 2004, 2009 and 2014. Dhlakama frequently threatened that Renamo would 'return to the bush' and in October 2012 he retreated to a rural stronghold in Gorongosa. Attacks on isolated government posts, road blocks, the burning of lorries and buses, the establishment of no-go areas in rural parts of the country, all create an atmosphere of political crisis which is accompanied by demands for negotiations and even for foreign mediation. On 19 March 2016 *Notícias*, a newspaper that generally supports the government, published an article which reflected on one such incident.

CAIA TO NHAMPAZA: TO TRAVEL WITH ONE'S HEART IN ONE'S HANDS

To start with, to one who is a Mozambican this title cannot appear strange, given that it is known in the country and abroad that Mozambique is living in a state of political and military tension which has required the reintroduction of convoys on some sections of the EN-1...

If a Mozambican should find this title strange then it is because he is one of those who wants, and always will want, there to be armed confrontations in the country in order to get some dividend from them. It is rather a title that is a cry of protest of a Mozambican citizen against what is happening at this moment in those regions which are important for the socio-economic life of the country....

During the passage of the convoy we were lucky not to be killed, since shots were fired from the dense bush, which provoked a general panic. Cries for help were heard and women wept demanding and appealing as mothers to the deepest sentiments of the politicians and governors of this country to put an end to the war. We experienced a moment of pure terror and chaos in which each person sought, in whatever way he could, to protect himself from the bullets. At last a scenario was enacted, unimaginable for a country which claims to be united and independent and which enjoys a democratic pluralism and was already considered an example for the world of reconciliation after a long and bloody war.... Even if some pretext can be found to justify the resort to arms, what most concerns us now, and is urgent, is that something must be done so that this tension finally ends .... The intelligence of Mozambicans is more than sufficient to resolve through agreement problems like this political-military confrontation.[12]

Since 2000 Renamo's demands have been focused on the idea that it should have the right to appoint governors in the provinces where a majority of voters had supported it. In 2016 it even went as far as to announce that it would take power in these areas with or without the government's consent. It demanded international mediation and in March 2016 Mario Rafaelli, who had been Italy's chief mediator during the negotiations which led to the 1992 Peace Accord, visited Mozambique. He and his team spent months holding talks with both sides before abandoning his efforts at the end of the year.[13]

After its boycott of municipal elections in 1998, and its poor showing in the 2004 and 2009 elections, many people predicted that Renamo was in terminal decline. They were surprised when the party began once again to poll strongly. In 2009 a structure of provincial assemblies was created and in 2014 a revived

Renamo won a majority in three of these (Sofala, Zambesia and Tete) while in Nampula and Manica it had parity with Frelimo, providing a basis for Dhlakama to demand that Renamo should be able to appoint the governors of all these provinces. Renamo's strong showing in the voting for the Assembly of the Republic in 2014 led one commentator to decide 'not only that targeted violence forced Frelimo into negotiations, but also that voters rewarded it [Renamo] for this.'[14]

The political realities that have re-established themselves after these elections show that Renamo has a large, and possibly growing, following—particularly among youth. This following is regionally based and reflects a generalised feeling that the central and northern regions have been neglected by a remote and even hostile central government. Renamo does not promise different policies from Frelimo, indeed it is even more patrimonial in its outlook, but its main attraction is that it is 'not the government'. The Economist Intelligence Unit commented in 2013, just before the elections, that 'many Mozambicans have been disillusioned by the ruling party's sense of entitlement and its failure to ensure that the poor benefit significantly from two decades of outstanding economic performance'.[15] Michel Cahen referred to Renamo in the 1994 election as a 'coalition of the marginalised'[16] and to some extent this has remained true. Political analysts too often assume that people vote for a political party or a political programme and in consequence direct their analysis that way. In fact voters are just as often inspired to vote by what they are against. Political parties and coalitions are made up of people who disagree on what they are for but are united by what they are against. Important also are community ties. Voting in the same way as one's neighbours is an important way of expressing solidarity with the community and adherence to communal values, and is not necessarily a result of *homo economicus*, beloved of some economists, making an informed choice according to individual economic self-interest. Viewed in this light the continued support for Renamo makes perfect sense.

On the positive side, Renamo claims to have been the real founder of democracy in Mozambique—'Frelimo brought national independence and founded the Mozambique state, Renamo brought democracy' is a formula to which many subscribe. As a political party, it is difficult to separate Renamo from its leader, Afonso Dhlakama. Dhlakama clearly possesses a certain charisma and has led Renamo since 1979. Although often dismissed as a man lacking political ideas and essential political skills, it is important to recall the positive impression he created on Michel Cahen who followed him during the campaign of 1994 and wrote very favourably of Dhlakama's rapport with ordinary people among whom he is believed to possess considerable power in the spirit world.[17] The question inevitably is asked— what will happen if and when Dhlakama goes—questions which surface every time there is a news report that he is ill and receiving medical treatment.[18]

Movimento Democrático de Moçambique (MDM)

If history seems to have created a two party system in national elections, third parties being squeezed as they so often are, in local elections a third party has nevertheless established itself. The Movimento Democrático de Moçambique was founded in 2009 as a breakaway from Renamo. In the two elections that followed its foundation it won 8 and 17 seats in the Assembly of the Republic but in municipal elections it proved much more successful, in 2013 capturing control of major municipalities, including Beira and Nampula, the second and third biggest cities in the country, and Quelimane. It also won 40 per cent of the vote in the capital—a very significant result given the fact that Maputo, with its large middle class electorate, is usually considered to be Frelimo's heartland and receives so many of the benefits of foreign aid and investment.

Between them Renamo and MDM, the anti-Frelimo parties, won or had parity with Frelimo in 6 of the 11 provinces in 2014 elections. It is clear that, taking into account the obvious manipulation of results by the government, the electorate is very evenly split between pro- and anti-Frelimo opinion. It is even possible that Dhlakama may actually have won the 1999 presidential election, which he firmly believes to have been the case. According to Joseph Hanlon, before that election Chissano had become very unpopular, and was widely believed to be corrupt—so that the 1999 election became a sort of referendum on Chissano's presidency.[19]

Coming to Terms with Traditional Society: New Land Regulations and Rural Development

Although Frelimo claimed to be a vanguard party defending the interests of workers and peasants, the party was in practice very suspicious of the peasantry, which it believed, not without reason, to be fundamentally hostile to the new order. When Frelimo took power in 1975 one of its major ambitions was to alter radically the basic structures of rural society and the rural economy. To achieve this the influence of 'traditional' authorities was to be replaced by administrators appointed by the central government. Alongside this radical measure, it was planned to collectivise the rural population and establish village co-operatives while at the same time pursuing policies which would undermine the influence of traditional healers and religious leaders. In practice Frelimo's administrators had to co-operate with the lineage and village heads, some of whom became active members of the dynamising groups and it was the higher levels in the traditional hierarchy, the *régulos* or *mambos*, who found their authority supplanted by government officials.

By the time the Peace Accord was signed, the general hostility to Frelimo's revolutionary project had allowed Renamo to establish itself throughout the centre and much of the north of the country. Although the scholarly community may have argued themselves into a stalemate over whether it was Frelimo's policies that were responsible for the rise and survival of Renamo, it is interesting to read what was said about this question by Frelimo itself in the Central Committee's report to the Sixth Congress in 1991.

> Today we can say that the essential errors we committed were linked to an overestimation of the degree of collective consciousness of the popular masses and to the conviction that a strong will could succeed in trans-forming society in a short period of time. We sought to generalise to the entire country the experiences and sentiments of the populations of the liberated zones, without taking into due account the economic and social complexity of the nation, the types of social relations, the dominant form of property relations, and the structural consequences of the colonial order. We disregarded the value of these experiences, and this permitted ruptures in the wider social base and in the alliances forged during the armed struggle, in particular with traditional leaders[20]

Following the implications of this report, once it had won the 1994 election, one of the Frelimo government's top priorities became a radical revision of rural policy. A number of issues had to be resolved. Rural communities needed to have their access to land enshrined in law, a system for managing the natural resources of the land had to be devised, provision had to be made for foreign investors to acquire land titles and an over-arching system of local government put in place which would include a role for 'traditional' authorities.

Corrado Tornimbeni describes the principles that underlay this new approach. 'The "empowerment of the local society" was, in theory, the driving concept of the new policies on local bodies and authorities, land, and forests and wildlife.'[21] As already indicated above, it was decided to exclude the rural areas from the new structure of municipalities on the grounds that 'only community-based policies could offer an opportunity for some kind of decentralisation in rural areas'. In other words, the rural population (75 per cent of the total population) were to be organised on a communal basis while in the urban municipalities individual citizens would elect their governors through the ballot box. The colonial term *regulado* was used to describe the communities that were now to be recognised.

The new structure of land management and rural government was elaborated in a series of laws passed between 1997 and 2000 covering land titles, forestry and wildlife and the legal status of 'traditional' authorities. With this legal structure in place community land maps were to be drawn up indicating the land reserved for each community, with the government issuing formal titles for these communities to use and profit by their land, although actual ownership of the land was vested in the state. Communities could claim rights to land that had been in use for 10 years and companies or individuals who wished to invest in agriculture would have to negotiate directly with the interested communities.

This new legal framework was, in general, supported by the donor community and was in part a response to the concerns it had expressed that the rural population were unrepresented and neglected by the government. However, implementing new arrangements was not straightforward.

The first problem was the mobility of the population. After the civil war large numbers of displaced persons tried to return to the land, while others followed a traditional pattern of seasonal migration in search of work. In frontier districts immigrants from across the border (for example from Zimbabwe during the troubles in that country) also arrived in large numbers. It became increasingly difficult to decide to which community people belonged and where they might claim to have access to the land. A system of identity passes, based on the *guias da mar-*

cha used during the civil war, was introduced in some areas—once more conjuring up memories of the *cadernetes* of the colonial past.

The second problem was caused by the overlapping claims of different communities and by disputes over who was the legitimate 'traditional' authority and who within the hierarchy of authorities should exercise which function. In some areas rival chiefs, supported by either Renamo or Frelimo challenged each other's credentials. *Régulos*, who retained much prestige and performed a cohesive role in conflict resolution at the local level, were now to become local agents of the government, as they had been in colonial times. After the official recognition accorded to them by the law of 2000, these 'chiefs' were granted a payment for the taxes collected in their areas—again reminiscent of colonial practice. This provided an incentive to encourage immigration and the settlement of outsiders.

The problems which threatened to nullify much of the new rural policy centred on the acquisition of land by large scale mining and agricultural business. As the development of coal mining became a major concern for the government, legal provision had to be made for the government to allocate land for mining, albeit with strong protection for the local communities embodied in a resettlement decree. In theory this gave the local communities the right to be resettled in an area where they could maintain their standard of living and customary agricultural practices. However, as with so many of the legal structures of modern Mozambique, there was often a huge disparity between what the law provided for and what actually happened in practice. Although rural communities were protected in many ways by the law, in practice they found it difficult to obtain redress.

Although the legal structures governing the access to, and use of, land provide a considerable element of decentralised control placed in the hands of rural communities, the central government still held the reins in its hands, as land titles, the recognition of authorities etc. all ended up as a government responsibility. There was relatively little opportunity for Renamo to use the system for its own patrimonial purposes.

Bringing Down the Frontier Barriers

Although, since its formation, the Organisation for African Unity (now the African Union) recognised that the colonial frontiers were sacrosanct in the post-colonial era, these frontiers have become increasingly lines on a map rather than effective frontiers between different nation states. Everywhere in Africa the frontiers have become porous as people and goods cross them almost at will and most states lack the capacity to police them even if they wished to do so.

For Mozambique this situation was not new and was an aspect of the continuity between the colonial and post-colonial present. During the colonial era Mozambique's frontiers scarcely presented any barrier to people crossing to escape taxation or forced labour, or in search of work, education or permanent settlement in the British colonies, or to people returning with goods purchased in the better stocked shops across the border. Indeed, as Corrado Tornimbeni has said, in many respects the internal frontiers between districts within Mozambique were more effective than the external borders.[22]

This situation did not change in any significant way after independence, although employment opportunities in South Africa began to dry up. During the civil war Renamo fighters crossed and recrossed the borders with Rhodesia, South Africa and Malawi as did refugees fleeing the fighting in Mozambique. South Africa's destabilisation campaign also recognised no borders. However, in one respect the civil war did respect the international frontiers and did not spill over into neighbouring countries. Renamo did not conduct military operations beyond Mozambique's frontiers even though it undoubtedly had the capacity to do so.

Since 1992 the movement of people and contraband goods across the frontiers continued, though against the grain of history much of this movement was into rather than out of Mozambique. The relative stability of Mozambique since the Peace Accord attracted immigrants from Zimbabwe (including a few of the white farmers expelled from their farms) and there was significant immigration of those fleeing the growing instability of West Africa and the Horn of Africa. Nampula, for example, acquired a large community of Malians as well as Eritreans and Somalis.

It might have been expected that the international community would have encouraged a strengthening of the international borders, as the prescriptions of the IMF and World Bank seem to require discreet national economies, subject to national policies and implemented by national governments. However, in one important respect the international community has not only encouraged, but even helped, to institutionalise the weakening and even the disappearance of national borders. In 2000, following extensive negotiations, the transfrontier parks were created. Two of these were created, the Great Limpopo Transfrontier Park and the Chimanimani Transfrontier Conservation Area. The first of these merged the Kruger National Park of South Africa with national parks in Mozambique and Zimbabwe to create a single park of 37,500 square kilometres, which became fully operational in 2002. The Chimanimani Conservation Area at 1,000 square kilometres was much smaller, but also included areas in both Mozambique and Zimbabwe.

The idea behind the parks was to help preserve Africa's wildlife by opening up larger areas for the migration of animals. The economic rationale was to encourage tourism. The schemes were strongly backed by international foundations, like the Peace Parks Foundation, concerned with the long-term future of Africa's natural resources. The governments of Mozambique, South Africa and Zimbabwe co-operated, as this became a condition for the continuation of international aid streams. There were, of course, implications for the communities living within the parks, which found they could not register land titles under the terms of the Land Law and became subject to the park administrations, with less control over their affairs than communities in other parts of the country. Indeed the park administration (in Mozambique a section of the Ministry of Tourism) put pressure on the populations within the parks, estimated at some 7,000 persons, to relocate. As has been pointed out, legislation designed to empower local communities and protect their rights was reversed in the parks, and resulted in greater state control of the land.

Fifteen years after their foundation, the fate of the Transfrontier Parks has not been entirely what had been anticipated. Opening the borders to the free movement of animals meant opening them to the movement of poachers and a regular war broke out between poachers and game wardens. In the early months of 2016 it was reported in the Mozambique press that at least fifteen poachers had been killed. It need hardly be said that these were extra-judicial killings.

In Chimanimani the growth of illegal gold prospecting, which became a virtual gold rush after 2006, and the ability of those washing for gold to operate freely either side of a non-existent international border, led to severe environmental degradation and the collapse of all the objectives identified in establishing the conservation area. Once again the Zimbabwe and Mozambique governments lacked either the will or the capacity to control the situation. Exactly the same can be said about the laws in place to licence fishing in Mozambique waters. According to the law all trawlers had to obtain licences but in practice illegal fishing continued unchecked. Once again events in Mozambique had demonstrated that it was one thing to pass laws that followed the dictates and fashions of the international community but quite another thing to enforce them.

The Trajectory of Modern Mozambican politics

Frelimo was founded in 1964 at a time when African nationalism held out high hopes for the future of the continent. Under Machel the party articulated a clear vision of the future of Mozambique, which would be cleansed of the corruption, superstition and exploitation of the colonial regime. These aspirations were enthusiastically echoed by friendly western commentators who saw in Frelimo (and in PAIGC) the harbingers of a new democratic and egalitarian society.

With Frelimo's assumption of power, African realities gradually asserted themselves, first when the guerrilla movement that had been so successful against the Portuguese colonial regime proved quite unable to respond effectively to the guerrilla army of Renamo raised against them. The Peace Accord, and aid bonanza that followed, rapidly transformed the Frelimo elite into a patrimonial political class which, in spite of the lip-service being paid to liberal democratic ideals, was determined to hang on to power at all costs. And the costs increasingly involved not only corruption, soon to achieve gargantuan proportions, but crime, fraud and political assassinations. Contemplating the history of the last fifty years, the ironies come thick and fast, as the accusations levelled so freely against the colonial regime in the early 1960s become a template for describing the regime that has inherited its power.

9

ECONOMY AND SOCIETY SINCE 1994

How Poor is Mozambique?

What happened to Mozambique's economy and society after the signing of the Peace Accord of 1992 and to what extent did the outcomes match the expectations of those involved? Nearly a generation later, the Human Development Index (HDI) for 2014 ranked Mozambique 180 out of 188 independent countries on its list. Above it were to be found such models of progressive development as South Sudan (ranked 168), Gambia (ranked 175) and Guinea Bissau ranked 178. 'Imagine that we are speaking of a sporting competition. To be in 180ᵗʰ position out of 188 international contestants is a very poor result' was how the monthly magazine *Exame—Moçambique* began its analysis in its March 2016 edition. The only sign of optimism, it concluded, was that the results were no worse than the year before and that, if the long term progress made since 1980 was considered, there had been a 75 per cent improvement in the country's 'score'. Nevertheless there was no denying that Mozambique was the worst placed of all the SADC countries and last among the former Portuguese colonies.

The overall scoring of the Human Development Index by itself meant little but the detail was more revealing. Life expectancy was 55.1 years where the regional average was 58.5 years. Among adults over 25 the average schooling received was 3.2 years as opposed to a regional average of 5.2 years, while only 50.6 per cent of those over 15 were literate. GDP was $1123 per person per annum, only a third of the regional average (although this had improved 107 per cent since 1980) and 60.7 per cent of the population lived on less than $1.25 a day. Unemployment stood at 22.5 per cent (double the regional average) while for youth it was 39.3 per cent (three times the regional average). And the World Bank, reporting in April 2016, painted a similar picture. 'The social progress index for access to improved sources of water and sanitation ranks Mozambique 128th and 119th, respectively, out of 135 countries. Indeed, Mozambique has one of the lowest levels of water consumption in the world.'[1]

So, why is Mozambique so backward and why are Mozambicans among the poorest people in the world?

How to Remedy Mozambique's Poverty

Reading these figures, it is difficult to believe that in the twenty years after the end of the war Mozambique experienced exceptionally impressive growth in its GDP, averaging over 7 per cent per annum and reaching a peak of 9.8 per cent in 1998. In spite of erratic rainfall, most of the country is relatively well watered and productive. Dams provide some areas with irrigation and hydroelectricity. There are valuable natural resources in the form of coal, graphite and natural gas. The long coastline has hundreds of miles of pristine sandy beaches attractive for tourists. The sea offers rich opportunities for fishing and the ports along the coast provide inland neighbours with access to the Indian Ocean. These natural advantages were exploited with some success by the Portuguese to produce a diversified economy, which largely paid its way, as far as this can be calculated for an economy that formed part of a unified Lusophone economic zone. Moreover, since 1992, Mozambique has enjoyed relative internal stability that compares favourably with many countries in Africa and is treated as a favoured son by the IMF and World Bank. In November 2012 the Economist Intelligence Unit posed the question in a simple form—why has 'Mozambique's outstanding economic performance ... failed to benefit the poor'?[2] And it is this question, and the way it has been understood by the government, by commentators and by the international donor community, which anyone visiting Mozambique, or hoping to do business there, needs to grasp.

Understanding this question, and suggesting some possible ways of answering it, depends very much on people's mind-set— the bundle of assumptions with which they approach Mozambique's recent history—and their preconceptions about what constitutes 'development'. For some, colonial rule can still be held responsible for the structural underdevelopment of the country. For others it was the experiment with a command economy, Soviet-style, that ruined the economy and led directly to the civil war. For others yet again the ten year civil war, and the massive destruction and loss of life that accompanied it, has meant that Mozambique has needed decades of rehabilitation just to return to where it was in 1980. Then, there are those who lay the blame firmly on the doctrinaire liberal economic policies, which were forced on the country by the IMF in the years immediately following the Peace Accord. Most informed observers would probably take some account of each of these explanations without finding any one of them entirely satisfactory.

A totally different approach is that taken by those who see 'underdevelopment' as in large part the product of Africa's patrimonial political culture. After all, in the HDI list of countries, the bottom twenty-five are (with the exception of Afghanistan) all in sub-Saharan Africa. 'Underdevelopment' may leave most of the population poor, or very poor, but it can enrich the ruling elites and their patrimonial client base. The elites benefit both directly and indirectly from the flow of aid, from collaboration with international capital and from the 'asset stripping' of a country's resources. It is now forty years since the end of colonial rule in Mozambique and twenty-five years since the Peace Accord, years in which the Frelimo elite have been in charge of their own destiny—ample time to have made a difference. But in the world of African patrimonial politics there are few if any rewards for making the poor less poor.

Since the end of the civil war Mozambique has been receiving aid averaging over one billion dollars a year, rising to two billion after 2010. Admittedly, as Hanlon and Smart point out, not all this aid is money that can be spent directly on developing the country's economy and relieving poverty. Much of it is debt relief or money spent on consultants while aid disbursed by NGOs often goes to pay the salaries and administration costs of the NGOs themselves. They estimate that only 58 per cent of aid is actually 'useable'.[3] Nevertheless this still makes Mozambique, over a period of nearly twenty-five years, one of the world's largest recipients of aid in the world. Yet Mozambique still remains among the poorest countries in the world. There appears to be a simple equation here, one that has led many people to question whether there is not some direct causal link between aid and poverty. Perhaps the country would be better off with less aid or with no aid at all. This idea has even been voiced by some members of the Frelimo elite, including former president Armando Guebuza himself, who is on record as saying that Mozambicans must cease simply 'holding out our hand begging' for aid.[4]

Why might aid produce poverty rather than development? Here the argument enters the highly controversial world of economic ideology which, during the Cold War, was inextricably linked to the struggle of the Eastern and Western blocs for world dominance and which, to some extent, has persisted to the present. To understand how this has affected Mozambique it is necessary to trace the continuities of the story back to colonial times.

A History of Development Policy

Under the Portuguese Mozambique was part of a single 'Portuguese' economic zone. It shared a common currency with Portugal and the other colonies, received much of its private and public investment from Portugal or Portuguese companies and had a protected market for much of what it produced, a factor of major importance for an economy struggling to achieve some form of development. After independence the government of Mozambique tried, understandably, to separate itself from its dependence on Portugal but its independence came at a difficult time, with a world wide depression following the 1973 Middle East War and a drastic cutting back of remittances from migrant workers in South Africa. As a result the Frelimo government tried to introduce a largely self-sufficient planned economy with central control of foreign exchange and investment (much as Portugal had done back in the early 1930s) and sought to join Comecon and benefit from being a member of another closed economic bloc.

Mozambique's application to join Comecon was finally turned down in 1981. By this time its planned economy was showing some signs of success (though this is disputed by some economists) but any economic recovery was soon wiped out by the escalating South African destabilisation policies and the civil war, as well as by natural disasters like the famine of 1983. The economy began to contract and soon had disintegrated entirely in many parts of the country. In order to survive, the Frelimo government, still led by the committed socialist and moderniser Samora Machel, became increasingly dependant on aid from Western countries, with Sweden, Italy and the Netherlands by far the largest of the donors. The financing of the government required that Mozambique join the IMF and World Bank, which it did in 1983. These organisations, dominated by the United States and its economic doctrines, became increasingly insistent that Mozambique adopt structural adjustment as a path to economic recovery and that it move generally in the direction of opening the economy to the free market. The first package, known as the Economic Recovery Programme, was adopted in 1987 and donor aid streams increased. Unexpectedly the Soviet Union in its dying days became Mozambique's largest bilateral donor—no doubt anxious to do something to retain a regional ally. Total aid, which in 1981 had been a modest $158 million, ballooned to $735million in 1987 and $1,061million in 1990.

By this time the functioning economy of the country had been virtually destroyed by the war and foreign aid accounted for 41 per cent of GDP. In 1986 industrial production was 20 per cent of what it had been in 1981 and exports were 28 per cent, while agricultural production had fallen by 50 per cent.[5] Then, from 1992 to 1994, the country was virtually taken over by ONUMOZ, the United Nations peace keeping project, and for three years the UN agencies were Mozambique's largest donors.

The aid that Mozambique received during this period had major long term consequences for the country. First, it helped to establish a relatively well-paid elite which received salaries and other 'perks' working for the United Nations or for the NGOs which now entered the country in large numbers. The political process leading up to the 1994 elections also saw funds channelled directly to Renamo, so that its personnel also briefly enjoyed the aid bonanza. The arrival of this aid, of course, nourished the patrimonial personality of the whole political process.

The other consequence of these enlarged flows of aid was that the government had to follow the precepts of economic liberalism as embodied in the Washington Consensus—a term which came into use after 1989 to describe the prevailing policies of the World Bank and IMF. These policies had their origins in Latin America but were soon applied wholesale throughout Africa and were coupled with demands for the introduction of liberal democratic constitutional freedoms and multiparty elections. Mozambique was not alone in having to implement these policies and the early 1990s saw elections and constitutional changes in all the former Portuguese colonies and throughout much of the rest of Africa.

The key features of structural adjustment, according to the Washington Consensus, were a reduction in the size of government, confining direct government activity to the maintenance of infrastructure and education; limiting or eliminating entirely government intervention in the economy, liberalising trade by the removal of tariffs on imports and the ending of subsidies on such things as food and fuel on which the poorest sections of the population depended. Devaluing the currency, it was hoped, would promote exports. State owned operations were to be privatised and barriers to inward investment, including the ownership of property, removed. The prevailing belief was that these measures would encourage inward investment and that the resulting growth in the economy would create jobs, encourage the creation of local SMEs and, in general, help a local entrepreneurial class to emerge. Meanwhile regular multiparty elections would serve to hold the government to account, check corruption and limit the diversion of resources to patrimonial networks.

The general direction of this prescriptive development policy was modified by the adoption in 2000 of the UN's Millennium Development Goals. These aimed to eradicate extreme hunger and poverty, achieve universal primary education, promote gender equality, reduce child mortality, improve maternal health, combat AIDS and malaria, and ensure environmental sustainability. These aims were, in one sense, a critique of the Washington Consensus policies since they implicitly recognised that economic liberalisation had not so far achieved progress towards any of the Millennium Goals, which now had to be addressed more directly by development economists and donors. It soon became clear that there would have to be a much greater role for government than had been envisaged by the World Bank and IMF in the immediate post-civil war period. Instead of structural adjustment, the new economic regime found expression in the Poverty Reduction Action Plans (PARP), the first of which was PARPA which covered the years 2001–05. This was succeeded by PARP/A-II for the years 2006–10 and then by PARP 2011–14. These formidable 'plans' were supported by a whole battery of reports, monitoring commissions, strategies and reviews. There was the National Planning System, the Medium Term Fiscal Framework, the Economic and Social Plan, the National Poverty and Wellbeing Assessment, the Strategy for Integrated Development of the Transportation System, and many others.

These plans were at least as much attempts to answer the criticisms that had been levelled at structural adjustment as they were serious attempts to relieve poverty. They played down, almost to invisibility, the original prescriptions of structural adjustment (although these remain lurking in the shadows) and instead shone the spotlight of their prose on governance, gender issues, the future of the family farm and the environment. For example, 'the challenge is to improve the sustainable management of natural resources; ... reduce conflicts between humans and wildlife; and address such problems as uncontrolled wildfires... and the illegal cutting and excessive consumption of timber', or 'one of the great challenges in the context of the reform of public finances now underway is to mainstream the gender perspective'. And there was a liberal sprinkling of phrases like 'pro-poor growth' and boosting the 'productivity of the family sector.[6]

The PARP 2011–14 directly addressed the issue of the causes of poverty and identified among the causes 'the low rate of growth in agricultural productivity', 'the vulnerability of the agricultural sector to climatic shocks' and 'the worsening terms of [international] trade'. As far as urban poverty was concerned it asserted that the 'informal activity (on which the majority of the poor depend) is predominant and access to formal employment is still very restricted, particularly for women'.[7] These are conclusions which solemnly proclaim the obvious—the poor are poor because they do not have jobs or they are victims of impersonal forces like the 'terms of trade' and 'climatic shocks'!

The PARP 2011–14 then embarks on its remedies and these turn into a kind of list of all that an enlightened government anywhere in the world should be doing. Everything is there—strengthening research services, providing incentives for local merchants to sell 'fishery inputs', 'promoting suppliers of services for mechanisation', creating 'business incubators' and 'industrial parks'. On and on it goes. Education—speed the construction of classrooms, 'implement programs to improve the quality of instruction', 'improve school management' make 'rational use of school facilities', 'continue efforts to retain children in school, with particular attention to girls' and 'together with stakeholders, prepare an integrated strategy for early childhood development'.[8]

Sometimes the recitation of the good and desirable simply dies away into such exhortations as 'revive rural commerce' or 'encourage the creation of employment'.

The problem with plans of this kind is that they have no focus. The authors try to include everything that they imagine a good government should be doing. The Mozambique government obediently responds to all these multiple issues but, even with the best will in the world, efforts by a government to pursue all these objectives would simply drain away into the sand. And there is no real indication that, if left to itself, the Mozambique government would select any of these as its priorities.

A SHORT HISTORY OF MOZAMBIQUE

Frelimo and the Donors

Unlike Angola whose oil wealth has enabled it largely to ignore donor pressures, Mozambique has had little choice but to follow, or appear to follow, the directions and changes of direction of the donors on whom it depends. As a result the aid has continued to flow. By 2006 this had risen to $1.6bn and in 2014 to over $2bn. Although President Guebuza voiced the opinion that Mozambique should become less dependent upon aid, there has been little sign of this happening and in 2015 aid made up 50 per cent of the state's annual budget.

Much of this aid was conditional. The government was expected to follow the prescriptions of the World Bank and the IMF and the changing fashions and emphases of the donor community—for example adopting the Millennium Development Goals or the conservation policies embedded in the creation of the Transfrontier Parks, responding to the PARPs or, more generally, conforming to Western practices of 'good governance'. Some of the aid arrives via NGOs concerned with issues of health, education, capacity training, rural development or the environment. These NGOs bring with them resources and provide some employment. They may work closely with the government, but sometimes they do not, and it has been suggested that overall their activities serve to weaken the authority of the government. In 2006 the American NGO Care had a budget bigger than the agricultural department of the province where it was operating.[9] In this way NGO activity (which is often funded only for a limited period) can undermine the government's capacity to pursue consistent long term policies.

On the other hand, Elizabeth Lunstrum has put forward the counterintuitive suggestion that the Transfrontier Parks, far from 'hollowing out' the government, in the manner of some other donor sponsored schemes, have actually allowed the government to reassert its control over significant areas of the country.[10]

Compliance can be largely a paper exercise. Mozambique, like other areas of the world, has environmental problems. Forests are being cut down and the native iron wood and ebony has been plundered uncontrollably; illegal hunting is emptying the game parks and illegal fishing is plundering the seas; the Zambesi dams are radically altering the ecology of the river valley and illegal washing for gold is destroying whole landscapes. Remedying this is among the priorities of donors and, at least on paper, of the government as well. 'Mozambique's reserves are increasingly the target of the secret activities directed against animal life, flora and the wilderness, depriving local communities of the fruits of these natural riches', said Celso Correia, Minister for the Environment and Rural Development, on the occasion of the graduation of seventy-six new park rangers in March 2016.[11]

A raft of legislative provisions have created game parks (including the Transfrontier Parks), and the Gorongosa park, famous in colonial times, is being rehabilitated and run with help from the Carr Foundation. A marine reserve has been declared around the Querimba Islands and there are forest reserves designed to create a sustainable management of timber resources. However, the capacity of the government to protect the environment, when plundering its resources is one of the most direct ways open to poor people to relieve their poverty, is simply inadequate and the patrimonial nature of politics means that officials at the highest level frequently turn a blind eye to what is happening while many benefit directly from it.

In colonial times the Portuguese authorities often adopted measures (for example against slavery or forced labour) *para os inglezes ver*—for the English to see—while the old practices continued behind this smoke screen of compliance. This is another cultural inheritance from colonial times. The Mozambique government complies on paper with the demands of the donor community and apparently tries to meet its concerns. In every day practice, however, little changes. The international donors get compliance only as long as Mozambique needs aid, a fact ruefully admitted by the Economist Intelligence Unit when in February 2013 it commented that the natural gas discoveries would probably lessen Mozambique's dependence on donor aid but that this would have the effect of weakening international pressure for 'good governance'.

In 2016 the façade of compliance was rudely stripped away when the clandestine loans contracted by members of the elite through paper companies and hidden from the IMF were rudely revealed. Corruption, rife among the Frelimo elite for decades, had always in the end been condoned because of the outward compliance of the government with IMF prescriptions, but this time the IMF threatened to withhold funding pending a full audit of the loans and the companies through which they had been channelled.

Big Projects and Employment

One major objective of structural adjustment and the policies prescribed by the IMF and World Bank was to increase Foreign Direct Investment (FDI). To encourage this, import controls were removed, Industrial Free Zones were established for Beira, Maputo and Nacala, and a Special Investment Regime was put in place for the Zambesi Valley with three years exemption from taxation. This policy resulted in over two billion dollars of FDI since 1998 when these policies came fully into effect. The benefits which it was imagined would flow from this were many and varied—increased government revenues (even though taxes paid were so limited), expansion of employment opportunities, improved infrastructure and spin offs in the form of education and capacity training provided by foreign companies.

From this flow of foreign investment have resulted a number of major projects, which have dominated the whole economic evolution of the country since the end of the war. These projects have been very much to the taste of the post-war Frelimo government, which in this respect is the heir of the previous regimes. 'The government preference for large scale capital intensive projects', wrote Anne Pitcher 'was not just a socialist preoccupation but a colonial obsession.'[12] The first of these to bear fruit after the civil war was the construction of the Mozal aluminium plant in Maputo, which started production in 2000. Built by a consortium backed by Australian, British, Japanese and South African capital, this massive development in 2013 provided more than 30 per cent of Mozambique's exports and consumed 45 per cent of the country's electricity output.

Among the other projects the most striking are the exploitation of the coal and natural gas reserves, the building of a new railway and the expansion of the port of Nacala, a proposed new dam on the Zambesi and investment in large scale commercial farming.

Natural gas and coal are Mozambique's most obvious marketable assets. Coal was discovered in the mid-nineteenth century and was exploited by the Portuguese during the colonial era, but the natural gas discoveries, the full extent of which was only determined in 2010, have been much more recent. Mozambique's gas reserves place it among the top ten countries in the world and investment to extract and liquify the gas began soon after 2011. However, large scale sales of liquefied gas are not scheduled to begin before 2020 at the earliest and the development of this industry (and the benefits expected to proceed from it) are affected by the uncertainties surrounding the price for oil. Moreover it appears that the government used the prospects of gas revenues to negotiate undeclared loans, which deeply compromised the country's public finances.

Coal is mined in Tete Province and, since colonial times, has been exported by rail through the port of Beira. The Moatize mines are controlled by the Brazilian Vale company and in 2010 a major expansion of coal production, the Benga coalfields, was financed by a Brazilian and Indian consortium which also announced plans for a coal fired power station in Tete Province. At the same time a new rail line, financed by the EU, was begun to link the coalfields to the port of Nacala, a route that would have to pass through Malawi but was less liable to flooding than the route to Beira. A coal handling terminal was built in Nacala and in 2016 a floating power station, owned and run by a Turkish company, arrived to boost the electricity supplies to northern Mozambique and Zambia. Exports of coal, like natural gas, have also been affected by falling prices but are projected to rise to 27.2 million tonnes by 2017 when coal revenues could account for 1.7 per cent of GDP. Meanwhile whole communities were displaced as increasing areas of land were allocated for open-cast mining and mining companies, government and local communities became mired in disputes over resettlement and compensation.[13]

The prospects for gas and coal exports, although important for Mozambique's future, hardly promise the bonanza which oil brought to Angola. This could mean that Mozambique will benefit significantly without experiencing the problems, often summarised in a kind of shorthand as the 'Dutch disease'. However, these industries are heavily mechanised and employ only limited numbers of technical staff. Their effect on the creation of employment is limited—the coal mines providing only 0.6 per cent of jobs in the Tete Province. The Economist Intelligence Unit warned that 'mining is capital intensive and it may sharpen inequality and increase frustration among the majority of people who will not benefit directly from it'.[14] Part of the problem it attributes to the fact that 'the labour market in Mozambique experiences significant skills gaps at all levels'.

The same would be true if China's investment in the new Zambesi dam goes ahead. While large numbers of people would be displaced, resettled and, in theory, compensated, little of the revenue generated would come back directly to the communities involved. China also funded the suspension bridge to link Maputo with Catembe and has projected a one billion dollar investment in a new port in southern Mozambique. Relatively few Mozambicans will find employment in any of these projects as China traditionally employs its own labour force in construction.

Among the major projects has been investment in commercial farming. Not all this can be described as foreign investment as significant areas of land, particularly in irrigated areas, have been acquired by Mozambicans. Commercial farming produces sugar, tobacco, citrus, bananas and biofuels, while cashew and cotton, which since colonial times have been peasant produced crops, are marketed and processed by concessionary companies who are granted monopoly rights in certain zones—a system reminiscent of that put in place by the Portuguese in the 1930s which has been the subject of so much criticism in the scholarly literature. Commercial farming probably makes a bigger impact on unemployment than mega-construction projects as it employs wage labour that supplements peasant income.

Commercial agriculture also contributes to diversifying Mozambique's exports. Ever since the end of the civil war Mozambique has run a large deficit on its balance of trade and payments—another reason for the continuing reliance on aid. Its main exports are aluminum, coal, hydro-electricity, lumber, cotton, prawns, cashew, sugar, and citrus but these do not begin to cover the cost of imports which include not only technical equipment of all kinds but also a wide range of consumer items including food. The shops of Maputo are well stocked but they are stocked with goods from South Africa. Mozambique simply does not have the industries to supply the consumer market and many people in the capital actually do their shopping across the border in South Africa.

So, a dispassionate observer might conclude, FDI has resulted in major expansion for Mozambique's GDP but most of the employment it creates is for foreign nationals and most of the profits of the enterprises accrue also to non-Mozambicans. The generation of FDI has been successful but the projected developmental outcomes have not materialised.

Peasants—the Family Farms

Central to the discussion of continuing poverty in Mozambique has been the policy adopted by successive governments since colonial times towards the peasantry, who are usually thought to make up 75 per cent of the population. Studies of this large sector of the population offer explanations for the failure of successive regimes not only to address the problems of rural poverty but even to understand them. However, in spite of these studies, solutions still prove elusive.

Exactly who are the 'peasantry'? As Merle Bowen put it, there has been 'a simplistic vision of agrarian class structure based on a dualist model of a traditional subsistence-oriented peasantry opposed to a modern large-scale commercial sector' when in fact the rural population is 'a regionally diverse and differentiated rural society.' Policies pursued since 1992 seem to have been guided by this misconception. Under pressure from donors the government has sought on the one hand to make provision for large scale private agro-business, while at the same time providing 'greater stability on land-ownership and the restitution of the *regulado* system' for the peasantry. In thrall to this dichotomy, policy-makers have failed to address the different needs of different sectors of rural society and have 'imposed a uniform strategy of national development upon a regionally diverse and socially differentiated rural society rather than considering peasant realities'. In particular the importance of wage labour in supplementing peasant incomes and enabling rural society to function has been ignored. She concludes that 'agricultural producers will need to reorganize themselves to assert and protect their rights to land... Equally as critical, they will need to demand the development of rural industries and a modern infrastructure in order to live and prosper in the twenty-first century'.[15]

Joseph Hanlon and Teresa Smart agree that it is impossible to find a policy where one size fits all. The different regions of the country have different problems, rural society is diverse and the needs of individual peasant families are not always the same. As a result there is a need for government policies to be flexible. The authors are largely concerned with pointing to the failures of the World Bank and IMF prescriptions—in particular those that limit the role of the state to developing human resources (education and training) and infrastructure. They emphasise the 'gaps' in the system where peasants who adhere to policies designed to increase production find there is no mechanism for marketing, for transport, or for financial and technical support. They advocate a 'new interventionist state' although they conclude that 'there are no detailed plans and the interventionist state will need to be flexible so that it can move in where help is needed'. In practice this means providing finance, technology, training and marketing opportunities, 'insurance, loan guarantees, guaranteed purchases, unemployment insurance' and offering 'income to poor rural people, through labour-intensive projects such as road building'. Meanwhile 'health and safety regulations, minimum wages, trades unions and arbitration committees for commodity prices' are all important and the interventionist state needs to become a 'learning state' which supports 'learning and experimentation [and] business development agencies that train, advise and support new business people'.[16] And they conclude that 'jobs are the top priority'. This all-inclusive list of good and desirable things is somewhat reminiscent of the recommendations of the PARPs and by including everything runs very close to focusing on nothing.

Hanlon and Smart's analyses are essentially the same as those of Bowen in that they recognize the 'depth and intractability of Mozambican poverty'[17] but Bowen realistically concludes that 'given the political and economic constraints existing in Mozambique and the multiplicity of demands on the postwar government, the chances of state assistance [are] slim.' In the end 'giving the poor cash is meeting their human needs and not giving "alms"'.

The peasants meanwhile regard changes of regime as 'so many storms in the political sky while the hard realities on the ground remained unchanged'.[18]

Employment

Everyone who has studied poverty in Mozambique, including the PARPs, has concluded, along with Hanlon and Smart that 'jobs are the top priority'. Ever since pre-colonial times Mozambican families have had a diversified domestic economy. In pre-colonial society, farming was supplemented by mining, weaving and iron working, and by incomes derived from hunting, trade, acting as carriers or boatmen, or as fighters. In the colonial period urban wages and migration to South Africa and Rhodesia supplemented family income. Peasants may have depended on their family farms for subsistence but they also sold surpluses into the market, sought seasonal wage labour or traded in the informal economy. This has remained true of the post-colonial period with the result that this mixed economy plays havoc with the exact meaning of employment statistics.

Nevertheless statistics that are widely accepted show that only 10 per cent of Mozambicans are in formal employment and that subsistence agriculture is still overwhelmingly dominant in the lives of the population. Employment in industry and construction accounts for less than 20 per cent of employment even in urban areas. Youth unemployment is significantly higher than unemployment in other age groups in the community and the proportion of the young in a rapidly growing population is getting larger. In urban areas unemployment among 15–24 years olds is running at 77 per cent.

In 2015 the population of Mozambique stood at 28 million having nearly doubled since the end of the civil war. Births are regularly three times the death rate and in some parts of the rural north the average family size is six children. The population has been growing at between 2 and 3 per cent per annum and 45 per cent of the population are under 15. Less than 3 per cent are over 65. The numbers entering the labour market grow at the rate of 3 per cent a year. It has been estimated that 'to absorb the current unemployed and take on board the new entrants to the labour pool, formal salaried employment would have to grow at 20 per cent a year for a decade'.[19] Given the scale of the problem and the history of the economy since the end of the civil war, it is difficult to think of any solutions that do not involve direct, state sponsored, job creation on a large scale.

Mozambique—'Modern' or 'Traditional'?

Mozambique is a young country and two thirds of the population have no experience or even recollection of the civil war. Nevertheless continuity with the past is a constant theme running through this book, and modern Mozambican social culture owes many traits to the pre-colonial past and to the colonial era. One notable feature is the importance of the creole element in the population—the Portuguese and mestizo descendants of the colonial population—though this group is smaller and less important than its counterpart in Angola. Many of those who stayed behind in 1975 did so through a commitment to Frelimo's revolutionary project and they have always been an important group within Frelimo. Marcelino dos Santos, the leading ideologue of Frelimo in its early days and, some would say, the real founder of the party, is a mestizo, while Mia Couto, the most prominent Mozambican writer and possibly the most influential writer in the whole Portuguese-speaking world, is of white Portuguese origin. His family have established and funded the Fundação Fernando Leite Couto, an important cultural centre in Maputo.

Although many of the physical structures of colonial Mozambique disappeared during the war or have been bulldozed during the massive building programme in the capital, and although many people argue that colonial buildings do not resonate with the culture of modern Mozambique, there are traces everywhere of the colonial past. In Maputo iconic colonial buildings have not only been preserved but have been impressively restored—the 'iron house', the natural history museum, the *fortaleza*, the town hall and the railway station, which is a magnificent *beaux arts* palace which gleams with fresh paint, even though there are now very few trains that depart from it. The colonial urban environment survives more completely in Beira where the streets are still lined with characteristic colonial architecture and the street names have not been changed. The port district is still dominated by the Casa Infante de Sagres which boasts its name in large characters and streets in the centre have names such as Rua António Enes and Rua Companhia de Moçambique.

Ilha de Moçambique is perhaps a special case. Declared to be a UNESCO world heritage site in 1991, it has struggled to conserve its colonial past. Various interests have clashed over its conservation and there have been disputes over who is responsible for administering the funds that become available. Some buildings are inextricably entangled in multiple ownership and much of the restoration that has taken place has not been done to the highest standards. Nevertheless the old colonial capital is gradually emerging from decades of neglect and resembles a sleepy rural Portuguese town. The other part of the island, the *macuti* town, still reflects the islanders' ancient urban way of life, which has a cultural depth deeper even than that of the colonial stone town. The great fort still stands empty with the eyes of the Unilurio University fixed ambitiously on it as a possible site for installing a faculty. Those interested in commemorating the slave trade have also cast their eyes on Ilha, determined to find there some physical traces through which to commemorate the fate of the thousands of slaves who were shipped from its port over the centuries.

There are colonial survivals in almost all the older towns—in the commercial and military buildings in Ibo and Inhambane and in the colonial cathedrals, which still dominate Nampula and Quelimane. For the most part statues of Portuguese personages have disappeared but in the courtyard of the National Archives in Maputo a statue of Salazar has been left, face to the wall, standing in the corner as it were, with no museum willing to find room for it.

The most obvious colonial inheritance is, of course, the language. Although Mozambique joined the Commonwealth in 1995, is a country where vehicles drive on the left and is surrounded by Anglophone neighbours, the Portuguese language is alive and well. It is not only the official language of government and business, but it is the language of the press and education—even of primary education.

Frelimo's mission was almost from the start a mission to modernise, and this mission fits well with the drive to attract Foreign Direct Investment. At the same time direct subsidies to support the living standards of the poor have been largely eliminated in conformity with the structural adjustment ideals of the IMF and World Bank. These policies do not pass without protest and in September 2010 there were serious riots in Maputo against rising prices, which forced the government temporarily to back down. After twenty-five year the most striking consequence of the government's policies is the huge disparity in living standards between rich and poor. A relatively small Mozambican elite, which includes many senior members of Frelimo and the foreign business, diplomatic and NGO communities, enjoy an exaggeratedly high standard of living. The modern buildings of Maputo are grand and even ostentatious, the city hotels are clad in marble with fountain courts and air conditioning. Expensive cars are parked outside to whisk businessmen to the ministries or the banks. Education and health for the elite is provided privately— and wealthy Mozambicans go routinely to India for medical treatment. In Beira luxurious gated communities provide housing for the rich. Anne Pitcher describes this as 'the de facto recreation of racial and ethnic hierarchies... in the social spaces of cities such as Maputo and Beira'.[20]

Outside these palaces of global capitalism live the poor. Although the informal market seems under some sort of control in the capital, the *barracas* are nevertheless everywhere in evidence and street sellers haunt the marginal and the beaches. In Beira the whole population seems to be engaged in selling on the street—hawking not only packets of crisps and cold drinks but even three piece suites and double beds. And around the cities are vast slum areas with only rudimentary services. In Beira, built in low-lying marshy country, the rainy season overwhelms the city's infrastructure. Some of the *bairros* (slums) become lakes with the wretched huts standing like islands in the water. And the streets, even in the capital, become huge lakes after rain, the water mixing with the mounds of garbage to make a sort of urban soup. Why is there this contrast between glistening high rise banks, ministries and hotels and the broken unpaved streets outside their entrances, undrained and strewn with litter? Unemployment is so high that it would be easy for the city authorities to engage workers, at the very least, to keep the streets clean. It seems the problem is as much cultural as practical. How better to show the gap between the 'modern' rich and the 'traditional' poor than to contrast the marble clad foyers of hotels with the litter strewn muddy life of the streets. And how better to show the visiting dignitaries of the IMF and World Bank that Mozambique is committed to 'small government'.

Large global corporations have imprinted their presence on the physical environment. 'Advertisements for rental cars and cell phones, insurance and bank loans, are the new icons' and have replaced the socialist poster art of the immediate post-independence period, observed Anne Pitcher.[21] And Vodaphone has found a particularly intrusive way of advertising its presence. By offering to paint people's houses for free, it has left the whole country incongruously strewn with bright red buildings bearing its corporate name.

In theory there is universal access to primary education (at least for a few years) and it is common to see school children in meticulously clean uniforms that must have cost poor families much of their income. However, as the rich do not use these schools, the standards of education seem to be of the lowest and, according to published statistics, most children only receive three or four years schooling. 'Post-secondary education' according to the Economist Intelligence Unit 'is poorly linked to private sector needs'.[22] The new university created in Nampula (Unilurio) seeks to address this and consists solely of technical and professional faculties. Even so, according to the vice-rector, most students still expect to get jobs with the government rather than with private industry. In the capital, although there are scholarships to enable poorer students to attend university, there is a major issue of students suffering from malnutrition.

While Frelimo, civil society and the international donors all pursue a modernising agenda, each in their own way, the culture of a pre-modern Africa is all around them and intrudes into the modern world in unexpected ways. Indeed there is no clear separation between the traditional and the modern. Not only have the traditional *régulos* been reinstated for political and administrative purposes but with them have returned communal ceremonies connected with the ancestors and the bringing of rain. In the northern half of Mozambique matrilineal family relations, which privilege the role of a woman's brother in family affairs, are still important in property matters, the organisation of agricultural labour and conflict resolution. Traditional *curandeiros* (healers) are still important in most communities as are the *mhondoro* spirit mediums. In a recent study of Manica, the Norwegian ethnographer, Bjorn Bertelsen, has stressed that the world of spirits is everywhere present in the lives not only of rural people but of the populations of towns—the *bairros*, he says, are characterised by 'non-cadastrialized paths versus the striated urban spaces of the state'.[23] In Manica it is widely believed that Dhlakama possesses rain-making powers and the ability to evade the ambushes laid for him by the government by turning himself into a partridge.[24] Moreover the elites of Frelimo and Renamo are deeply influenced by these beliefs. It is now known that Frelimo, the great exponent of modernisation, regularly consulted the *mungói* medium 'during the war for help in fending off Renamo attacks'.[25] As Bertelsen puts it 'the state is engaged in a battle to control the unruly field of the spirits'.[26]

And stories circulate of practices that bring the world of the occult closer still to everyday life and blur the distinctions between the 'traditional' and the 'modern'. Early in the twenty-first century there were numerous reports in the press of trafficking in body parts, though no one seemed quite sure whether this was connected with an international trade in transplant organs or with traditional medicine. Some sceptics doubted whether these practices really existed, but in March 2016 *Magazine Independente* repeated a report that had originally appeared in the Beira paper *Diário de Moçambique*. 'The Mozambican police last week detained three young men in possession of the severed head of a 12 year old child.... They are facing charges of murder and trafficking in human body parts.' The arrests had taken place when the three were on the way to meet the man 'who had promised to buy the head'. Whatever the reason for this killing, it was presumably not linked to international trade in body parts for transplants![27]

Intriguing also were the reports from Mueda in the far north of the country, that between July 2002 and May 2003 at least fifty deaths occurred, attributed to lions but which were in fact carried out by groups of men who either dressed as lions or, as some local people believed, turned themselves into lions. These killings were studied by Paolo Israel who unpicked an elaborate tangle of traditional beliefs in magic and sorcery, the trade in body, parts, social tensions, local political rivalries and the impact of global economics, all of which came together to produce this outbreak of murders and lynchings.[28] And Bertelsen reports similar events in Manica where predatory lions are, somewhat incongruously, linked to Germans active in the area as aid workers.[29]

These mysterious episodes should remind one that many Mozambicans interpret the bewildering changes that have been inflicted on their country through their own inherited logic as often as they do through the 'modernising' logic of international donors and the 'new men' hopefully called into existence by Samora Machel's revolution.

FURTHER READING

This list of books is not intended to be a bibliography of Mozambique's history. It is merely some suggestions for further reading.

General histories

W.G. Clarence Smith, *The Third Portuguese Empire, 1825–1975*, Manchester University Press (Manchester, 1985).

David Hedges, Gerhard Liesegang (et. al.), *História de Moçambique*, 3 vols (Maputo, 1993).

Malyn Newitt, *A History of Mozambique*, Hurst (London, 1995).

Pre-1900

Valentim Alexandre, *Velho Brasil, Novas Áfricas, Portugal e o Império (1808–1975)*, Afrontamento (Lisbon, 2000).

Filipe Gastão de Almeida de Eça, *História das Guerras no Zambeze*, 2 vols, Agência Geral do Ultramar (Lisbon, 1954).

Eric Axelson, *Portuguese in South-East Africa 1600–1700*, Witwatersrand University Press (Johannesburg, 1960).

Eric Axelson, *Portugal and the Scramble for Africa 1875–1891*, Witwatersrand University Press (Johannesburg, 1967).

Eric Axelson, *Portuguese in South-East Africa 1488–1600*, C. Struik (Cape Town, 1973).

Patrick Harries, *Work, Culture and Identity. Migrant Laborers in Mozambique and South Africa, c.1860–1910*, Heinemann (Portsmouth NH, 1994).

S.I. Mudenge, *A Political History of Munumutapa c1400–1902*, Zimbabwe Publishing House (Harare, 1988).

Malyn Newitt (ed.), *Treatise on the Rivers of Cuama*, Oxford University Press for the British Academy (London, 2009).

Malyn Newitt (ed.) *A Journey from Tete to Zumbo by Albino Manuel Pacheco*, Oxford University Press for the British Academy (Oxford, 2013).

C.E. Nowell, *The Rose-Colored Map*, Junta de Investigações Cientificas do Ultramar (Lisbon, 1982).

Hilary C. Palmer and Malyn Newitt, *Northern Mozambique in the Nineteenth Century. The Travels and Explorations of H.E. O'Neill*, Brill (Leiden, 2016).

René Pélissier, *Naissance du Mozambique*, 2 vols (Orgéval, 1984).

Carlos Serra, *Como a Penetração Eestrangeira transformou o modo de Produção dos Camponeses Moçambicanos*, 2 vols (Maputo, 1986).

c1900 to 1975

Eric Allina, *Slavery by Any Other Name*, University of Virginia Press (Charlottesville, 2012).

Thomas Henriksen, *Revolution and Counterrevolution. Mozambique's War of Independence 1964–74*, Greenwood (London, 1983).

Allen F. Isaacman, in collaboration with Barbara Isaacman, *The Tradition of Resistance in Mozambique: Anti-Colonial Activity in the Zambezi Valley, 1850–1921*, Heinemann Educational (London, 1976).

FURTHER READING

Allen Isaacman, *Cotton is the Mother of Poverty: Peasants, Work, and Rural Struggle in Colonial Mozambique, 1938–1961*, James Currey (London, 1996).

Eduardo Mondlane, *The Struggle for Mozambique*, Penguin (Harmondsworth, 1969).

Jeanne Marie Penvenne, *Women, Migration & the Cashew Economy in Southern Mozambique 1945–1975*, James Currey (Woodbridge, 2015).

Leroy Vail and Landeg White, *Capitalism and Colonialism in Mozambique*, Heinemann (London, 1980).

Post-1975

Merle Bowen, *The State against the Peasantry. Rural Struggles in Colonial and Postcolonial Mozambique*, University Press of Virginia (Charottesville, 2000).

João Cabrita, *Mozambique*, Palgrave (Basingstoke, 2000).

Michel Cahen, *Les Bandits: Un Historien au Mozambique*, Fundação Calouste Gulbenkian (Paris, 2002).

Stephen Chan and Moisés Venâncio, *War and Peace in Mozambique*, Macmillan Press (Basingstoke, 1998).

Mustafa Dhada, *The Portuguese Massacre of Wiriyamu in Colonial Mozambique, 1964–2013*, Bloomsbury (London, 2016).

Stephen A. Emerson, *The Battle for Mozambique: the Frelimo-Renamo struggle, 1977–1992*, 30° South Publishers, (Pinetown, South Africa, 2013).

Margaret Hall and Tom Young, *Confronting Leviathan. Mozambique since Independence*, Hurst (London, 1997).

J. Hanlon and T. Smart, *Do Bicycles Equal Development in Mozambique*, James Currey (Woodbridge, 2008).

Carrie Manning, *The Politics of Peace in Mozambique. Post-conflict Democratization, 1992–200*, Praeger (Westport Conn., 2002).

Mozambique to 2018. Managers, Mediators and Magnates, Chatham House Report (London, 2015).

Barry Munslow (ed.), *Samora Machel: An African Revolutionary*, Zed Books (London, 1985).

Anne Pitcher, *Transforming Mozambique: the Politics of Privatisation 1975–2000*, Cambridge UP (Cambridge, 2002).

Richard Synge, *Mozambique. UN Peacekeeping in Action 1992–94*, United States Institute of Peace Press (Washington DC, 2005).

Alex Vines, *Renamo: Terrorism in Mozambique*, James Currey (London, 1991).

NOTES

1. THE MOZAMBICAN ENVIRONMENT AND ETHNOGRAPHY

1. Patrick Harries, *Work, Culture and Identity. Migrant Laborers in Mozambique and South Africa, c.1860–1910*, Heinemann (Portsmouth NH, 1994), 5.
2. Charles Ley, *Portuguese Voyages 1498–1663*, Dent (London, 1947), 14.
3. João dos Santos, *Etiópia Oriental e Vária História de Cousa Notáveis do Oriente*, (originally published Évora, 1609) Comissão Nacional para as Comemorações dos Descobrimentos Portugueses (Lisbon, 1999), 247.
4. Santos, J. Norberto R., 'Mutilações dentarias em pretos de Moçambique', *Garcia de Orta*, 10 (1962).
5. For an elaboration of the following discussion see Malyn Newitt, 'Kinship, Religion, Language and Political Control: Ethnic Identity among the Peoples of the Zambesi Valley', in Alexander Keese (ed.), *Ethnicity and the Long-Term Perspective*, Peter Lang (Bern, 2010), 67–92.
6. Santos, *Etiópia Oriental*, 204.
7. Harries, *Work, Culture and Identity*, 3; Terence Ranger, 'Missionaries, Migrants and the Manyika: the Invention of Ethnicity in Zimbabwe', in Vail (ed.), *The Creation of Tribalism in Southern Africa*, 118–150, esp 121. See also Elisabeth MacGonagle, *Crafting Identity in Zimbabwe and Mozambique*, University of Rochester Press (Rochester, 2007), 16.
8. Manuel Barretto, 'Informação do Estado e Conquista dos Rios de Cuama', in G.M.Theal (ed.), *Records of South Eastern Africa*, Struik

(Cape Town, 1964), vol. 3, 480; A.C.P. Gamitto, *King Kazembe*, trans. Ian Cunnison, 2 vols, Junta de Investigações do Ultramar (Lisbon, 1960), vol. 1, 92.

9. António Bocarro, 'Livro do Estado da Índia', in Theal (ed.), *Records of South Eastern Africa*, vol. 3, 254–435. Passage from pp. 357–8.

10. S.I. Mudenge, 'The Rozvi Empire and the Feira of Zumbo', unpublished PhD thesis (London University, 1972); Inácio Caetano Xavier, 'Notícias das Domínios Portugueses de África Oriental 1758', in A.A. Andrade, *Relações de Moçambique Setecentista*, Agência Geral do Ultramar (Lisbon, 1955), 145.

11. Malyn Newitt, 'The Early History of the Maravi', *Journal of African History*, 23 (1982), 145–62.

12. Gamitto, *King Kazembe*, 63–4.

13. Gerhard Liesegang, 'Nguni Migrations between Delagoa Bay and the Zambesi, 1821–1839', *African Historical Studies*, 3 (1970), 317–37.

14. R.C.F. Maugham, *Zambezia*, John Murray (London, 1910), 276.

15. E.A. Alpers, 'Towards a history of the expansion of Islam in East Africa: the matrilineal peoples of the southern interior', in T.O.Ranger and I.M. Kimambo (eds), *The Historical Study of African Religion*, Heinemann (London, 1972), 172–201.

16. Santos, *Etiópia Oriental*, 225.

17. Bocarro, 'Livro do Estado da Índia', 392.

18. Santos, *Etiópia Oriental*, 226.

19. Allen and Barbara Isaacman, *Slavery and Beyond. The Making of Men and Chikunda Ethnic Identities in the unstable world of South-Central Africa, 1750–1920*, Heinemann (Portsmouth, NH, 2004), 6.

20. See 'Ethnologue languages of the world. Mozambique', https://www.ethnologue.com/country/mz/languages (last accessed 21 February 2017). Also Michel Cahen, Philippe Waniez and Violette Brustlein, 'Pour un atlas social et culturel du Mozambique', *Lusotopie* (2002/1), 229–30.

2. THE SIXTEENTH TO THE EIGHTEENTH CENTURIES

1. The contents of this chapter is largely based on Malyn Newitt, *A History of Mozambique*, Hurst (London, 1995) and the sources quoted therein.

2. Santos, *Etiópia Oriental*, 319.

3. Harry Langworthy, 'A History of Undi's Kingdom to 1890', unpublished PhD thesis, Boston University, 1969, 38–9.

4. The best account of the 'Monomotapa Empire' is S.I. Mudenge, *A Political History of Munumutapa c1400–1902*, Zimbabwe Publishing House (Harare, 1988).

5. S.I. Mudenge, 'The Rozvi Empire and the Feira of Zumbo', unpublished PhD thesis, London University (1971); Malyn Newitt (ed.), *Treatise on the Rivers of Cuama*, Oxford University Press for the British Academy (London, 2009).

6. Eugénia Rodrigues, 'Mercadores, Conquistadores e Foreiros: A Construção dos Prazos nos Rios de Cuama na Primeira Metade de Século XVII', *Vasco da Gama Homens, Viagens e Culturas*, Comissão Nacional para as Comemorações dos Descobrimentos Portugueses, vol. 1 (Lisbon, 1999), 466–7.

7. Mauriz Thoman SJ., *Reise und Lebensbeschreibung* (Augsburg, 1788), chapters 7–9.

3. THE NINETEENTH CENTURY: AFRICAN AGENCY IN THE CREATION OF MOZAMBIQUE

1. Quotations from Malyn Newitt, 'Drought in Mozambique 1823–31', *Journal of Southern African Studies*, 15 (1988), 15–35.

2. Ibid.

3. Richard B. Allen,'The Mascarene Slave-Trade and Labour Migration in the Indian Ocean during the Eighteenth and Nineteenth Centuries', in Gwyn Campbell (ed.), *The Structure of Slavery in Indian Ocean Africa and Asia*, Routledge (Abingdon, 2003), 33–50. See also Richard B. Allen, 'The Constant Demand of the French: The Mascarene Slave Trade and the Worlds of the Indian Ocean and the Atlantic during the Eighteenth and Nineteenth Centuries', *Journal of African History*, 49 (2008), 43–72. This article is particularly useful for its comprehensive survey of the historiography of the subject.

4. Ralph A. Austen, 'The 19th Century Islamic Slave Trade from East Africa (Swahili and Red Sea Coasts): a Tentative Census', in William Gervase Clarence-Smith (ed.), *The Economics of the Indian Ocean Slave Trade in the Nineteenth Century*, Routledge (London, 1989), 21–44.

5. Pedro Machado, 'A forgotten Corner of the Indian Ocean: Gujerati Merchants, Portuguese India and the Mozambique Slave-Trade, c.1730–1830', in Campbell (ed.), *The Structure of Slavery in Indian Ocean Africa and Asia*, 17–32.

6. Gerhard Liesegang, 'A First Look at the Import and Export Trade of Mozambique 1800–1914', *Proceedings of the Symposium on the Quantification and Structure of the Import and Export and Long Distance Trade of Africa in the 19th Century (c.1800–1913)*, (St Augustin, 1983), 452–523.

7. For a detailed account of the events leading up to Portuguese abolition see João Pedro Marques, *Sounds of Silence. Nineteenth-century Portugal and the Abolition of the Slave Trade*, Berghahn Books (New York and Oxford, 2006).

8. Quotation from Hilary C. Palmer and Malyn Newitt, *Northern Mozambique in the Nineteenth Century. The Travels and Explorations of H.E.O'Neill*, Brill (Leiden, 2016), 133.

9. Harries, *Work, Culture and Identity*, 4.

10. Quotation from Palmer and Newitt, *Northern Mozambique in the Nineteenth Century*, 124.

11. Malyn Newitt (ed.), *A Journey from Tete to Zumbo by Albino Manuel Pacheco*, Oxford University Press for the British Academy (Oxord, 2013).

12. Newitt, *A Journey from Tete to Zumbo by Albino Manuel Pacheco*, 111.

13. The classic account of the Zambesi Wars is Filipe Gastão de Almeida de Eça, *História das Guerras no Zambeze*, 2 vols, Agência Geral do Ultramar (Lisbon, 1954).

14. For the complexities of the market in Madagascar see Gwyn Campbell, 'The East African Slave Trade, 1861–1895: The "Southern" Complex', *International Journal of African Historical Studies*, 22 (1989), 1–26.

15. W.P. Johnson, *My African Reminiscences, 1875–1895*, UMCA (London, 1924), 62–3.

16. Quotation from Palmer and Newitt, *Northern Mozambique in the Nineteenth Century*, 138.

17. Ibid., 143.

4. THE INTERVENTION OF EUROPEANS AND THE SCRAMBLE FOR AFRICA

1. A.C.P. Gamitto, *O Muata Cazembe e os povos Maraves, Chevas, Muizas, Muembas, Lundas e outros da Africa austral: diario da expedição portuguesa comandada pelo Major Monteiro*, 2 vols, Agência Geral das Colónias (Lisbon, 1854), Ian Cunnison (ed.), *King Kazembe: and the Marave, Cheva, Bisa, Bemba, Lunda and Other Peoples of Southern Africa, Being the Diary of the Portuguese Expedition to That Potentate in the Years 1831 and 1832*, 2 vols, Junta de Investigações do Ultramar, Estudos de Ciências Politicas e Sociais, nos. 42 and 43 (Lisbon, 1960).

2. Valentim Alexandre, *Velho Brasil, Novas Áfricas, Portugal e o Império (1808–1975)*, Afrontamento (Lisbon, 2000).

3. C.E. Nowell, *The Rose-Colored Map*, Junta de Investigações Cientificas do Ultramar (Lisbon, 1982).

4. Marquês de Lavradio, *Portugal em África depois de 1851*, Agência Geral das Colónias (Lisbon, 1936), 117.

5. A reconstruction of the intended first volume was published in Palmer and Newitt, *Northern Mozambique in the Nineteenth Century*.

6. For the last stages of the Zambesi Wars and much else see René Pélissier, *Naissance du Mozambique*, 2 vols (Orgéval, 1984).

7. Eric Axelson, *Portugal and the Scramble for Africa 1875—1891*, Witwatersrand University Press (Johannesburg, 1967).

5. PORTUGUESE COLONIAL RULE TO 1919

1. W.G. Clarence-Smith, *The Third Portuguese Empire, 1825–1975*, Manchester University Press (Manchester, 1985), 85.

2. António Ennes, *Moçambique*, (Lisbon, 1913), 1.

3. Caroline Brettell, *Anthropology and Migration*, Altamira (Oxford, 2003), 12.

4. Eric Allina, *Slavery By Any Other Name*, University of Virginia Press (Charlottesville, 2012), 23.

5. R.C.F. Maugham, *Africa as I have known it*, John Murray (London, 1929), 215–16.

6. In Palmer and Newitt, *Northern Mozambique in the Nineteenth Century*, 169.

7. Ibid., 314.

8. R.C.F. Maugham, *Zambezia*, John Murray (London, 1910), 118.

9. Marco Fortunato Arrifes, *A Primeira Grande Guerra na África Portuguesa.* Edições Cosmos (Lisbon, 2004), 122.

6. COLONIAL MOZAMBIQUE 1919 TO 1975

1. This period is covered in detail in David Hedges, Gerhard Liesegang et. al. (eds), *História de Moçambique* (Maputo, 1993), vol. 3.

2. Quoted in John P. Cann, *Counterinsurgency in Africa: The Portuguese Way of War 1961–1974*, Greenwood Press (Westport Conn., 1997),14.

3. Quoted in Filipe Ribeiro de Menezes, *Salazar*, Enigma Books (New York, 2009), 91.

4. A typed copy of this diary was given to me in 1998 by his son, Ian Spence. It is entitled 'The Diary of a Trip through Portuguese East Africa October and November 1943'.

5. C.F. Spence, *The Portuguese Colony of Moçambique, An Economic Survey*, A.A. Balkema (Cape Town and Amsterdam, 1951), 8.

6. C.F. Spence, *Moçambique. East African Province of Portugal*, Howard Timmins (Cape Town, 1963).

7. 'The Diary of a Trip through Portuguese East Africa', Wednesday 20 October.

8. C.F. Spence, *The Portuguese Colony of Moçambique*, 61.

9. 'The Diary of a Trip through Portuguese East Africa, Friday 22 October.'

10. Eric Allina, *Slavery by any other Name*. Corrado Tornimbeni, '"Working Boundaries": Boundaries, Colonial Controls & Labour Circulation in Beira District, Mozambique, 1942–1960s', in Malyn Newitt (ed.) with Patrick Chabal and Norrie Macqueen, *Community and the State in Lusophone Africa*, King's College London (London, 2003), 137–182.

11. Jeanne Marie Penvenne, *Women, Migration & the Cashew Economy in Southern Mozambique 1945–1975*, James Currey (Woodbridge, 2015).

12. Merle Bowen, *The State against the Peasantry Rural struggles in Colonial and Postcolonial Mozambique*, University Press of Virginia (Charlottesville, 2000), 35.

13. Claudia Castello, *Passagens para África*, Edições Afrontamento (Lisbon, 207), 97.

14. Ibid, 216.

15. Margaret Hall and Tom Young, *Confronting Leviathan. Mozambique since Independence*, Hurst (London, 1997), 13.

16. João Cabrita, *Mozambique*, Palgrave (Basingstoke, 2000), chapters 1 & 2.

17. *História da Frelimo*, Frelimo Colecção Conhecer (Maputo, 1978), 8, 17.

18. *Eduardo Mondlane*, Panaf (London, 1978), 29, 26.

19. Eduardo Mondlane, *The Struggle for Mozambique*, Penguin (Harmondsworth, 1969), 163.

7. INDEPENDENCE AND CIVIL WAR

1. Much of this section is taken from Malyn Newitt, 'Os partidos nacionalistas africanos no tempo da revolução', in Fernando Rosas et al., *O Adeus ao Império*, Nova Vega (Lisbon, 2015), 25–43.

2. Quotations from Barry Munslow (ed.), *Samora Machel: An African Revolutionary*, Zed Books (London, 1985), 2, 5, xxii.

3. Quotations from Samora Machel, *Mozambique. Sowing the Seeds of Revolution*, Committee for Freedom in Mozambique, Angola and Guiné, London, 1975), 16–17.

4. Amílcar Cabral, *Revolution in Guinea: An African Peoples' Struggle*, Stage 1 (London, 1969), 70.

5. Machel, *Mozambique. Sowing the Seeds of Revolution*, 16.

6. Quotations from Munslow, *Samora Machel. An African Revolutionary*,130–31, 113.

7. *Moçambique. Marcha para a Independência*, (Lourenço Marques, 1974), 27.

8. Quotations from Munslow, *Samora Machel. An African Revolutionary*, 136,137.

9. Carrie Manning, *The Politics of Peace in Mozambique. Post-conflict Democratization, 1992 200*, Praeger (Westport Conn., 2002), 43–4.

10. See especially Newitt, *A History of Mozambique* and Bjorn Enge Bertelsen', *Violent Becomings. State Formation, Sociality and Power in Mozambique*, Berghahn (New York and London, 2016).

11. Stephen Chan and Moisés Venâncio, *War and Peace in Mozambique*, Macmillan Press (Basingstoke, 1998), 14.

12. Roberto Morozzo della Rocca and Luca Riccardi, 'The Peace Process in Mozambique', in Malyn Newitt (ed.), with Patrick Chabal and Norrie Macqueen, *Community and the State in Lusophone Africa*, King's College London (London, 2003), 127–136. Quotation on page 131.

13. Richard Synge, *Mozambique. UN Peacekeeping in Action 1992–94*, United States Institute of Peace Press (Washington DC, 2005), 148–9.

14. Ibid., 6.

15. Ibid., 10.

8. MOZAMBIQUE AFTER THE CIVIL WAR

1. Victor Igreja, 'Memories as Weapons: the politics of peace and silence in post-civil war Mozambique', *Journal of Southern African Studies*, 34 (2008) 539–56. Quotation from 552.

2. Manning, *The Politics of Peace in Mozambique*, 8.

3. EIU February 2010.

4. *Mozambique to 2018. Managers, Mediators and Magnates*, Chatham House Report (London, 2015), 18.

5. Manning, *The Politics of Peace in Mozambique*, 8.

6. *Magazine Independente*, 22 March 2016.

7. Manning, *The Politics of Peace in Mozambique*, 136.

8. Quotations from Simone Montanari, 'Dominance and Belonging: The FRELIMO Party in Massingir, Mozambique', in Corrado Tornimbeni (ed.), *Working the System in Sub-Saharan Africa*, Cambridge Scholars Publishing (Newcastle-upon-Tyne, 2013),166–8.

9. EIU, February 2016.

10. *Zambeze*, 24 March 2016.

11. Synge, *Mozambique. UN Peacekeeping in Action 1992–94*, 148.

12. *Notícias*, 19 March 2016.

13. *Zambeze*, 24 March 2016.

14. *Mozambique to 2018, Managers, Mediators and Magnates*, 19.

15. EIU December 2013.

16. Quoted in Manning, *The Politics of Peace in Mozambique*, 66.

17. Michel Cahen, *Les Bandits: Un Historien au Mozambique*, Fundação Calouste Gulbenkian (Paris, 2002).

18. For example see *Zambeze*, 24 March 2016.
19. J. Hanlon and T. Smart, *Do Bicycles Equal Development in Mozambique*, James Currey (Woodbridge, 2008).
20. Quoted in Manning, *The Politics of Peace in Mozambique*, 131–2.
21. Corrado Tornimbeni (ed.), *Working the System in Sub-Saharan Africa*, 12.
22. Corrado Tornimbeni (2005), 'The State, Labour Migration and the Transnational Discourse—A Historical Perspective from Mozambique', in Veronika Bilger, Albert Kraler (eds), *African Migrations. Historical Perspectives and Contemporary Dynamics*, Stichproben. Wiener Zeitschrift für kritische Afrikastudien/Vienna *Journal of African Studies*, special issue, no 8 (2005), Vienna, 307–328.

9. ECONOMY AND SOCIETY SINCE 1994

1. World Bank Overview (Mozambique) April 2016 www.worldbank.org/en/country/mozambique/overview (last accessed 20 February 2017).
2. EIU Nov 2012.
3. Hanlon and Smart, *Do Bicycles Equal Development in Mozambique*, 11.
4. Quoted in ibid., 201.
5. Figures from Manning, *The Politics of Peace in Mozambique*, 122.
6. *Republic of Mozambique: Poverty Reduction Strategy Paper*. IMF Country Report No 11/132, (henceforward PARP 2011–14), 11, 15, 8.
7. PARP 2011–14, 7.
8. PARP 2011–14, 22.
9. Hanlon and Smart, *Do Bicycles Equal Development in Mozambique*, 22.
10. Elizabeth Lunstrum, 'Green grabs, land grabs and the spaciality of displacement. Evictions from Mozambique's Limpopo National Park', Royal Geographical Society, 2015 (Wiley Online Library).
11. *Diário de Moçambique*, 25 March 2016.
12. Anne Pitcher, *Transforming Mozambique: the Politics of Privatisation 1975–2000*, Cambridge UP (Cambridge, 2002), 237–8.
13. Discussed in *Mozambique to 2018. Managers, Mediators and Magnates*, 4–6, 9, 17.
14. EIU, Nov 2011.
15. Merle Bowen, *The State against the Peasantry. Rural Struggles in Colonial*

and *Postcolonial Mozambique* University Press of Virginia (Charlottesville, 2000), 205, 209, 207, 210.

16. Hanlon and Smart, *Do Bicycles Equal Development in Mozambique*, 200–7.
17. Ibid., 205.
18. Bowen, *The State against the Peasantry*, 209.
19. *Mozambique to 2018. Managers, Mediators and Magnates*, 39.
20. Pitcher, *Transforming Mozambique*, 237.
21. Ibid
22. EIU October 2011
23. Bertelsen, *Violent Becomings*, 124.
24. Ibid., 109–11.
25. Manning, *The Politics of Peace*, 65.
26. Bertelsen, *Violent Becomings*, 115.
27. *Magazine Independente*, 22 March 2016.
28. Paolo Israel, 'The War of the Lions: Witch Hunts, Occult Idioms and Post-socialism in Northern Mozambique', *Journal of Southern African Studies*, 35 (2009), 155–174.
29. Bertelsen, *Violent Becomings*, 103–4.

INDEX

INDEX

INDEX

INDEX

INDEX

INDEX

INDEX

INDEX

INDEX

INDEX

INDEX